Woody Allen and
Charlie Chaplin

ALSO BY JILL FRANKS

*British and Irish Women Writers
and the Women's Movement:
Six Literary Voices of Their Times* (McFarland, 2013)

*Islands and the Modernists:
The Allure of Isolation
in Art, Literature and Science* (McFarland, 2006)

Woody Allen and Charlie Chaplin

Little Men, Big Auteurs

JILL FRANKS

McFarland & Company, Inc., Publishers
Jefferson, North Carolina

ISBN (print) 978-1-4766-7792-7 ∞
ISBN (ebook) 978-1-4766-3619-1

LIBRARY OF CONGRESS AND BRITISH LIBRARY
CATALOGUING DATA ARE AVAILABLE

LIBRARY OF CONGRESS CONTROL NUMBER: 2019942373

© 2019 Jill Franks. All rights reserved

No part of this book may be reproduced or transmitted in any form or by any means, electronic or mechanical, including photocopying or recording, or by any information storage and retrieval system, without permission in writing from the publisher.

Front cover images: Charlie Chaplin, circa 1936 (Photofest); Woody Allen, 1972 in *Everything You Always Wanted to Know About Sex * But Were Afraid to Ask* (United Artists/Photofest); background © 2019 Shutterstock

Printed in the United States of America

McFarland & Company, Inc., Publishers
Box 611, Jefferson, North Carolina 28640
www.mcfarlandpub.com

To my mother,
Mary Harris Franks

Table of Contents

Preface	1
Introduction: Little Men as Tramp and Schlemiel	7
1. Modern and Postmodern Circuses in *The Circus* and *Shadows and Fog*	29
2. Technology and Alienation in *Modern Times* and *Sleeper*	51
3. Master/Slave Dialectic in *The Great Dictator* and *Zelig*	78
4. Getting Away with Murder in *Monsieur Verdoux* and *Crimes and Misdemeanors*	99
5. What Is Love in *Limelight* and *Manhattan*?	124
6. Nobility and Ambiguity in Modern and Postmodern Endings	149
Appendix: Sex Scandals and the Role of the Critic	161
Chapter Notes	171
Bibliography	185
Index	191

Preface

This book arose from a desire to investigate the genres of Little Man comedy and absurdist humor as they evolve over the course of the twentieth century in accordance with historical and cultural changes. Specifically, how does the Little Man change as human experience shifts across the mid-century divide, and whole new dimensions of potential alienation open up in postmodern times? Charlie Chaplin and Woody Allen are exemplars of Little Men at the same time they are Big Auteurs. Their names come to the forefront of any discussion on film comedy auteurs due to their control of their product (they are writer/director/star of most of their films) as well as their genius for creating original but entirely relatable personae, their innovative construction of the *mise-en-scène*, and their keen sense of comic timing and engaging subject matter. This book also explores their respective abilities to walk the line between comedy and tragedy, creating an in-between genre that is very difficult to achieve or even define. It is my contention that their comic tones—the particular ways in which they create their clowns with-*gravitas*—produce a more engaging type of comedy than that of their peers.

Woody Allen and Charlie Chaplin: Little Men, Big Auteurs is a comparative analysis of ten films. Five films by Allen are paired with five by Chaplin, the selection of which is based on common themes. Principles of modernism (for Chaplin) and postmodernism (for Allen) influence the very different plots, resolutions, and characterizations that their films contain. The differences in the Chaplin and Allen personae and plots epitomize the shift in the role of the protagonist in modern versus postmodern narratives, from a noble individual fulfilling some kind of personal quest (Chaplin) to one flawed, average city dweller who reaches the end of the story with the same problems as those with which he started (as in *Annie Hall, Manhattan, Husbands and Wives, Deconstructing Harry*, and many others). My conclusions about these films' different modes of modern and postmodern narration emphasize the role of film as a medium that powerfully conveys and reflects the culture in which it is produced.

In discussing the films, I explain and apply various theories that will be familiar to film studies, literature, and cultural studies scholars, including those of Mikhail Bakhtin, Roland Barthes, Karl Marx, Jacques Lacan, Sigmund Freud, G. W. F. Hegel, Friedrich Nietzsche, and Laura Mulvey. Psychoanalysis, feminist theory, gender studies, and film theory constitute the bulk of my theoretical approach. This work places primary emphasis on narrative analysis, though in the course of my discussions of the films, attention is also paid to framing, camerawork, sound tracks, editing, and other elements of film production.

By choosing to work on Woody Allen and Charlie Chaplin, I am seeking to fill a gender gap and offer a new kind of voice in the field. My thesis addresses the auteurs' relation to their times, and their dance on the line between comedy and tragedy; these are not explicitly feminist arguments. I do, however, approach all art through the lens of feminism; feminist theory informs my thinking; and Chapters 3 and 5 in particular make feminist arguments.

A survey of the critical literature reveals that Allen and Chaplin scholarship is dominated by men. In Charles Silet's 2006 collection of scholarly essays about Woody Allen's films, the ratio of male to female essayists is twenty-one to four.[1] In Peter Bailey and Sam Girgus's 2013 collection on Allen, the ratio is improved, at eighteen to ten.[2] The disproportionate number of men to women in Chaplin scholarship is greater. In a 2004 collection of essays on *The Great Dictator*, the ratio is eleven to one.[3] On the website charliechaplin.com/books, the ratio is forty-one males to ten females. In addition to this large disparity, the women whose works do appear on this website tend to co-author their articles and books with men. A few excellent woman-authored studies do exist. Donna Kornhaber's groundbreaking *Charlie Chaplin, Director* came out in 2014, Lisa Stein Haven's *Charlie Chaplin's Little Tramp in America, 1947–77* in 2016.[4] Female-authored books on Allen date from an earlier era: Nancy Pogel's monograph for Twayne's Filmmakers Series in 1987 and Mary Nichols's refreshing *Reconstructing Woody* in 1998.

Perhaps women have shied away from writing about Allen because of the abuse scandal surrounding him. Especially at the present moment, women may be disincentivized to work on his films. But for me, writing about him is especially interesting in the current climate of concern generated by the Mia/Dylan/Woody scandal that arose in 1992, resurfaced in 2014, and reappeared in 2017. Any discussion I have had with friends, colleagues, students, and family over the course of years in which I have been writing this book has necessarily addressed—and usually started with—the question of whether he molested Dylan Farrow, and whether that makes a difference in my willingness to work on his films in an extended research project. The critic's role in such a case constitutes such an important and involved topic that it merits a separate essay, which is found as an appendix. This essay both summarizes the events pertaining to the scandal and reviews the literature—books, articles, websites, videos, interviews, and blogs—whose creators have weighed in with evidence and opinions. In answer to the second question—no, the existence of the scandal has not lessened in any way my desire to work on this project. If anything, it has motivated me to explore many biographies and memoirs in order to understand all aspects of the scandal, including public opinion and the ways in which celebrities' personal lives affect the reception of their work in America.

Chaplin was not immune to sex scandals either. He was prosecuted under the Mann Act for meeting—at her insistence—with an ex-lover in New York City. Though he was acquitted, she later sued him for support of a child that was not his. The court granted a decision in her favor, ordering Chaplin to pay $75.00 a week till the child's age of majority. Public opinion raged against Chaplin due to the young ages of his wives. Two were sixteen, and one was eighteen; the auteur was twenty-nine, thirty-five, and fifty-four, respectively, when he married them. Chaplin paid the price for his sexual proclivities and his defiance of moral order. Forty years after his death, sufficient time has passed to lessen critical emphasis on his morals and to focus it instead on his work.

But the opposite is true of Allen. With the #MeToo movement's inception in October 2017, the subject of sexual abuse by men in the entertainment industry is brought up almost daily in news and editorial venues. Dylan Farrow has explicitly asked actors to boycott Woody Allen in support of her claim that he molested her as a child. Yet I am not willing to boycott one of my favorite film artists, nor do I believe that boycotting is a useful response for a critic. The appendix, "Sex Scandals and the Role of the Critic," elucidates the reasons I feel it is important to separate the art from the artist.

I am by no means the only feminist who loves Woody Allen films. Besides Pogel and Nichols (mentioned above), there are several female critics, some of whom are detectably feminist, who have written incisive, sympathetic analyses of the films, including Iris Bruce, Ruth Perlmutter, Ruth Johnston, Hannah Arendt, Joanna Rapf, Renée Curry, Katherine Fusco, Cynthia Lucia, Diane Snow, and Monica Osborne. Many of these critics have noticed that Allen is interested in female perspectives on life and love. If he privileges the male viewpoint, he nonetheless affords the female lead a role of equivalent importance, or at least equal screen time, to the one the male counterpart holds. As in Shakespeare's plays, the women in Woody Allen films often have more integrity and wisdom than the men they love (Tracy in *Manhattan*, Treva in *Oedipus Wrecks*, Hattie in *Sweet and Lowdown*).

My feminist analysis pertains not only to ways in which the filmmakers structure narratives that give males agency while females depend on them, but also to patterns in male criticism that reveal their phallocentric assumptions about the gender roles assigned by patriarchy. Another subject that warrants a feminist analysis is the historical shift in attitudes about gender equality that occurs between Chaplin and Allen's times. Chaplin begins his career at the height of first wave feminism, a time when women fought for and gained the right to vote (1920 in America). Feminists at that time constituted a very small proportion of the populace compared to what they would become during second and third wave feminism. On the one hand, Chaplin's female characters fit many of the traditional stereotypes of the vaudeville genre in which he was trained. If they are strong and opinionated, they are likely to be shrill harridans such as the battle-axe wives that keep their husbands under control. In contrast, many of his ingénues are demure and submissive. On the other hand, Chaplin worked with three strong women whose independence he emphasized when creating their movie characters: Mabel Normand, Georgia Hale, and Paulette Goddard. The suffragette movement, flappers, and women entering the workplace (Mary Pickford was one of the actor/directors with whom he co-founded United Artists in 1919) were influences that opened Chaplin's mind to the possibility that strong women roles could enhance his movies. His wife, Paulette Goddard, acted as a comrade to the Tramp instead of merely a love object. The trend of strong women continues up to his last film, *A Countess from Hong Kong* (1967), in which a vibrant Sophia Loren steals scenes from Marlon Brando.

Chaplin worked during the peak of first wave feminism, whereas Allen was more influenced by the second wave. The early and middle periods of Allen's career (which are the focus of this project) coincide with the height (1968) and aftermath (late 1970s) of second wave feminism. His films investigate—without lamenting—the changes that women's liberation brought to the power dynamics and expectations within romantic partnerships. Most of the various Woody personae's girlfriends are educated, middle-class, white women who are as intelligent as he is, but whom he often derides for being pseudo-intellectual. Perhaps due to his insecurity, the Woody character feels uncomfortable with these women's tendencies to intellectualize or show intelligence. Allen's films sometimes appear to be women's stories when they are actually framed by male storytelling, as in *Melinda and Melinda*, where male writers are crafting the lead female character in their minds.

Numerous detailed monographs have been written about Allen and Chaplin (separately), including biographies, reception studies, film analyses, cultural studies about the role Chaplin played in American cultural history, and defenses of aspects of their work that have previously received negative criticism. For instance, Donna Kornhaber's book, *Charlie Chaplin, Director*, defends Chaplin's directing aptitude against charges that his style is antiquated because he never gave up the stylistic elements of classical editing (long takes, few edits, minimal use of close-ups). Mary Nichols's *Reconstructing Woody* defends Allen against charges of excessive pessimism; she believes his films demonstrate an attempt to improve contemporary life and fight amorality. Over the course of forty-two years, Eric Lax has maintained a friendship with Allen; he followed the director on set, interviewed him and his colleagues, and wrote four books about his life and work. Lax's books are detailed, elegant, and authentic, since they are based on deep friendship and respect for Woody Allen. For historical and biographical background, I find the following especially helpful: Charles Maland's *Charlie Chaplin and American Culture: The Evolution of a Star Image*; David Robinson's definitive biography and Richard Carr's political biography of Chaplin; and John Baxter, Eric Lax, and David Evanier's biographies of Allen.[5]

This book does not aspire to the level of archival or primary-source scholarship of these works. This book is intended for a general readership that may be interested in a comparison of the two directors' major themes and works with regard to the many ways in which these reflect historical events, modern and postmodern styles, and cultural attitudes. I combine my insights with those of other critics, biographers, and theorists to achieve a new and nuanced reading of the ten selected films.

No good book is written in isolation. I wish to acknowledge the assistance I received while writing this one. I am deeply grateful to Austin Peay State University's administration and professional development committee for awarding me a sabbatical leave during which to finish the manuscript. James Kelly, Humanities Research Librarian at the W.E.B. Du Bois Library at University of Massachusetts Amherst, generously provided me access to the extensive film studies resources available in the Five College Consortium. Missy Roser, Reference Librarian at Frost Library, Amherst College, graciously helped with technical fine points. Students in my Woody Allen/Charlie Chaplin seminar helped me become aware of how these "old" filmmakers read today, requiring me to reconsider many of my unexamined assumptions about what constitutes funniness, or how *funny* means different things to different people. Students in my London film class shared the excitement of spotting plaques, statues, and other Chaplin monuments while living and walking in the Kennington neighborhoods where Chaplin was born and raised. The course featured a trip to The Cinema Museum in London, where museum director Martin Humphries gave generously of his time and resources, including screenings of *The Immigrant*, a guided tour of the museum, and lectures pinpointed to the needs of my students.

Friends who have read and commented on drafts helped me to hone ideas and clarify my expression, including Kitty Florey, David Neelon, Richard Randall, and Dr. David Guest. Richard Godsey may be the most fanatic Woody buff I have ever met; his interest in my project energized me.

I am grateful to my editors at McFarland, David Alff and Layla Milholen, who facilitated the production of this book. Thanks to Dr. Marty Norden for the invitation to present a lecture about Allen's career in his University of Massachusetts film class and to Natane Halasz for a similar opportunity at Leverett Library in Leverett, Massachusetts. Professors Shawn Shimpach at University of Massachusetts, Robin Blaetz at Mount Holyoke College, and Josh Guilford at Amherst College all engaged in meaningful discussions about the scope of my project. Philosopher Michael Millner helped clarify the theories of Hegel and Kant, specifically the categorical imperative, when he entered into discussion of my plans to wax philosophical in Chapter 3. Dan Kamin is an expert on Chaplin's ways of moving, dressing, and speaking. He offered helpful suggestions and insights on early chapter drafts. Professor Sam Girgus shares my psychoanalytical interest and approach to Allen's films. He helped me by reading the early chapters and commenting graciously on their attributes. I am especially grateful to Professor Peter Bailey for his careful reading of several chapter drafts and his valuable advice for improving the book. Peter's shared love of the filmmakers and his writing guidance made this a better book.

Introduction:
Little Men as Tramp and Schlemiel

> "Woody Allen is the foremost popularizer of The Absurd in the latter half of the twentieth century and over a decade into the twenty-first. The silent film comedians were avatars of the absurd long before it became a philosophical ideology."[1]

Woody Allen and Charlie Chaplin have in common a love of the absurd. From Chaplin's slapstick to Allen's metaphysical wit, the concept of absurdism—our tendency to seek value and meaning in life despite our inability to find them in an irrational universe—underpins their best comedy. This book brings together the films of Charles Chaplin (1889–1977) and Woody Allen (b. 1935) in order to explore their love of the absurd and to contrast its expression in the two distinct eras to which they belong, the modern and postmodern. Reflecting modernist faith in individualism, the Tramp films present his victory against the cold, cruel world. The endings of the films either reward him, or at least show his pathos and the heroism of his struggle. Reflecting a postmodernist sense of contingency, Allen's schlemiel only survives his ordeals by luck, if at all. As Gerald Mast writes, "Allen is such a spectacular combination of post–Freudian complexes and insecurities that the very notion of heroism and its opposite has no place in his world."[2] Although the schlemiel (fool) is Jewish (usually played by Allen), the appeal of this persona is universal. We recognize ourselves in his feelings and situations: bad luck in love, the fruitless search for meaning, and the depressing effects of American materialism, consumerism, and the culture of narcissism that peaked in the 1970s and '80s. Absurdism is an appropriate genre in which to express a sense of catastrophe regarding twentieth-century events because it mixes serious responses to the depressing state of the world—awe, terror, disbelief—with comic relief, expressed through irony, nonsense, and hyperbole.

The Chaplin films analyzed herein date from the beginning of the sound era until 1952 (constituting the second half of his career); they occupy an era of modernism during which expression of the absurd arises as a response to catastrophic events such as the Great Depression, the First World War, and the spread of fascism. Chaplin directly addresses these events in films such as *Modern Times* (1936) and *The Great Dictator* (1940). Scenes such as the Tramp acting mechanically, like the machine in the factory where he is employed, or the Dictator ordering his henchman to kill all the striking factory workers because he "doesn't want any of his workers dissatisfied," express the dehumanization of the mechanized world and the inhumanity of fascist dictators. These phenomena belong to the realm of the absurd, illustrating the irrationality and cruelty of the world. These films also affirm the value of pointing out the absurdity dramatically, of satire for the purpose of social amelioration.

The selection of Allen's films range from 1973 to 1991 (the first half of his career) in the postmodern era; his expression of the absurd reflects events and phenomena such as the Cold War, the arms race, the Holocaust, and nuclear weaponry. *Sleeper* (1973) expresses Allen's sense of the absurdity of a world in which technological developments distance humans from one another rather than bringing them closer. Allen's brand of humor takes ideas to a silly extreme, or *reductio ad absurdum*. In *Sleeper*, even the bananas we eat are three times larger than ourselves. In pursuing our goal of efficiency, our use of technology outstrips human dimensions and fails to satisfy true human needs. Chaplin exerts a powerful influence on Allen, who is grateful for the "genius" of his predecessor and also aware that his own comedy expresses the different concerns of a later era. Allen defines his difference from Chaplin by saying: "I came along after Freud when the playing field had shifted to the psyche. It was interior. What was interesting to people suddenly was the psyche."[3] Instead of the chases and butt kicks which were uproariously funny gags during Chaplin's period, now the wild goose chases of the chaotic postmodern mind provide entertainment for those who recognize in Allen's characters their own mental contortions. Unlike Chaplin's films, Allen's convey no sense that the cinematic texts constitute solutions to the postmodern conflicts they invoke.

Although funny, the comedy of the absurd also contains serious aspects that tend to elevate it above other forms of humor. Monty Python's troupe of merry pranksters makes fun of our pretenses of civility, suggesting that the whole structure of civilization rests upon hypocritical platitudes. Samuel Beckett's characters mock our need to find meaning, while at the same time they dramatize our inability to live without it. *Absurdism* can be defined as an awareness of the human propensity to seek meaning in a meaningless, indifferent, irrational universe. There are at least three serious aspects to such a proposition: (1) humans are doomed to failure in their spiritual/emotional quests, (2) humans are aware that their quests are futile but continue to seek meaning anyway, regardless of this awareness, and (3) the world's fallen condition is sad, since humans can conceive of a safer world with kinder people, but remain unable to construct it. Many comedians have a strong sense of the absurd, but as William Hutchings wrote, Allen is the foremost popularizer of the absurd during postmodern times, as Chaplin was an avatar of the absurd during modern times. Whether in the physical modes of Charlie Chaplin or the metaphysical modes of Woody Allen, any comic writer/director who wants to deliver a serious message amid hilarious jokes about the human condition faces large challenges.

Chaplin struggled to integrate his social messages with his comic business; the greatest challenge of his craft was blending genres. Although he was tremendously gifted at creating pathos (*City Lights, Limelight*) and humor (*The Pilgrim, The Circus*, and the many one- and two-reel shorts), and even produced a compelling serious drama (*A Woman of Paris: A Drama of Fate*), he was less adept at attaching democratic sentiments to his plots in convincing ways, although this was his stated intention (*Modern Times, The Great Dictator, Monsieur Verdoux*). The problem was related to his working across the transition period from silent films to talkies. His background training in vaudevillian theatre and early short films made him an expressive pantomimist in a compelling persona. Moving to the sound era as writer and actor required a new characterization of this persona, one who could no longer be the silent Tramp whose eloquence of gesture produced a universal appeal. Speaking detracted from that universality. Writing speeches that conveyed a social conscience challenged and changed Chaplin's concept of the Tramp as a scofflaw underdog. The Tramp was a worldwide phenomenon with a huge fan base; it was difficult, if not ultimately impossible, for Chaplin to leave him behind without losing his own identity and success. From *Modern Times* to *Limelight*, Chaplin struggles for a convincing way to develop the Tramp into a citizen with a social conscience. *The Great Dictator* and *Monsieur Verdoux* have immense appeal because of their comic characterizations of evil individuals (a dictator and a serial killer) as well as their sophisticated parallel editing of plots and subplots (*Dictator*) and multiple simultaneous marriages (*Verdoux*); however, they lack credibility as social-message films because of their failure to integrate their comedy with their serious components.

Being trained in physical comedy is not, however, the only reason for Chaplin's writing difficulty. His art was limited by its focus on himself; any social message that he wanted to express was constrained by having only himself as its mouthpiece.[4] Furthermore, his narcissism and sensitivity sometimes caused him to react strangely, or perhaps overreact, to events in his life that he then transmuted into art. *Monsieur Verdoux* is such a case. Because of Chaplin's pro–Russian speechmaking in 1942–43, his friendships with exiled Communists, and his failure to become a U.S. citizen, the FBI was convinced he was a Communist, and baited him accordingly. In the same period, aspiring actress Joan Barry won a paternity suit despite the fact that blood tests proved that her child was not sired by Chaplin. The two situations deeply embittered Chaplin to America and to women. *Monsieur Verdoux* is the product of the emotional abyss into which he sunk. In "Notes for Verdoux," he wrote the following propositions:

> When all the world turns against a man he becomes holy.
> It is more important to understand crime than to condemn it.
> Good is in everything—even evil. Evil has its attendant good.
> Violence is patience's last resort.
> A reputation is the concern of cooks and butlers.[5]

Although it is interesting for a certain kind of artist to explore the psychopathology of a criminal mind, Chaplin did not explore psychology, but rather proselytized against abstract enemies. Verdoux was the "holy man" of the first proposition above, who did evil for the sake of the greater good. Specifically, he killed women so that he would be able one day to say on the witness stand that America is the greatest murderer of all. Since it was America that had turned against Chaplin, it was America that Chaplin must pillory, using the strongest weapon he possessed, his art. Using art for revenge is never the recipe for a good film, and *Verdoux* suffers because of it.

On the other hand, Allen achieves a desirable integration of comedy and serious messages, or comedy and substantive drama, in several key films of his canon (*Crimes and Misdemeanors, Shadows and Fog, Annie Hall, Manhattan*). There are many reasons for this difference, but I will focus on two at present: one having to do with the appearance of the two personae, and the other, the different ways in which their directors construct plots. First, Chaplin's persona combined elements of vulnerability and strength that showed in his walk, posture, and gestures, but he was not very humorous in speech. In contrast, Allen's persona showed funny and serious elements in the way that he moved *and* talked. It is very funny to hear profound pronouncements about the futility of life delivered by a nerd in a stuttering Brooklyn accent. In his writing, Allen combines funny and sad in classic two-part sentences such as, "God is silent; now if only man would shut up." Chaplin's Tramp was humorous in appearance and movement; Allen's schlemiel was funny in appearance, movement, and speech.

Second, whereas Chaplin writes classical-style linear plots centered on the plight of an individual (usually played by himself), Allen writes postmodern-style plots that compare the problems of two or more people. The double plot (one comic, one serious) is his most effective device for achieving this blend. For example, *Shadows and Fog* (1991) contrasts the Woody character being persecuted by fascists with a lighter subplot involving the love problems of a clown and a sword swallower. *Crimes and Misdemeanors* (1989) juxtaposes a tragic murder plot with a comic misdemeanors subplot, one which comments on the main action by insinuating that crimes begin with misdemeanors—we all have the capacity and tendency to commit evil or harmful acts. The prologue of *Melinda and Melinda* (2004) states Allen's intention to compare comic and tragic visions of life as two artists discuss their different choices of genre. The film proceeds to cut between two plots using the same characters and situation, which come out differently based on the director's choice of tragedy or comedy. *Manhattan* (1979) pits the Woody character's infatuation with a young girl and his desire for monogamy against his best friend's messy adulteries and willful disregard for the health of his marriage.

This graceful blending and counterpointing didn't come to Allen immediately or easily. It took ten years of filmmaking before he began to understand how to blend serious and comic elements. His early career consists of silly comedy; his middle period contains romantic comedies, chamber films, and existentialist dramas; in his late career, he turns to darker comedy and several dramas on the recurring themes of murder, betrayal, and depression. In the early period, from *What's New Pussycat* (1965) to *Love and Death* (1975), some of the movies contain serious themes, as the title of the latter indicates, but he didn't know how to integrate them with comedy. Allen spoke to Richard Schickel about his struggle: "*Love and Death* was a film in which I wanted to talk about love and death in a comic way. But I failed to communicate that to an audience because I chose a very broad format.... There is a certain sense of the futility of life and the ... the transience of love, and the inconstancy of love and the difficulty of love, and the pathos and tragedy of death and, and how it haunts all our affairs.... But the film was too light and silly for anyone to respond to that aspect of it."[6]

Allen actually prefers tragedy to comedy for its capacity to make a greater impact on the audience. "When comedy approaches a problem, it kids it but it doesn't resolve it. Drama works through it in a more emotionally fulfilling way.... There's something immature, something second-rate in terms of satisfaction when comedy is compared to drama."[7] Exploring his taste for seriousness, Allen wrote and directed three chamber films between 1978 and 1988: *Interiors, September,* and *Another Woman.* As with *Love and Death,* however, he felt that audiences did not understand his dramatic vision, blaming it on his own inexpertise. In 2007, reflecting on the chamber films, he enumerates his mistakes: the films were too cerebral and lacked action, the characters were too cold, and he didn't exploit his medium of film but instead wrote them as if they were stage plays.[8] Fundamentally, the problem of the chamber films is that they don't contain his authentic voice—which is best suited to expressing such depressing situations in a hybrid seriocomic tone.[9]

Starting with *Annie Hall* (1977), Allen finds his stride in the proper vehicle for him: blended comedy and substantive drama in which he starts with a serious premise and lightens it with frequent jokes of a verbal, visual, and situational kind. In that film, the sting of Alvy Singer's failure with Annie is not exactly compensated for, but at least made tolerable, by the character's reaching out to the audience (in speeches made directly to the camera) to share his very human ambivalence about whether relationships are worth the pain they cause. The comedy of this film is situated not only in clever narrative devices such as satirizing "date talk" (by showing in subtitles what the characters are really thinking) but also in the Aristotelian sense of ending on a happy note: Alvy enjoys a friendly reunion with Annie and vows to continue looking for love.

In addition to their love of the absurd and their penchant for tragedy, Chaplin and Allen are linked by their identities as true auteurs. The phrase "big auteurs" in this book's subtitle refer to the fact that they are the best-known auteurs in all of American comedy. Auteurs are filmmakers who are said to author their films because they control all or most aspects of the work: they are director and writer, and sometimes star and producer. It is unusual for writer/directors to also star in their pictures, but doing so puts a definitive personal stamp on their work. Auteurs are recognizable by their unique style and their thematic preoccupations.[10] Chaplin's recurrent theme is the dignity of the Little Man, or commoner, in the face of upper-class condescension. Allen's is the difficulty of psychic survival (especially for Jewish urban intellectuals) in a world that is utterly indifferent to individuals' wellbeing.

During their decades-long heydays, Allen and Chaplin wrote, directed, and starred in most of their films.[11] Both insisted on creative autonomy and got it, Chaplin at First National and United Artists studios and Allen at United Artists, Orion, and now at Gravier and Perdido Productions. By writing and directing, they control the images and ideas that they wish to portray; by acting, they become a popular persona that is repeated, with changes, throughout their careers. Long exposure to these personae helps audiences to know and sometimes adore them—although some of the Woody personae are more relatable than adorable. Their names are bywords for certain personality traits and classic situations in which they find themselves; they are easily recognizable icons of popular culture. "Charlie Chaplin" calls to mind a shabby Tramp kicking someone in the rear, pretending he didn't as he saunters away nonchalantly. "Woody Allen" might conjure up a worried face looking directly at the camera while whining about how difficult it is to find meaning and satisfaction in this chaotic world. In his early career, Chaplin was arguably the most recognizable person in the whole world.[12] Allen's audience is more urban than Chaplin's, which limits his audience somewhat; therefore, his films are not as widely known as were Chaplin's in his time.[13]

Chaplin and Allen, along with Buster Keaton, Spike Lee, Jerry Lewis, and Mel Brooks, are the half-dozen American comedy auteurs who embody true auteur status[14] by being actors, directors, and writers of their material— what I'll call the trifecta of auteur filmmaking. Unlike Keaton (twenty-one trifectas), Brooks (twelve trifectas), Lewis (ten trifectas) and Lee (nine), Chaplin and Allen produced dozens of films in that capacity. Chaplin directed, wrote, and starred in sixty-six films, including one- and two-reelers and feature length. Allen had directed and written forty-nine films at the time this book went to press, of which he starred in thirty-one.[15] These tallies don't count the films in which they filled one or two of the capacities and not the third. Other auteurs usually fill two of the three roles, such as Judd Apatow, the Coen Brothers, and Steve Martin, but Chaplin and Allen are the only ones who consistently perform all three roles over decades' worth of work.

Even in Europe, Allen and Chaplin are virtually unrivalled in this regard, possibly only by Jacques Tati, whose Monsieur Hulot pictures he scripted, acted in, and directed. Roberto Benigni co-wrote, starred in, and directed *Life Is Beautiful* (1997), giving a Benigni stamp to the work, but one such film does not an auteur make. As for the silent era, during his fertile period of the early 1920s, Buster Keaton wrote, directed, and starred in all of his work: twenty-one short films. His persona, known as The Great Stone Face, had in his heyday nearly as much popularity as Chaplin's Little Tramp. He continued to direct and star, but did not write his feature-length films of the later 1920s. By signing with Metro-Goldwyn-Mayer Studios in 1928, Keaton lost control of his product, being allowed minimal writing, directing, or producing tasks. His popularity didn't last as long as Chaplin's, and did not carry over as successfully into the sound era. Silent stars Harry Langdon, Harold Lloyd, and Fatty Arbuckle also created memorable personae but their careers also lost momentum with the arrival of the talkies.

Besides being true auteurs, Allen and Chapin share the quality of being the Little Man, a persona that each adopted and perfected in his own way. Their popular comic personae are based on a sense of marginality. The Little Man is a comic archetype: he is an unimportant person but one who is imbued with a special aura of defiance and creativity.[16] The Little Man became a favorite character from the very beginning of filmmaking (and is, of course, carried over from the literary medium).[17] Outlaw, oddball, or loner, he entertains by appealing to our repressed anti-cultural desires.[18] The Little Man appears "eccentric, childlike, mad, and/or creative and fantasizing."[19] As such, he expresses our desire to transcend hardship, suffering, and persecution.

Chaplin's Little Man persona was called the Tramp, a character who is always getting in and out of trouble, who loves and helps ladies, asserts his dignity against all slights, and is ever resourceful, even when inebriated. The Tramp's innate dignity and humanity contrast with the soulless toffs and brutal he-men he meets. To get out of a scrape, or just to have fun, he can impersonate most anyone (cops, women, toffs, preachers) and anything (a tree in *Shoulder Arms*, a porcupine in *Behind the Screen*, a giant chicken in *The Gold Rush*, a mechanical doll in *The Circus*). His stunts push the laws of physics to the very limit, as when a small log cabin he shares with Big Jim becomes a seesaw balancing on the edge of a precipitous cliff while they slip back and forth across the floor. He will do anything to assist a lady: street cleaning and boxing an opponent twice his size to earn money for the Flower Girl in *City Lights*, or the ultimate noble act of procuring the promise of the girl's suitor to marry her in *The Circus* (when he himself was in love with her). His dignity can be funny, as when he is offended by Merna's lack of table manners in *The Circus*, or it can be moving, as in *The Gold Rush*, when he prepares for the date that Georgia promised him by earning money to buy supper for her and her three friends, fixing a humble meal, and waiting past midnight while she gallivants with others, having totally forgotten the promise. When he locates her at the tavern, he does not get angry (exhibiting true dignity); instead, he promises her he'll come back a millionaire.

Allen's Little Man has similar pretenses to bigness, but they are verbal rather than physical, and soon squelched when he faces another man who is large or carries a weapon (*Love and Death*, *Bananas*, *Take the Money and Run*). Early in his career, Allen's Little Man was a *schlemiel*, a Yiddish word for a clumsy, awkward, unlucky person: a fool. However unlucky, this fool is endearing because he maintains hope and faith in the goodness of the world, despite all evidence to the contrary. Allen's schlemiel is a lascivious man who is always on the lookout for sexual relationships. He is handicapped by any number of unpleasant conditions and personal tragedies, including unemployment, illness, and the unkindness or downright cruelty of bosses, exes, and family members. Like the Tramp, he is indomitable; he falls down and always gets back in the saddle. Also like the Tramp, he goes to great lengths to win a girl's heart, including fighting dictators (*Bananas*, *Sleeper*, *Love and Death*), trying to impersonate Humphrey Bogart (*Play It Again, Sam*), and risking arrest by making love in public places for the sake of his wife's sexual perversion (*Everything You Always Wanted to Know About Sex*).

As the Woody persona grows from innocence to experience over the course of Allen's film career, his schlemiel gradually morphs from what Menachem Feuer calls the "unabashedly lighthearted" to the "serious and lighthearted." In his later work, Allen leaves the schlemiel behind altogether, assimilating this Jewish archetypal figure into mainstream culture, even casting WASPy men such as Kenneth Branagh and Owen Wilson to play his part. When his protagonists "achieve a type of freedom that lacks any form of irony," then, according to Feuer, the films end with "non-Jewish humor."²⁰ In such films, Allen loses his distinctive postmodern sensibility as he defaults to his nostalgia for innocence and romance (and perhaps desire for assimilation), thus losing the bite that makes his work distinctive.²¹ In order to examine the mixture of comic and serious modes, I have chosen Allen's middle-career films—such as *Shadows and Fog* and *Zelig*—that contain the more serious schlemiels. After this period, from about 1992 on (the start of Allen's sex scandal), the persona loses the lightheartedness and can be downright negative, such as the misogynistic writer Gabe in *Husbands and Wives* (1992), narcissistic Harry in *Deconstructing Harry* (1997), and cynical Boris Yelnikov (Larry David) in *Whatever Works* (2009).

No matter how bleak the worldview of some of the Woody personae, they all have in common a black humor that mitigates their pain by pointing out the ironies in their respective situations. Allen's humor is characterized by the juxtaposition of the metaphysical with the mundane: for example, his parents' values are "God and carpeting." One of his characters muses, "what if everything is an illusion and nothing exists? In which case, I definitely overpaid for my carpet."²² Even the most sensitive topics receive this treatment: "How the hell do I know why there were Nazis?" Mickey Sachs's father thunders, "I don't know how the can opener works."²³ The effect of such juxtapositions is to make fun of human striving for transcendence of the everyday. However much we aspire, we are mired in the material realities of existence, and limited by human frailty. Allen's protagonists would like to believe in God, but are underwhelmed by the evidence: "If it turns out that there is a God, I don't think he is evil. I think that the worst you can say about him is that basically he's an underachiever" (*Love and Death*). Allen applies the same deflating mechanism to every human aspiration, including love and art. This does not mean that his personae don't continue to strive for something better. Indeed, it is the continued aspiration of the persona for love and art, all the way from 1965 to 2019, that keeps audiences watching. Being able to create a *Wonder Wheel* at age eighty-two proves that Allen is still in love with the magic of the medium and the beauty of living, despite his heightened awareness of suffering—much intensified by scandal.

Chaplin and Allen's Little Men personae share a pariah status due to their ethnic and economic characteristics. Chaplin's penniless Tramp was defined by his defiance of social order, Allen's schlemiel by his angst over an absurd universe that has no moral order, and is particularly unkind to Jews. Young Chaplin's sense of marginality originated in a poverty-stricken, fatherless childhood in South London; Allen's originated in an emotionally scarring upbringing, especially by his Jewish mother, in Midwood, Brooklyn. As Hannah Arendt wrote: though not Jewish, Chaplin was often mistaken for and scapegoated as a Jew because of the pariah qualities of his Tramp figure and rumors about his ancestors.²⁴ His paternal grandmother was a gypsy, and gypsies were often presumed to be Jewish at the time of the Holocaust. Morris Dickstein said that Chaplin may as well have been Jewish for all he suffered: "Chaplin's early life was so painful he didn't have to be Jewish; the memory of indignity was enough to fuel his genius."²⁵ For Arendt, the Tramp and the Jewish pariah are linked because they are both suspect persons in a world whose social benefits are denied them due to their looks and background. For Dickstein, the "Little Yid" and the Tramp are linked by the fact of their dwelling in a modern urban setting where they can pass as something other than what they are. The anonymity of urban living means that they can try on different roles, which they do in order to pass as Gentile (Allen) or middle class (Chaplin): "The Tramp's fluidity, protean nature, and adaptability are also characteristic of the Jew who is trying to pass."²⁶ Allen's persona does not attempt to disguise his Jewishness, but does yearn for assimilation. He dates Gentile women and likes to parody Jewish stereotypes. He shares the artistic tastes and intellectual preoccupations of a certain set of privileged upper-middle-class New Yorkers living on the Upper East Side, the wealthiest neighborhood of Manhattan that was traditionally dominated by WASP families.²⁷

Because early childhood experiences set the stage for conflicts that artists attempt to work through, it is helpful to learn about the filmmakers' early lives. Charles Spencer Chaplin was born April 16, 1889, in South London to Hannah and Charles Chaplin, Sr., both music hall performers. Chaplin Sr. was a popular performer, but his job involved drinking with the customers, and he soon became addicted to drink. When their father left the small family (Hannah, Chaplin, and his older brother, Sydney), Chaplin was a toddler of two. He lived with his father again only briefly (two months) at the age of nine. This experience provided a painful education about the life of a raging alcoholic and his co-dependent mistress. Drink would never become a problem in the auteur's own life. Meanwhile, Hannah lost her singing voice and she struggled to maintain herself and the children with nursing and sewing jobs. Chaplin and Sydney took whatever work they could find, but ended up in Lambeth Workhouse when Chaplin was seven. Hannah developed mental illness that was aggravated by malnutrition. She was confined to Cane Hill Asylum when Chaplin was nine; the experience of losing his mother and watching her lose her mind were major traumas of his youth. In the majority of his films, he would repeat the theme of a young man saving a desperate woman, because in real life, according to psychobiographer Stephen Weissman, Chaplin was working through the helpless feeling of being unable to save his mother.²⁸

Young Chaplin's sense of helplessness was compounded by the fear that he would inherit her mental illness.²⁹ This fear contributed to the depression and anxiety that plagued him throughout his long life. At age five, Chaplin stood in for his mother when she lost her voice on stage. At age nine, he decided to become an actor. His father found him a job clogging with the Eight Lancashire Lads. On the road with this troupe, Chaplin experienced more homesickness. Back in London, he auditioned for the play *Sherlock Holmes*, in which he made a name as a funny pageboy. Sydney got a job with Fred Karno's comedy company and secured his little brother an audition when Chaplin was eighteen. With his small, erect stature, his comic timing and agility, Chaplin was funnier than the average vaudevillian, so he was selected to tour on the North American vaudeville circuit. During a New York performance he was discovered by a Keystone Studio representative and offered a $150-per-week contract to act in one-reel films. By the time of his second film, Chaplin had already picked out the Tramp's outfit and the idiosyncrasies that would last for the rest of the Tramp's lifetime of nearly thirty years. It was the bigness of the shoes that required him to turn out his toes, making his walk a waddle. The tightness of the jacket perhaps reminded him to constantly puff out his chest, suggesting the dignity of the little man within. The bamboo cane he twirled like a big swell. With these simple accoutrements, the elegant homeless man was born.

Allan Stewart Konigsberg was born December 1, 1935, in Brooklyn, New York, to Nettie (bookkeeper) and Martin Konigsberg (jewelry engraver and jack of all trades). Allen still seems disturbed by not knowing exactly what his father did for work.[30] Allen's grandparents immigrated to the Lower East Side from Austria (Nettie's side of the family) and Russia (Martin's); they spoke Yiddish, Hebrew, and German. As in *Radio Days*, Allen's childhood home was filled with many relatives and a lot of yelling. But Allen did not become unhappy until he was about five, when he suddenly realized that life ends in death.[31] The point is nicely dramatized in *Annie Hall* when little Alvy's mother takes him to a therapist because he has stopped doing homework. When asked why, he responds that the universe is expanding, and one day it will explode, so what's the point? The fact that young Allen was nearly strangled to death by a babysitter (his relative) did not help his existential feeling of radical uncertainty and distrust.[32] Allen's parents fought constantly, creating an unstable environment; he and his sister, Letty, expressed fear that the parents would separate, leaving them bereft of their home. However volatile, it was still their family, and, like any other children, they needed a home.

In Robert Weide's *Woody Allen: A Documentary* (2012), Nettie Konigsberg admits on camera that she did not behave warmly towards the young Allen, and in fact, she beat him every day. He was an active, inquisitive boy, and she said she didn't have the right personality to handle him. By his own choice, he took his meals alone in the basement. He began acting out at school, disengaging from all subjects except those that held an intrinsic interest, such as playing the clarinet, playing baseball, and learning magic tricks.

Starting at fifteen, he wrote gags for an agent who sold them to newspapers. He changed his name to Woody Allen, and was already earning more than his parents' wages combined. From then on, he was steadily employed for the rest of his life. From the outset an independent type, seventeen-year-old Allen hired a professional jazz musician, Gene Sedric, to give him clarinet lessons in his own bedroom.

At nineteen, Allen married his first wife, Harlene Rosen, for two reasons: to have sex, and to get out of his parents' house. The marriage lasted for three years. Harlene introduced Allen to philosophy by sharing her college reading list. Allen began the film programs at New York University and, later, at City College of New York, but dropped out from lack of interest. Besides sharing intellectual interests with Harlene, Allen married because he wanted intercourse, and as he tells the camera in Robert Weide's documentary: in those days, marriage was the only way to have it. After you'd been to the ball games, been to the restaurants and the movies, there was nothing left to do but get married. Yet sex with Harlene became the source of many of the unkindest jokes in his comedy routine; she eventually sued him for calling her "Quasimodo." There ensued a bitter divorce. Allen's youth is characterized by ambition, sorrow, independence, creativity, and a sense of persecution—all the ingredients for the black humor that defines him to this day.

As with any artist, our two filmmakers are constantly using art to work through childhood issues. In a long-distance analysis of the person through examination of his art and persona, Sigmund Freud said that Chaplin, even more clearly than most, is working out his childhood scenario of poverty, helplessness, and indignity throughout his oeuvre, trying to compensate for the humiliation these conditions caused.[33] Although most of his films were shot in his Hollywood studio, their urban settings are reminiscent of his South London childhood, where he had to learn how to scam for money (think, for instance, of the Tramp's smashing windows so that he can repair them for pay, in *The Kid*). Young Chaplin also had to learn how to dodge the police. It is a comedy cliché that the police are stupider than the criminals they're meant to catch, but Chaplin adds to the trope his peculiar ability to cajole and befriend authority figures.

Another frequent theme is the pursuit of a sweetheart he believes is pure and innocent (Georgia in *The Gold Rush* was anything but pure, though naïve Charlie does not know that). For this purpose, the younger the girl, the better. Weissman believes that Chaplin's first brief romantic relationship with another vaudevillian, Hetty Kelly, when he was nineteen and she fifteen, set the tone for his love ideal for all time.[34] Although the unconscious element of his attraction toward young women was emotional—a longing for his own lost innocence—he described the attraction as primarily physical. Hetty was "a slim gazelle, with a shapely oval face, a bewitching full mouth and beautiful teeth."[35] In his 1964 autobiography, Chaplin wrote, "Although I had met [Hetty] but five times, and scarcely any of our meetings had lasted longer than twenty minutes, that brief encounter affected me for a long time."[36] She turned down his marriage proposal because she was too young to marry. In Chaplin's films, the Tramp pursues his love interest aggressively, often forcing the girl to say *yes*, as when he pulls a demurring Edna Purviance by the crook of his cane into the Town Hall for a license (*The Immigrant*). In real life, Chaplin also called the shots. He seduced his second wife, sixteen-year-old Lita Grey, by arranging for her to take a steam bath in his mansion.[37]

Chaplin worked through feelings of injustice, abandonment, and inadequacy (which he denied), by giving his Tramp wiliness, survival skills, charm, unexpected success with the ladies, and a physical ability to escape all threatening situations. Allen in turn worked through his own psychological issues in his films. In Allen's view, the world is a terribly unkind and unpredictable place without any moral structure or other kind of meaning. Growing up in the shadow of the Holocaust, Allen felt that all people are potential enemies until they do something to earn his trust. Famously, he said of the Holocaust that it was not surprising that such an event could happen, only that it hadn't happened sooner.[38] This view was born and cultivated in the bosom of his family, and accentuated by Allen's reading of existentialists, absurdists, and other alienated men (some favorites were Dostoyevsky, Tolstoy, Kafka, S.J. Perelman, Robert Benchley, Saul Bellow, J.D. Salinger, Kierkegaard, Sartre, Camus).[39] In Allen's personal philosophy, the best one can do in the face of the cruel universe is to hope for luck, which, in his mind, means finding women who say *yes* to sex and love, and finding work consistent with one's artistic principles and values (in accordance with the existentialist principle of authenticity). Film after film shows the Woody persona quitting (or wanting to quit) his day job to pursue his art (*Manhattan, Anything Else, Shadows and Fog, Midnight in Paris*). Each film also features the persona getting very attractive, young, and smart women to love him and go to bed with him.

Both Allen and Chaplin's personae are comical because the physical appearance of each actor seems to contradict his success, making the persona's achievements seem improbable. But this is the combination that appeals to every admiring viewer. We relate to the ordinary person who shouldn't be able to succeed, but does (a projection of ourselves). Chaplin's Tramp is dirty, penniless, and homeless, yet often manages to charm people and get the girl. Allen's schlemiel is nerdy, needy, and depressed, yet manages to make friends and conquests, and even attain fame. Despite this penchant for success, time and again, Chaplin leaves his Tramp outside the circle of mainstream bourgeois contentment represented by marriage, kids, and the white picket fence (*City Lights, The Kid, The Circus, Modern Times*). Central to his identity is the fact that the Tramp never settles down. Nor is Allen's persona content with the girl he gets. As Douglas Brode remarks, "Woody very often gets the girl in the end, but that only adds to all his problems.... [He] may win so far as the world is concerned, but remains the loser inside his psyche."[40] There are at least two reasons for this refusal of romantic conventionality. First, the unhappy achiever trades on the appeal of a seriocomic persona. A sad clown is much more interesting than a cheery one. The pathos element gives the work its seriousness. To be able to capture both the comic and tragic elements of life in one film is rare, although it is artistically desirable to portray the full emotional range of human experience.

Second, the Tramp and the schlemiel aren't happy characters because their creators are not happy men. Traumatized in youth, Chaplin's depression and anxiety pursued him throughout his long lifetime. His first son said his father was aware of the tragedy of happenstance in life: one wrong turn and you ruin your life.[41] Biographer Richard Carr said that having his mother wrenched away at an early age "led [Chaplin] to keep all future relationships at something of a safe distance."[42] Biographer Simon Louvish could be describing Chaplin's melancholic core with this fine description of his alter ego: "The Tramp, it appears, cannot abide reality, with all its dangers, its trammels, its looming disappointments. Outwardly indomitable, and able to survive the slings and arrows, there is nevertheless a defeated soul inside."[43] In Allen's case, depression and anxiety are so central to his worldview that he intensifies the feeling into several suicidal characters among his films (Mickey in *Hannah and Her Sisters*, Duane in *Annie Hall*, Boris in *Whatever Works*). "I think I've burned over a low flame of depression my whole lifetime … like the pilot light's always on," Allen told Eric Lax.[44]

Chaplin and Allen's childhood developments share many features. Both were melancholy, had precarious home lives, troubled parents, schoolyard bullying due to their small stature, and early existential traumas (Chaplin watching his mother go insane, his life in the poorhouse and on the streets; Allen watching his parents fight every day, his perception that life is meaningless). But their differences are as interesting as their similarities. The primary aspect of their comic execution that sets them apart is that Chaplin, in the tradition of vaudeville and slapstick, excels in physical comedy, whereas Allen excels primarily as a verbal, intellectual jokester who was galvanized by the sexual liberation movement of the 1960s. Yet each tried to master the other half of the comic toolkit: Chaplin took on intellectual comedy and Allen, physical. With the encouragement of his manager, Jack Rollins, Allen overcame his early aversion to acting and speaking in front of an audience. He used to be so petrified of "dying" during his act (in the comedy sense of failing to amuse) that he would vomit before taking the stage. But Rollins saw in Allen a great actor with a unique comic voice.

In his early movies, Allen brought to life a postmodern form of slapstick. Only occasionally (*Sleeper*) does he rely on old formula gags like slipping on a banana peel. There is an intellectual aspect to Allen's slapstick when the persona gets involved with machines and political organizations that are maniacal and beyond his control. In *Bananas, Everything You Always Wanted to Know About Sex, Love and Death,* and *Sleeper,* Allen accentuates the physical awkwardness of his character by getting him into adventures that are over his head. Fielding Mellish has to lead a gang of guerrillas to overtake a Central American dictatorship. Boris Grushenko tries to kill Napoleon because his wife desires it. And Miles Monroe tries to overthrow the dictatorship of the Central Federation of States because it will please Luna Schlosser (Diane Keaton), and perhaps give them a habitable environment that is not a technocracy. Although decreasing in frequency as his career progresses, and sometimes overlooked in film criticism, Allen's physical comedy is very funny. His persona acts out the inner klutziness of every viewer: humans undergoing their most-feared humiliations. The words "awkward" and "shame" take on new meaning in the Woody persona's social and physical bumbling. But with *Annie Hall* in 1977, Allen began to adopt a new kind of humor that was far less reliant on physicality and more on the characters' emotional states. Plots became more realistic, less fantastical, and locations were closer to home, often recognizably New York.

Similarly, when Chaplin emerged into the world of talkies around the mid–1930s, he had a great desire to be taken seriously. This required that he and the persona verbalize his ideas. He began to write screenplays based on one-theme social messages such as these: The Machine Age is killing our collective soul (*Modern Times*). Fascist regimes are led by incompetent, insecure bullies (*The Great Dictator*). Capitalism kills (*Monsieur Verdoux*). The Red Scare is a heinous abuse of power (*A King in New York*). As the prevalence of physical comedy in his films decreased, Chaplin's urge to make a social difference increased. Although he excels at creating pathos in a Tramp who maneuvers on the margins of society, Chaplin is not as adept as Allen at integrating comedy and tragedy, or comedy and social criticism. In eloquent silence lies the essence of the Tramp's charisma. Yet his stunning pathos carried his genre experiments over several bumps. As his *Great Dictator* costar, Jack Oakley, said of Chaplin: he had created a new genre, the "dramady."[45] Chaplin's son concurred: "Dad has always managed carefully to keep his comedies balanced on the very borderline of tragedy."[46] But talking and speechifying had the tendency to reduce the pathos inherent in the Tramp's character.

Each auteur was a man of his time, skilled in the comic modality that best expressed the issues of that period. Chaplin's physicality expressed a sense of physical danger and physical pleasure as these were understood in the early twentieth century, with its material conditions of hardship, such as the Depression, starvation, unemployment, and fighting in World Wars I and II. On the other hand, Allen's wit expresses the sense of intellectual and moral decay that constitutes the artistic preoccupation of the second half of the century. The sexual revolution posed a threat to constancy in sexual relationships. Awareness of the Holocaust and anti–Semitism permeates several of his films. The surveillance and alienation of the Digital Age loom large. Nuclear annihilation is always a possibility. Self-hating Jews and a Jewish sense of separation from God and the religious tradition of their people are also key late twentieth-century issues, as more Jews assimilate into mainstream culture. With intellectual comedy as his milieu, Allen was able to lighten the tone by the mere physical presence of his funny nebbish: a little man who fights an extremely large universe, which is ever indifferent to his plight.

The objective of this book is to explore Chaplin and Allen's appreciation of the absurd, to evaluate their blending of serious and comic elements, and to contrast their expression in the two distinct eras to which they belong, the modern and postmodern. To lay a foundation for this endeavor, the remainder of this introduction will describe historical events and cultural phenomena that give rise to ideological aspects of modernism and postmodernism.

Modernism has a close link with film history, as they are born at approximately the same time, the mid–1890s.[47] Film was one of the myriad new technologies that expressed people's enthusiasm for a brave new world in which technology's applications would make life not only easier but also more fun. This new form of entertainment was cheap and could reach the masses. Modernism also shares a philosophical kinship with auteur theory, which assumes our faith in the artist's ability to convey his or her message; faith in the individual's (character's) ability to make meaningful choices; and access to some sort of absolute reality beyond the representations on celluloid. Film was meant to portray life.

In contrast, postmodern film "undermines the image's reference to reality" and heightens the self-reflexive aspects of the medium.[48] Self-reflexivity in this context means that the film calls attention to the construction of the image and its relation to other images in media rather than to external reality. Self-reflexivity in auteur films also means making reference to the filmmaker's other films, and even to his or her own life, as Allen's films often do. Postmodern films make extensive use of homage, pastiche, and intertextuality, assuming that at least some members of the audience know the other films and cultural events to which the movie refers. Postmodern films embrace contradictions of all sorts, including the characters' morals.[49] For example, in an Allen film, the persona is likely to have moral defects, such as his sex-obsession and penchant for young girls, while at the same time his overall moral integrity may be stronger than that of the minor characters. Moral relativity is a preoccupation of the postmodern.

The modernist movement stems from a desire to "make it new," borrowing Ezra Pound's famous epigram. Coming at the end of the Edwardian period in England, and the Gilded Age in America, modernism was a response to world crises that deeply affected our sense of tradition, meaning, and art. If the world was to change so much and so fast, art too must change to accommodate a new reality. World War I is the largest world crisis of the time that gives rise to new art forms. Not only did it obliterate thirty-seven million people, it wiped out the belief of many, especially artists and intellectuals, that war was fought for moral reasons. The war to protect the rights of small nations turned out to be a way for imperial powers to extend their jurisdictions. Awareness of class distinctions within military units disturbed many people: the working class died on the battlefront while the upper class led, often from positions of safety. With their men away fighting, women took charge of their homes and gained outside employment, upsetting the balance of patriarchal power when men came home.[50] Suffragettes won the vote for women. Women smoked, danced, and discussed politics in mixed gender settings. Technological developments, such as the telephone, the airplane, poison gas and explosives, the internal-combustion engine, the large-scale production of electricity, the increased efficiency of industrial organization, all contributed to the commoditization and bureaucratization of modern life and institutions.

How did narrative art respond to such drastic change? By turning the lens inward to reflect human subjectivity, to explore how individuals cope with changing social roles, changing perceptions of human nature, and the ever-increasing sense that God is absent, or somehow insufficient to promote morality in the world. Artists look for God-substitutes, or metanarratives, to explain or contain the world in its chaotic state. For modernists, Art was God. It justified suffering, created meaning, and above all, placed value on the individual's quest for wholeness in a world without eternal verities. In modernism, there was still a sense of individual autonomy, which would be undermined after World War II.

As a narrative artist, Chaplin demonstrates a mix of Victorian and modernist values. His films are Dickensian in their sympathy for the social underdog who fights a brutal class system to earn a few small rights. Chaplin's films do not call for widespread social change; rather, they champion the lone individual who maintains personal dignity in the face of indifferent or cruel institutions. In *Modern Times*, *The Great Dictator*, and *Limelight*, the hero earns dignity at the end when he escapes the authorities (*Modern Times*), speaks truth to power (*The Great Dictator*), and turns in the superb final performance of his life (*Limelight*). In modernism, the universe is not meaningless, compared to how it will seem after the detonation of the atom bomb in 1945. In contrast to postmodern narrative, modern narratives are often closed, with finite, understandable endings, and focused on a few individuals. These individuals might be symbolic or allegoric, as in *The Great Dictator*, but we tend to relate to them as individuals whose successful quests to be taken seriously are meant to provide satisfactory endings of their films. Chaplin demonstrates modernist values by positing the worth of one individual struggling to survive and find meaning, even if it is only the safety of love and a warm place to sleep.

Modern art itself offered a warm place to sleep, in the metaphorical sense that it posited the existence of morality. Frederic Jameson's Marxist critique of postmodernism makes favorable references to the relative morality of modernity. Modernist art "uses parody to imply a moral judgment or a comparison with societal norms"; but postmodernist art "uses pastiche and other forms of juxtaposition without a normative grounding."[51] Jameson writes, "whereas modernism was still minimally and tendentially the critique of the commodity and the effort to make it transcend itself," postmodernism is "the consumption of sheer commodification as a process," or, the victory of commodification over all other spheres of life.[52] Commodification is the transformation of goods, services, ideas, and people into objects of trade. Allen's melancholic voice persistently complains about this flattening of the affect of the postmodern world with its narcissistic, materialistic pursuits: His joke, "Does art imitate life, or does life imitate TV?" expresses the shallow quality of contemporary life. "Not only is there no God, but try getting a plumber on weekends," suggests (to me at least) that a life of material ease and convenience could somehow compensate for the lack of God, but even such a life is not easily attained. Although Allen doesn't pinpoint capitalism per se as the nemesis of the human spirit, his perennial complaint (godlessness equals a lack of morality) relates to the commoditization of contemporary life.

Postmodern narrative imitates the explosion of the A-bomb; it is fragmentary, shattering, and the only tone it can afford to take is one of ironic detachment. The individual is powerless to create meanings, though doing so is one's only hope. Human beings keep trying to make sense of the world, even when they know it is beyond their comprehension, or worse—there is no sense to be made. This is the essence of theatre of the absurd, made famous in plays such as Samuel Beckett's *Waiting for Godot* and Harold Pinter's *The Birthday Party*. In postmodernism, there is a sense of the vastness of world crisis, of its global rather than local or national ramifications. There is no escape from the problems human beings have created on this planet, only temporary diversion through activities such as art, sex, or playing games. Language is slippery; each word or sound means different things to different people. Religion is only a metanarrative told by capitalists to keep the working class docile. Science is also in the service of capitalists. Love is a fraught term, marriages last for shorter periods, and sex is an open topic for discussion and public display. Preteens, teens, and politicians photograph and display their genitalia using smartphones. Artificial intelligence and information technology dominate everyday life: we rely on them in order to execute most of our tasks and to communicate with other human beings. As Miles Monroe indicates in *Sleeper*, the political solution is only temporary; the scientific solution is political. And love? As his affair with Luna Schlosser demonstrates, it is more physical than spiritual, and thus doomed to short duration.

Allen's films bring these postmodern crises to our attention with a mix of seriousness and comedy that does provide momentary relief, if only in the solace that perhaps our fears are universal, or at least shared by the director of the film. We feel less alone and less strange when watching his familiar schlemiel. Allen's quester, the various incarnations of the Woody persona, is unlike Chaplin's persona insofar as he constantly speaks of world crisis, or he speaks of his personal crisis in global terms. Here is Boris Yelnikoff on religion (*Whatever Works*): "It's not the idea behind Christianity I'm faulting, or Judaism, or any religion. It's the professionals who've made it into corporate business. There's big money in the god racket, big money." Or Alvy Singer talking about depression (*Annie Hall*): "I feel that life is—is divided up into the horrible and the miserable. The—the horrible would be like, um, I don't know, terminal cases, you know, and blind people, crippled. I don't know how they get through life. You know, and the miserable is everyone else." Or Harry Block on dishonesty (*Deconstructing Harry*): "All people know the same truth. Our lives consist of how we choose to distort it." An awareness of the doomed state of the world is key to Allen's postmodern style.

Each of the following five chapters pairs a Woody Allen film with a Charlie Chaplin film that addresses a similar theme. Chapter 1, "Modern and Postmodern Circuses in *The Circus* and *Shadows and Fog*," compares Chaplin's *The Circus* and Allen's *Shadows and Fog* to investigate the role of the carnivalesque (reversal of social hierarchies and revelry in the grotesque body) in each director's vision. Carnival gives the upper class the chance to go slumming, and the lower class the opportunity to be appreciated. Because of his time period, we might assume that Allen enjoys greater license to pursue bawdy humor in physical and verbal ways that were off limits to Chaplin. Reading the Tramp's movements carefully, however, we notice a strange anality that subverts conventional representations of bodies, sexuality, and manners. In contrast, Allen's film presents a strange orality suggesting the threat of late capitalist consumerism and voracious desire.[53]

Chapter 2, "Technology and Alienation in *Modern Times* and *Sleeper*," compares threats associated with the Machine and Digital Ages. Both films depict their creators' fear that our ever-increasing use of technology makes incursions upon our humanity. Whereas the Machine Age posed the possibility of man's superannuation by machines (depriving humans of employment and the physical necessities for survival in the Depression economy), the Digital Age as seen through Allen's creative vision translates into a loss of control over one's mental faculties. By computerizing our basic chores, entertainments, and institutional functions, we may gain efficiency, but we lose individualism, critical thinking, and the potential for intimacy and meaning.

Chapter 3, "Master/Slave Dialectic in *The Great Dictator* and *Zelig*," applies Hegel and Nietzsche's philosophies of dominance and submission to films whose protagonists epitomize these extremes. The Dictator of the eponymous film is Master. In Allen's film, the epitome of a Slave is Zelig, an ordinary man who is afraid of everyone and who capitulates to the perceived wishes of each person he meets. Hegel theorizes that the world can progress only by the collision of people, their fight for power, and their eventual creation of symbiosis. Only people's mutual recognition of the other as a human subject like themselves (instead of an object) can elevate them to the next level of development. Chaplin creates a Master and Slave dynamic by playing both parts: this doubling sends the message that we each contain both parts within ourselves. Allen demonstrates the same idea by showing the little tyrant inside the slavish personality.

Chapter 4, "Getting Away with Murder in *Monsieur Verdoux* and *Crimes and Misdemeanors*," explores the origins of morality and conscience in sources other than Church and God. Using recent psychoanalytic theory on pre–Oedipal bonding with the mother, it compares the personality structures of Verdoux (a serial lady-murderer) and Judah Rosenthal (a man who orders a hit on his mistress). This chapter explores the question whether anyone really gets away with murder, even a sociopath like Monsieur Verdoux. The murder theme of these films may speak to the existence of deep-seated aggression or unconscious rage in their creators, which are valid and common responses to the difficulties of the human condition, as well as to the particular challenges of being a celebrity movie director.

Chapter 5, "What Is Love in *Limelight* and *Manhattan*?," explores the stigma around May-December romances and various motives for people to engage in them. Despite their own relationships and marriages with much younger girls and women, Allen and Chaplin break up the romances in these films. Laura Mulvey's theory of the male gaze sheds light on this type of narrative decision, suggesting ways in which gender conditioning creates the male partner's uneasiness in each of the relationships depicted in the films. Chaplin's traditional view of heterosexual marriage as the only vehicle for love contrasts with Allen's more nuanced offering of a variety of romantic combinations that are possible in the postmodern age.

Chapter 6, "Nobility and Ambiguity in Modern and Postmodern Endings," concludes the argument with a comparative analysis of the ten films' endings.

Chaplin and Allen share thematic concerns—how to find love that lasts, how to resist the dehumanization of their times, and how to survive in a world that is grossly unfair—expressed in accordance with their own historical Zeitgeist. Chaplin adopts a comical physicality to resist reification of the individual; he critiques mechanical takeover of basic human functions and bureaucratic indifference to human dignity. Allen issues a metaphysical complaint against the dehumanization inherent in our godless, technocratic, commoditized world. Even though each one draws on his profound experience of dread, both auteurs make these twentieth-century critiques supremely funny. John Lahr wrote, "Both are comic geniuses who give life without actually loving it."[54] Yet for all their similarities, Allen and Chaplin appeal to us in fundamentally different ways. As comedy historian Gerald Mast notes, "the Tramp displays a greater human sensitivity, Allen's persona a greater perceptivity, intellectual awareness, and psychological astuteness."[55] The Tramp's sensitivity demonstrates the power of the individual to resist the slings and arrows of outrageous fortune, as though determination and a good soul are all it takes. The Allen-persona's traits are adaptive to the postmodern experience, for which a sharp intellect and psychological acuity are felt to compensate—though they never really can—for so much that is missing in the realm of spirit and faith. Each filmmaker's persona was a metaphor for his era.

1

Modern and Postmodern Circuses in *The Circus* and *Shadows and Fog*

In film and literature, circuses are rich in symbolism. A writer may use a circus to stand for either the ultimate Real (place of death, id, the unknown) or the paradigmatic Imaginary realm (a space of images, imagination, and deception).[1] A Bakhtinian reading of circuses in these films incorporates all three Lacanian orders of the psyche: the Imaginary, the Symbolic, and the Real. In reversing their hierarchy, Bakhtin's carnivalesque plays havoc with Symbolic boundaries of class. Carnival's revelry in the grotesque body implies Real order categories of id and horror, while carnivalesque practices of illusion belong to the Imaginary order. Elements of carnival can be found in festivals as early as classical times; they acquire different characteristics in different historical moments.

A modernist carnivalesque works within different cultural parameters than a postmodern version. In the modern world of Chaplin's films, sex (and the nude body) can be neither shown nor discussed, only intimated, euphemized, or idealized. By the time of Allen's *Shadows and Fog*, American censors had been allowing sex scenes in films for thirty years.[2] During his initial celebration of this freedom, Allen turned sex into jokes (sex with a sheep in *Everything You Always Wanted to Know About Sex*, sex with soy sauce in *Love and Death*, sex with a machine in *Sleeper*). By the late seventies, however, he had exhausted this vein; his sex jokes took a more philosophical look at human sexuality. The sexuality discourse in *Shadows and Fog* (1991) ranges from the grotesqueness of perversions, to the objectification of women, the destructive nature of lust and the excesses to which it leads, and the deflation of love's spiritual and relational qualities. Whereas modernist film held the idea of sexual consummation outside of the frame as a drive or desire that motivates the characters within, postmodernist film deals with the aftermath of sexual consummation, the post-coital depression of having had too much, too soon, of the wrong thing—only to need more. Postmodernism reveals and critiques the use of people as objects of trade.

The Circus (1928) and *Shadows and Fog* (1991) present circuses as places of opportunity for their protagonists, the Tramp (aka "Charlie") and Kleinman the schlemiel.[3] For the Tramp, the circus is a place to find work and love, although ultimately he chooses to leave because of his essential outsider status. For Kleinman, the circus is a place to escape anti-Semitic persecution and Death itself—clearly impossible feats. In *Shadows and Fog*, the real (non-circus) world is akin to the Holocaust, making the circus a lifeline, whereas in *The Circus*, the circus *is* the real world, defined by competition and class hierarchy. The narrative arc of Chaplin's film fosters our identification with the alienated artist: though inept at performing cliché circus acts, Charlie is brilliant at improvisation. A sentimental melodrama, *The Circus* pits a noble individual with good values against a cold, hierarchical world. Charlie's selfless renunciation of a companion makes him a hero in a modern age. In contrast, postmodern *Shadows and Fog* offers limited opportunities for heroism in a world with insurmountable existential problems. The best one can do is to survive—or merely prolong survival awhile longer—with a little help from magic. While Chaplin's film ends with its hero walking away from the circus, Allen's hero runs to the circus to save his life. These differences in structure and theme align with the different symbolic meanings that the circus contains for each character, and with the different possibilities for narrative resolution available in modern and postmodern modes.

The Circus begins with an equestrienne (Merna Kennedy) missing a jump through a hoop and receiving a rebuke from her stepfather, the Ringmaster (Al Ernest Garcia), who intends to starve her until she performs perfectly. Another hungry person (Chaplin) is watching the sideshows when a thief decides to frame him as a pickpocket. In his flight from the police, the Tramp winds up in the Big Tent, unwittingly performing an act that is funnier than the actual show. The Ringmaster auditions Charlie to play a clown, but Charlie is inept, so he is hired as a lowly property man instead. Ironically, Charlie is so funny as a property man botching his simple tasks that attendance at the circus begins to increase. By now half in love with the endearing misfit, Merna complains that her father is using him for profit. Charlie stands up to the big boss and gets a raise.

When dashing tightrope walker Rex, King of the Air (Harry Crocker), arrives for a job, Merna instantly falls in love. A psychic predicted that she would marry a dark, handsome stranger. Charlie is so depressed by Merna's defection that he can no longer be funny; as a result, the circus loses business, and the exasperated Ringmaster is ready to fire him. One day when Rex is absent, the Ringmaster demands that Charlie replace him. Charlie pays a property man to belay him with an invisible wire and harness, delighting the audience with his supernatural prowess. Charlie appears to float up the ladder, bottom up, and does hair-raising feats on the wire. Then the property man drops the rope, leaving Charlie untethered. Monkeys get loose and attack him, ripping off his pants and biting his nose. Charlie survives this ordeal, only to get fired.

Later that night, the Tramp is camping in the woods. Angry with her father, Merna runs away from the circus, finds Charlie, and asks if she can join him on his travels. Knowing he can't support her, Charlie refuses to take her on the road. He implores Rex to marry Merna. After their wedding the next day, her father asks them to re-join the circus. Merna will only accept if the Ringmaster hires Charlie too. Merna invites Charlie to join her and Rex in their wagon as the circus leaves town, but he refuses, saying, "Two's company, three's a crowd." The Ringmaster tells Charlie to hop on the end wagon. Instead, Charlie remains seated on a crate in the middle of the now abandoned circus ring, watching the wagons roll away. He pouts, contemplating the torn paper star from Merna's broken hoop. Then he crumples it, stands, and kicks it away with his signature back-kick. As the film irises out, the Tramp waddles alone toward the horizon, twirling his cane and giving an insouciant hop.

Whereas *The Circus* establishes setting by bursting *in medias res* through Merna's hoop into the circus ring, *Shadows and Fog* (1991) starts not with the circus itself, but with the town it is visiting. From that point on, the circus (together with its counterpart, the brothel) shares roughly equal screen time with the town's dangerous streets. It is a foggy night in a forlorn Middle-European town, late 1920s.[4] The choice of black-and-white film stock and high-contrast lighting alludes to both film noir and German Expressionism. Diegetic sounds include foghorns, wails, and indistinguishable cries of cats, hyenas, or dying humans. Wisps of fog drift across establishing shots of a tower, a crescent moon, a carriage, and smokestacks half obscuring a huge suspended clock face. Non-diegetic carnival songs written by Kurt Weill for Bertolt Brecht's *The Threepenny Opera* (1928) accentuate the grittiness of the setting. Suddenly, we are thrust into a circle of light over Kleinman's bed as he awakens to thumps on his door. Highlighted by the iconic unshaded light bulb of film noir, groggy Kleinman awakes "from a deep sleep" to confront a gang of vigilantes. His repetition of this phrase raises the question of whether the following sequence of events is a nightmare or reality. As in Kafka's *The Trial*, Kleinman is awakened to learn that he is a wanted man. In *The Trial*, the ruffians charge Josef K with an offense they refuse to name, so he spends the rest of the novel trying to figure out what his crime might be. *The Trial* allegorically expresses a widespread Jewish experience of wariness toward a world that might at any moment persecute you. The same menacing atmosphere applies to Kleinman in his Prague-like town. Although it is set at a time prior to the Holocaust by roughly twenty years, the insidious anti-Semitism of *Shadows and Fog* foreshadows the later event, heightening the film's tone of danger and inhumanity.[5]

Like Josef K's, Kleinman's crime is being Jewish. He doesn't have to do anything wrong in order to attract the attention of the authorities. As Hannah Arendt points out, the pariah figure is always suspect, whether or not he has committed a crime.[6] The vigilantes are searching for a serial killer who is afoot in the town. Kleinman is being tested to see if he will resist the Aryan power structure, but the vigilantes refuse to inform him of his role in the plan. As the film progresses, we learn that the killer is a personification of Death itself—this is why he can't be captured. Iris Bruce asserts that the Killer represents Hitler,[7] and I can detect several parallels between them: his ubiquity, his near-absolute power, and the incomprehensibility of the nature of his evil. Although Kleinman is weak and cowardly, the gang suspects him of treachery, an indication that the Killer is not the only problem in town. In addition to being about a poor clerk striving to get by, *Shadows and Fog* is an allegory about the Holocaust.[8] The title recalls the night-and-fog laws that enabled Nazis to round up Jews under cover of darkness; it also alludes to Alain Resnais' film about concentration camps, *Night and Fog* (1956). The policeman's reference to poisoned-well-theory references an actual historical belief that Jews caused the Black Plague.

Seven minutes into the film, we cut to the parallel plot. The same high-contrast lighting, the dying campfires, and the debris around the circus wagons indicate an ambience as bleak as the death-haunted town. An extreme close-up of the mouth of Paul the Clown (John Malkovich), reflected in a mirror, establishes the uneasy tone of the scene in Paul and Irmy's wagon. Irmy (Mia Farrow) is Paul's sword-swallowing mistress, who wants to quit the circus and have a baby. Paul protests that artists are special people who must not be tied down by family responsibilities. In a snit, he goes to visit the high-wire performer, Marie (Madonna), who seduces him. Irmy bursts in, argues violently with Paul, strikes him, and runs away.

Meanwhile, Kleinman is looking for answers to the questions, what is my job in the vigilante gang, and what is the meaning of life? Hoping to find reasonable answers from the town Doctor (Donald Pleasence), Kleinman instead finds an unbalanced obsessive who anticipates dissecting the Killer's mind to discover the nature of evil. Kleinman thinks the physical body is only one aspect of human existence, asking, "But isn't it possible that under the microscope there's something you could never see?"[9] The Doctor derides him for needing to believe in the existence of the soul or God. As he leaves, Kleinman passes a signboard with a giant eye painted on it, signifying the surveillance of the Jews.

1. The Circus *and* Shadows and Fog

Running away from the circus, Irmy meets a prostitute, Jenny (Lily Tomlin), who has been soliciting in a dark tunnel but readily leaves her "track" to take Irmy home for a meal. Stepping into the brothel is like entering another film; it is full of light, warmth, and people having fun. The ladies banter cheerfully about the weird johns they service, unquestioningly welcoming another female into their midst.[10] Irmy gets drunk and succumbs to the blandishments of philosophy student Jack (John Cusack), who pays her $700 for sex.

Back in the streets, Kleinman witnesses the eviction from their home of a family called the Mintzes. Inquiring of a bystander, he learns they are considered "social Undesirables; they may be linked to the killings." Kleinman inquires at police headquarters about the eviction, but far from being protectors of the innocent, the police support the persecution of Jews. The police and townspeople believe that the Killer is haunting their town because Jews are present. Irmy has been arrested for prostitution without a license, and has to pay a fine. Irmy and Kleinman leave together, pausing for a moment of stargazing, in which Irmy experiences peace, while Kleinman feels only anxiety. Irmy donates the money she made from prostitution to a beggar woman with child.

The vigilantes hire Spiro the Sniffer, who smells something fishy about Kleinman—his Jewishness. Spiro incites the mob to lynch him. Kleinman rushes to the home of his ex-fiancée, Alma (Julie Kavner), but she orders him to leave—or else she will kill him. Years earlier, Kleinman had jilted her at the altar while having sex with her sister in a broom closet. His apology is insincere; he is incapable of taking sexual betrayal seriously.

Bereft of his partner, Paul the Clown stumbles into a bar where he meets Jack, who soliloquizes about the Sword Swallower he bought at the brothel (Irmy), saying that she was a "tigress" in bed. Knowing that the tigress is his own lover, Paul chooses not to fight Jack, but instead to fight with Irmy. In the postmodern world of *Shadows and Fog*, positive attributes of masculinity are either absent or contingent (unlike in the modernist universe of Chaplin's *The Circus*, where chivalrous attributes make the Tramp a hero). The coos of an abandoned baby forestall Paul and Irmy's altercation. Irmy convinces Paul to adopt the baby, and they return to their circus wagon.

As Kleinman flees the vigilantes, he encounters his coworker Simon Carr (Wallace Shawn) who insults him, but does at least tell him in which direction Irmy was headed. He arrives at the circus just in time to save Irmy from the Killer. The previously cowardly Kleinman now hoists a mallet overhead to strike at the Killer, but the mallet head flies off when swung. Running for his life into the Big Top, Kleinman discovers Irmstedt the Magician drunk on the floor. Irmstedt magically removes himself and Kleinman to safety inside a mirror, where the Killer can see but not touch them. The Magician entraps the Killer in massive chains, from which he soon escapes. After a botched magic-trick tryout (like Charlie's in *The Circus*), Irmstedt nonetheless invites Kleinman to become a magician's apprentice, and he joins the circus. As the Killer lurks, Irmstedt makes himself and Kleinman vanish through the mirror.

In *The Circus* and *Shadows and Fog*, circuses have figurative significance with both negative and positive values. The circus provides an ideal setting for Chaplin to display the Tramp's physical virtuosity while charming a member of the fair sex. At the circus, he attains a higher social status by earning a raise and wearing a tux, enabling him to woo the Ringmaster's daughter. In contrast, *Shadows and Fog*'s circus is a place where lust replaces romance. The scene between Marie and Paul exaggerates sexual desire and fetishizes sexual incorporation (the taking into one's body of another's body parts), thereby likening sex to eating. On the positive side, Allen's circus is a place where magic actually works; it saves the hero from death by vanishing him into a mirror. Circuses are rough places in both films; the rules of genteel living do not apply. Yet a circus is also an environment in which magic happens and outcasts can find a place of belonging.

Allen's circus setting and major elements of the plot, including the sinister doctor and murderous wanderer, pay tribute to Robert Weine's German expressionist classic, *The Cabinet of Dr. Caligari* (1920). Circuses and carnivals, though commonly associated with fun, are (in literature and film) also fitting venues for the exploration of more sinister aspects of human behavior. In *Strangers on a Train* (1951), Hitchcock uses a visiting carnival as a crime scene, the darkness and noise providing cover when a killer attacks his victim. The murderer's flight from the police ends on a carousel careening wildly out of control when its operator is shot. In Kafka's "The Hunger Artist" (1922), the misunderstood faster resents the forty-day fasting length imposed by his manager, when he knows he could do it for longer. The public's loss of interest in him, a mere wraith, in favor of carnivorous animals, emphasizes carnival as a place to vicariously indulge our predatory instincts.

Circuses or carnivals enjoy a long history in literature as places of excess and horror. Carnivalesque is a term coined by Russian critic Mikhail Bakhtin in *Rabelais and His World* (1965) to describe a literary mode that incorporates the topsy-turvy world of festivals, in which people from all walks of life celebrate momentary liberation from social strictures. The word *carnival* derives from the Latin *carne vale*, or farewell to the body. The festivities preceding Lent allowed for one's indulgence of the senses in order to prepare one for the forty days' abstinence to follow. Such festivals occurred in both ancient Greece (described by Socrates and Menippus) and medieval Europe, where they were called Feasts of Fools. One type of fooling involved low-ranked church officials making fun of the Church, exposing what Barbara Tuchman calls "the lout beneath the cassock."[11] Carnival is a time when excess is encouraged, especially eating, drinking, and sex. Women and men dance suggestively and may wear scant clothing or be naked—sexual display that often leads to violence. In Rio, the number of sexual assaults spikes during Carnival week. Carnival can also lead to illicit but consensual couplings; in Venice, where masks and cloaks are part of Carnival costume, sexual innuendos and anonymous unions abound. Several films capitalize on the potential of Carnival for spectacle and drama, such as Fellini's *Casanova* (1976) and Kubrick's *Eyes Wide Shut* (1999), in which members of a secret sex society wear Venetian masks to disguise their identities.

The rite of carnival has both physical and ideological components: the liberation of the body functions as a metaphor for the breakdown of social hierarchy. Festivals level class distinctions: the poor dance with the peer, the upper class gets down with the low. Carnivalesque is an indulgence of both sexual and political fantasies, wedding the sacred and profane. It is an opportunity to express the id in a punishment-free zone. By exaggerating bodily functions, carnivalesque privileges the grotesque body, Bakhtin's term for the degradation of the culturally high (such as ideals, abstractions, officialdom) to the level of the low, figured as the body and its typically shunned functions. The grotesque body has both positive and negative values: "The grotesque body is a comic figure of profound ambivalence: its positive meaning is linked to birth and renewal and its negative meaning is linked to decay."[12] The openness of the body through its orifices fascinated Bakhtin as a metaphor for the link of the individual to the outside world, since outside things can come into these orifices. The mouth is the gateway to the interior of the body; Allen uses extreme close-ups on mouths in *Shadows and Fog* to accentuate the grotesque.

The inside of the body is seen by many as sacred, even as a temple for the soul, so it follows that any intrusions into that space can be seen as grotesque, profane, and exceptional. Such intrusions include excessive amounts of food and drink, body parts, and instruments such as swords— as in the case of Irmy in *Shadows and Fog* and Stella the Sword Swallower in *The Circus*. Throughout history, sword swallowers are typically male; however, it is not difficult to understand why Chaplin and Allen chose to reverse genders. With its allusion to fellatio, the image of a female engaged in this act is highly sexual, almost pornographic, expressing the liberation associated with Carnival. Interestingly, in neither film do we see a live female engaged in the act. We only hear about Irmy's job, in *Shadows and Fog*, and we only see a poster of Stella swallowing a sword, in *The Circus*. The verbal suggestion (*Shadows*) or two-dimensional image (*Circus*) is enough to elicit a sensation for the audience, which also allows Allen to forego hiring a stuntwoman to stand in for Mia Farrow.[13]

The circus is replete with Bakhtinian carnivalesque, with its freak shows (three-headed persons, dwarves, fat ladies), junk food (cotton candy, candied apples, popcorn), large game animals (lions, tigers, elephants, and bears), and sexual suggestiveness (sword swallowers, trapeze acts, and the hypersexual costumes these performers wear). Both elements of carnivalesque are found in circuses: a reversal of social roles, and indulgence and display of the grotesque body. As for social reversal in *The Circus*, even though the Ringmaster claims the top of the hierarchy, it is the clowns, magicians, and trapeze artists who rule the ring with their talents. Clown acts take down persons of high status and elevate clownishness above dignity. Freak shows topple social rules by showcasing instead of hiding deformities, excessive appetite, and risky practices like sword swallowing. This social reversal aspect of circus is thematically central to both movies. While Charlie the Tramp and Kleinman spend time in and around circuses, they are able to escape momentarily their underdog status (Charlie's as a tramp, Kleinman's as a hunted Jew).

Indulgences of the grotesque body are particularly prominent in Allen's film, but are alluded to more subtly in Chaplin's due to stricter social regulation in his time. Incorporation of food is an important theme of the Bakhtinian grotesque body. Doing funny things with food happens in many Chaplin pictures; *The Circus* has a particularly creative relationship with food. In an early scene, the Tramp steals a hot dog from a baby, not by grabbing it out of its hand, but by flirting with the baby so that it eventually feeds Charlie from its own hand. We laugh at this bit of comic business because Charlie breaks the cardinal rule against stealing food from children, but does it so charmingly that it ceases to be a robbery. In turn, the Girl steals a slice of white bread from Charlie, who becomes indignant, but gradually relents because she is pretty. Undercranking, a technique that speeds the action of a film, makes the Girl's wolfing of the bread more humorous. Because she is female, Charlie is offended by her crudeness. Being

"Mind your manners!" Merna Kennedy and Charlie Chaplin in *The Circus*, 1928 (Charles Chaplin/Photofest).

effeminate himself, he is proud of his table manners, even when the food is stolen and the dining conditions improvised. He instructs Merna to eat graciously, which advice she ignores behind his back, till a fit of hiccups seizes them both and equalizes their status as grotesque bodies. Hiccupping is a paradigmatic example of the grotesque. An aberration of the usual way of breathing, it defies social conventions with its loud, uncontrollable noise-making. Slapstick artists like to introduce uncontrollable bouts of hiccups in formal settings: Charlie hiccups at a swanky party in *City Lights*, made louder by the fact that he has swallowed a whistle.

Using bodies and body parts in ways in which God didn't intend them is one of slapstick's stock gimmicks, and Chaplin is particularly fond of making comic transformations of one thing into another.[14] In *The Circus*, Charlie uses an unconscious man's body as a footstool so that he can reach a peephole in the Big Tent to spy on the Girl. As in the case of eating the baby's food, this is funny despite and because of its socially taboo nature. Even though the act shows thoughtlessness toward a disadvantaged person, at the same time it is so expedient to Charlie's appetite (this time his desire for the Girl), and so resourceful, that we momentarily disregard the footstool's humanity and regard him as the object that Charlie takes him for. Swallowing non-food items is another slapstick trick; in this case, Charlie is ordered to blow a pill the size of a ping-pong ball through a foot-long tube stuck down a horse's throat. Instead, "the horse blew first," causing Charlie, instead of the horse, to swallow the huge pill. A swift kick in the butt from the trainer eventually solves the problem, but before he is cured, Charlie forgets all about this relatively minor health risk when he gets locked inside a cage with a lion. Chaplin skillfully structures comic sequences in such a way that suspense builds throughout a series of gags. One mishap leads to another of greater proportions. Knowing that Charlie has swallowed a ping-pong-sized pill ups the ante the whole time that we watch him trying to get out of the lion's cage.

The most comic scene in *The Circus* shows the grotesque body at both ends. In "Charles Chaplin and the Annals of Anality," William Paul explicates Chaplin's oft-dismissed vulgar humor "of the lower body" (anal and genital). Slapstick places great emphasis on people's posteriors, which are funny because they house the anus, a body part that society would rather ignore or deny. The Tramp often gets kicked, or kicks someone else, in the rear. His pants have a hole in the seat just where the anus would be; Charlie gets impaled through this aperture in *City Lights*. In William Paul's view, this situation points to a thinly disguised homosexual theme.[15] In *The Circus*, the exposure of Charlie's lower body happens in a high place, where the audience can literally look up his undershorts. At the same time that his rear end and genitals are quasi-exposed, his mouth is penetrated by the most unlikely and disgusting of non-food items—a monkey's tail.

The monkey sequence goes like this: after a few self-training sessions, Charlie substitutes for Rex on the high wire. He is safe for as long as his invisible harness and tether hold, but after they break, he is in genuine peril. In conceiving of the film, the tightrope sequence was the central kernel around which Chaplin planned the plot. In other words, he worked from the gag backward to the sentimental narrative. Chaplin wrote to his friend Henry Bergman (who plays a Clown): "I have an idea I would like to do a gag placing me in a position I can't get away from for some reason. I'm on a high place troubled by something else, monkeys or things that come to me and I can't get away from them."[16] This is a common formula: put a clown in a dangerous spot, then throw sequentially more risky situations at him. In *Safety Last* (1923), while Harold Lloyd climbs a 12-story building, seeds are spilled on him, attracting pigeons to land upon his head and shoulders and make it impossible to see or to climb. Yet Chaplin goes further, touching on the absurd. Unlike Lloyd's pigeons, Chaplin's monkeys are made to seem human, and to act with humanlike ingenuity to add challenges to Charlie's ability to stay on the wire. Like a gang of Curious Georges, these beasts act not out of

The last straw. Charlie Chaplin in *The Circus*, 1928 (Charles Chaplin/Photofest).

malice but only out of intense busyness and curiosity, even about his nose, which they repeatedly bite.

Monkeys might not be such a problem if Charlie had hands free to brush them off. The secret to this gag is that both hands and feet are occupied, so that Charlie cannot defend himself: feet are precariously perched on the tightrope, hands holding the balancing pole, which is about three times the length of Charlie's body. If he were to drop the pole into the audience to deal better with the monkeys, it would probably impale the Mayor. One of the monkeys tears open Charlie's pants, which drop down to his ankles. Though ditching his pants was part of the original act, the walker was supposed to wear tights underneath his trousers, which Charlie didn't have time to don in the haste of his last-minute substitution for Rex. Exposing the lower body in boxer shorts and garters was scandalous in his day, and sufficient reason for the Ringmaster to fire Charlie, if the cheat harness, the wild monkeys, and the flying butt-upwards were not cause enough already. The most original gag of this sequence is literally a gag: it is the accidental penetration of various monkeys' tails into Charlie's mouth. This image conjures up both phallic and furry sensations: the act appears scandalous because of the tail's shape, and we shudder at the thought of sucking fur. Last of all, a monkey drops a banana peel on the rope, and Charlie trips. Despite being the most clichéd gag in slapstick, the banana peel is more than usually funny because of sequencing: it is last in a series of increasingly dangerous events. No wonder the audience enjoys Charlie's act better than Rex's; its danger and degradation keeps them on the edge of their seats. The grotesque body is not only ravenous and excretive; it is also prone to mishaps of a bizarre nature.

While Chaplin makes fun of the propriety of adequate clothing and social mores, Allen's post-sexual-revolution version of the circus comments audaciously on sexual incidents and perversions. A whorehouse is a classic venue for exploration of the grotesque body, but in *Shadows and Fog*, it is figured as a safe, friendly community, even while the whores tell tales of their clients' perversions, such as being ridden, being tied, and using twins. Although she feels guilty later, Irmy enjoys her night of prostitution. In other ways, too, the movie trivializes the job. During her one trick, Irmy becomes a sensuous woman capable of intense enjoyment of sex with a stranger. Jack describes her to Paul as a voracious tigress who clawed his back and yelled for more.

Back at the circus, Paul and Marie act out their own version of naughtiness. They talk about sex as though it were eating:

> PAUL: The most voluptuous woman in the circus is married to the Strongman—just my luck. You're so ... edible.
> MARIE: How hungry are you now?
> PAUL: I'm always famished after a performance. And you?

MARIE: I can never sleep on an empty stomach [high lighting on her melon-like breasts, while her face is in deep shadow].
PAUL: Do you have a taste for anything special?
MARIE: I'm not fussy. I eat what you put in front of me.

Even after Irmy interrupts this preprandial dialog to beat up her boyfriend, Marie and Paul continue their word play. It is this legerdemain of words, rather than physical chemistry, which links them:

PAUL: We were just talking about acrobatics.
MARIE: I was showing him how to do a backbend.

The scene is carnivalesque in its equation of sex with eating. Copulation, which high culture has imbued with noble, loving properties, is likened to a function as impersonal and necessary as eating; this levels the high ideal down to the ground. Throughout his oeuvre, Allen typically deflates sexual idealism by using absurd one-liners that juxtapose love with small, mundane, unrelated details, very often to do with food. In *Love and Death*, when Sonja suggests they go upstairs to make love, Boris replies, "Nice idea! I'll bring the soy sauce."[17]

Allen's comic treatment of the grotesque body may provide some insight into the public scandals regarding his alleged sexual abuse. Throughout his career, his treatment of sex has been light, schlemiel-like, and mockingly perverse (in *Sleeper*, Miles says he is a good man, who "would never force myself sexually on a blind person"). The Woody persona of the early films is the nebbish who either can't get the girl, or who surprisingly gets the girl but cannot hold her because he isn't sexy. In bedroom scenes, Allen-the-actor plays the fool, typically by not removing his large, black-framed glasses during the act of love, and giving non-erotic, frenetic caresses. In *Everything You Wanted to Know about Sex*, Fabrizio clumsily pats his wife's body, commanding, "Excite, excite, excite!" until he falls asleep from boredom. There is nothing threatening about Allen-the-actor in these scenes. It is Allen-the-writer's verbal banter about sex that raises questions about his perversions. Since perversity is the butt of the joke in Allen's work, however, it seems wrong to judge the writer as perverse. Even in artwork as seemingly confessional as Allen's, we should not mistake the art for the artist, as discussed in the appendix to this book. The schlemiel persona is an artistic construction. It is more productive to contextualize Allen's onscreen treatment of sexual perversity as a product of comedy history. Starting out as a stand-up comedian in the early 1960s, Allen fully realized the potential of the period's new artistic freedom by joking about sex, sexual hang-ups, and sexual perversions, and has continued to cash in on that popular sex-crazed persona until the present day.

In *Shadows and Fog*, the non-sexual aspects of the carnival grotesque are actually more interesting than the sexual—perhaps because the sex talk is riddled with cliché. For instance, the Doctor's fascination with psychological autopsy is novel. In his underground autopsy lab, ceiling mirrors placed over operating tables reveal corpses undergoing dissection. The camera pans around to show myriad jars of human body parts in formaldehyde, arranged categorically on shelves. The Doctor believes that, if he tears apart dead bodies, he can discover the true moral nature of human beings. Just as the circus characters equate sex with eating, this Doctor equates the physical parts of human bodies with the sum total of what it means to be human. When Kleinman challenges him, the Doctor scorns the idea that there is anything beyond the physical realm of existence. The Doctor's obsession illustrates the grotesque body par excellence; far from being a temple of one's soul, the body is only a frail container of slimy parts. So little regard does the Doctor have for idealized humanity that he casually gestures toward Kleinman with a dead man's heart, as though it were a piece of steak.

Steaks also function as payment for casual sex, when Kleinman disappears at the very moment of his wedding to copulate with his fiancée's sister in the broom closet. Attempting to calm an irate Alma (with a pistol in her hand), Kleinman promises that her sister didn't really like him; she was only doing it for the steaks that he offered as compensation. We might also hear "stakes," and be reminded that the stakes for sex are very low in Allen movies. Because sex is treated as no more than a bodily function, Kleinman doesn't think Alma should be upset about his having a little tryst with her sister. Sister betrayals are another recurring theme in Allen's films; again, they are low stakes for the men, who either disregard or diminish the added perversity of destroying a sister bond in the course of adultery (*Hannah and Her Sisters, Interiors, September, Deconstructing Harry*). This recurring theme may symbolically reflect Allen's deep distrust of family loyalty (though he gets along famously with his own sister). The sexual betrayal theme underlines his inability to see sexual situations from a woman's viewpoint.

In addition to their exploration of the grotesque body, Allen and Chaplin's circus films adopt the carnivalesque politics of social reversal, in which power relations temporarily shift to allow outsiders the spotlight and to deflate the higher status of insiders. On the tightrope, the Tramp outdoes, at least by comedic standards, the performance of the elegant, patrician Rex. He gets the Girl, though he does not take her when offered. In contrast, Kleinman does not get the Girl, although he does stand up to Death for the Girl's sake. Refreshingly, the schlemiel is not trying to get any girls during this nightmare interlude. Kleinman outwits both Death and the vigilantes-cum-Nazis when he escapes into the mirror of illusion in the last frame. The circus is good to Kleinman. Unlike the townspeople, who persecute him for being Jewish, the circus appreciates him for his desire to be a magician rather than for his actual talent (he repeatedly botches a simple coin trick). Both films end with qualified victories for their protagonists. Charlie proves himself to be the noble Tramp by relinquishing the Girl. Kleinman finds the courage to leave so-called real life and take a low-paying job with the circus, in order to embrace his dream and venture onto the unknown and dangerous road of circus life.

Besides the high and low social structures relevant to a Bakhtinian analysis, it is also useful to consider the two-dimensional geometry of circles, lines, and triangles in evaluating the meaning of circus in these two films. The etymology of the word *circus* prompts geometric visualization. The word *circus* derives from Greek *krikos*, meaning circle or ring. All circuses are performed in rings, and vary in size from one to three rings. Circles are symbolic in literature, mythology, film, and Jungian psychoanalytic theory. The circle may have been the first symbol ever created by humans, when our forebears told stories about the various orbs in the sky. Although the circle has many symbolic meanings, I will focus on two of these: wholeness and inclusion. Jungian mandalas are circles with pictures inside their borders. Carl Jung's therapeutic drawing of mandalas to cure problems ranging from sadness to psychosis was based on the concept of wholeness. Jung observed that circles were the first shape that infants were attracted to, and the first thing that children drew. Jung and his patients drew mandalas to work out conflicts. The circular mandala represents the self in the world, combined with the essence of the universe, the seasons, cycles of nature, and the infinity of energy. A mandala is both a macro and micro view of existence: it interprets the vast mysteries of the universe on a more manageable scale.[18]

Circuses in film and literature can be metaphors for both life and an escape from life, as they are in the two films under discussion. Writers often describe characters wanting to "run away with the circus" as a metaphor to denote their utter disconnection from the world they inhabit, and their desire to escape to some fanciful place of magical entertainment. One dreams that one will be made whole by allowing fantasy to play a part in real life. An imagined circus is also a place of inclusion, in which performers are linked by their outsiderness. All circus performers are freaks or misfits in some capacity, for if they were normal actors or acrobats, they would choose the so-called legitimate stage or sports arena. In the circus, there is something childish and rebellious (Chaplin traits par excellence) that legitimate theatre does not share. The vaudeville theatres in which Chaplin received his training resemble a circus. Vaudeville features short acts of slapstick, broadly drawn archetypal characters, and dangerous acrobatics (Buster Keaton's father, for instance, used his four-year-old son as a human floor mop, dragging him upside down across the floor and tossing him into the wings when he was through).

In *The Circus*, Chaplin uses the circle literally and figuratively to denote inclusion and exclusion. The film opens and closes with ring shapes: in the opening, Merna jumps through a hoop, then misses one, which angers her father, initiating the dramatic action. She is unable to jump into the hoop of his fatherly love. In the closing scene, Charlie sits within the circular boundary of the circus tent trench, after the circus proper has decamped. He sadly watches as the caravan takes away his beloved Merna. At this moment, though he sits within a dirt circle, it is a mere ghost of the erstwhile circus, and Charlie is now excluded from the warmth and acceptance that his friendship with Merna represented. When he leaves the ghost of a circus to strike out for new adventure, however, Charlie effectively asserts the linearity of his itinerant life as a positive value. He is independent, and will start again.

Not all critics agree with this positive interpretation of the ending. Stark Young sees the ending as a "willed pathos" that mars the rest of the film, rather than a natural closure.[19] Kyp Harness describes the images ending the film as glimmering "not with the sad sentimentalism of pathos, but an even deeper sadness, the futility of all things … as Charlie makes his way into an unimaginably vast emptiness."[20] Richard Carr believes the ending "cheats the audience" by having the Tramp walk away twirling his cane "as if happy to be back on the open road."[21] The ending might be read autobiographically as a melancholy commentary on Chaplin's personal troubles of 1926–27, when he was thrust outside the protective embrace of marriage and fandom. The American public reacted vehemently to his second wife Lita Grey's accusations of his adultery, selfishness, and sexual perversion. Charles Maland reads the evil brutality of the Ringmaster as a sign that Charlie was getting in touch with his own brutality and bad temper, both on the set and in his marriage.[22]

My reading of a happy ending derives from both a visual interpretation of signs and an appreciation of the genre in which Chaplin works, which is linear and episodic, carrying the Tramp from one movie to the next. The Tramp is a persona who, across many films, repeats his efforts to be accepted by the mainstream world of work and domesticity, but whose outsider status asserts and reasserts itself as the nobler identity. At the end of *City Lights*, we do not know whether the flower-seller will love Charlie when she discovers he is poor, but if she does not, we also know that she is not worth having. In *The Kid*, Charlie is invited into the new home of his adopted son, but he is unlikely to inhabit a meaningful place in that home, since he has no relationship with the boy's mother and no legal status as the adoptive father. In *The Circus*, it is noble to relinquish the love of a good woman, whom the Tramp cannot financially support. True to modernist form, the good individual is the lone individual, who is rejected and misunderstood by the mainstream but who understands life better than the toadies in the middle. When Charlie refuses to board the last wagon of the caravan offered by the evil Ringmaster, it might signify that he refuses to play second fiddle—or to come last—in any relationship or group. Charlie's attitude about social circles may in this sense be the very opposite of the one that the Woody persona claims in the beginning of *Annie Hall*: "I would not want to be a member of any group that would have me as a member." Alvy's self-hating persona cannot tolerate acceptance because he doesn't feel good enough to deserve it. Conversely, Chaplin's Tramp might be refusing the offer of inclusion in the circus because he is better than that offer. Rejoining the circus would make him the second-best friend of Merna, and lousy performer of circus acts. On the road, the Tramp is free of the hierarchy.

In *Shadows and Fog*, circles can be either sinister, or soothing, or both. This film's postmodern sensibility breaks down any easy moral binaries. In several of the town sequences, cinematographer Carlo Di Palma uses high-contrast circular lamp lighting to denote entrapment rather than inclusion. When the vigilantes interrupt Kleinman's deep sleep, they surround him underneath the circle formed by a ceiling lightshade, launching a political interrogation to find out whether he's with them (anti–Semitic) or against (a self-loving Jew). Once again they surround him in the dark streets, employing Spiro the Sniffer to sniff out Kleinman's essential (Jewish) otherness.

The happy whorehouse. (From left) Lily Tomlin, Jodie Foster, and John Cusack as whores and a client in *Shadows and Fog*, 1991 (Orion/Photofest).

On the other hand, the circle reappears in a somewhat confused but mostly positive gathering of sisterly whores around a dinner table as they share food, laughs, and support in the warm, welcoming atmosphere of the brothel. It is difficult to tell what Di Palma's camerawork means to suggest by careening around this circle, sometimes taking in faces but, just as often, the walls of the brothel dining room.[23] Perhaps this reeling motion represents Irmy's point of view, since she is getting drunk on wine and the adulation of one cute student. The reeling effect might also refer to Irmy's unsettling discovery that whores are much like other women, needing to bond together in order to process their experiences of men's perversities. The dizzy camera might also refer to the confusing, topsy-turvy war between the sexes. During this scene, each prostitute describes both the baffling fantasies that clients pay her to enact, and also her conviction of the impossibility of having non-transactional relations with men. For instance, Jodie Foster's prostitute says there's only one kind of love in this world—unrequited. Prostitute Lily Tomlin's husband left her when he discovered that she paid for his life-saving operation by whoring. Lily Tomlin's character claims that any potential harmony between men and women is based only on luck rather than on anything inherently harmonious between the sexes. By "luck," she means the lucky pairing of a man and woman with symbiotic sexual perversions.

In contrast to the professional whores, Irmy forms a meaningful center to this dizzy circle, when she drunkenly psychoanalyzes Paul: "He's really sweet ... but when I see him out there in his makeup just getting knocked around, falling into a tub of water with all the people laughing, I can only think he must have suffered so to act like that." Irmy and Paul's relationship follows a cyclical pattern of conflict followed by forgiveness. Rather than give up or opt out of this hellish circle, Irmy compassionately considers the childhood causes of Paul's acting-out behavior. Instead of finally leaving him for his cheating or his narcissism ("I am a great Artist"), she chooses to raise a child with him.

Besides the group of whores, the other positive circle in *Shadows and Fog* is the circus ring, where Kleinman finally finds courage and acceptance by others, just before vanishing into the mirror of illusion. Of course it is difficult to imagine that Kleinman (or any character played by Woody Allen) is courageous; his boss describes him as "a cringing, slimy worm." At the end of the film, circumstances necessitate that Kleinman run away from the town. It is not out of bravery that he does so. We know that the Killer can never be caught, because he is Death itself. The vigilantes will always need their scapegoats to explain the Killer's evil psyche, and Kleinman, being Jewish, will continue to serve that function. Kleinman's bravery consists in deciding to follow his passion (performing magic) instead of running away to be a clerk in some inevitably similar town with similar anti–Semitism. In the allegorical mode, as in other types of literature, we often wish for the protagonist simply to run away to escape trouble. In allegory, there is no escape from the moral degradation of one community by choosing another, because the community represents one's psyche itself. On the other hand, for Kleinman to choose the circus, and the identity of artist over "wretched clerk," is to take an existential stance, to make a personal choice instead of being the pawn of other people. The escape to magic does not, however, solve Kleinman's problem of dreading the "constant uncertainty and change of the world." It is, at best, a temporary solution. Yet Kleinman is so positively encircled in the final few minutes of the film—by the circus people, the circus ring, and finally the mirror framed by a crescent moon—that we feel the kind of momentary wholeness that only art can give.

While circles create meaningful symbols of inclusion and wholeness, the triangle is the more familiar term for discussing human relations. Both films capitalize on the narrative opportunity of romantic triangles. Chaplin resolves the romantic triangle by breaking off its third part (Charlie), but Allen's geometry is more complex. First, he doubles the love triangle of Irmy-Paul-Marie by creating an intersecting second triangle of Jack-Irmy-Paul. This second triangle momentarily equalizes Irmy's extramarital sexual experience with her husband's, but it is an unstable configuration. Because of Irmy's newfound sexuality (from turning a trick, improbable as this may seem), Irmy and Paul are now capable of re-forming the only kind of "safe" love triangle there is, the holy one comprised of Mother, Father, and Child. Although we like to believe that having children stabilizes a marriage, the experts say it does not. But it does make for a satisfactory film ending.

In human terms, the triangle formation causes more tension than the circle and is more likely to break. Charlie shows his understanding of this principle when he tells Merna that "two's company, three's a crowd." Allen's complex story line, with characters' rapidly shifting allegiances and their inability to rely on coupling as a lasting or meaningful event, reflects the cynical post-sexual-revolution world that postdates Chaplin's experience. Part of the appeal of *The Circus*, in a narrative sense, is the simple logic by which threesomes are unstable. Romantics and modernists alike should find satisfaction in the Tramp walking off into the sunrise at the end of *The Circus*: romantics, because Merna is married to her proper social match, and modernists, because Charlie is off on another adventure as the noble Little Man against the cruel but funny world. Such an ending affirms the individual's power to make meaningful choices, even without a penny in his capacious trousers.

While inclusion and wholeness are positive ideals of human fulfillment, the individual also needs to leave the circle in order to find authenticity when living in a corrupt, modern world. A modernist attitude implies that only in individuals and their individualism lies the possibility of truth. Consider the words of D.H. Lawrence's Rupert Birkin, in *Women in Love*: "Humanity is less, far less than the individual, because the individual may sometimes be capable of truth, and humanity is a tree of lies."[24] As Charlie leaves the dirt circle made by the departed circus, he makes a beeline for the horizon, a linear journey away from the promise of that particular circus. But we know that the Tramp will enter a new circle in his next film—in this case, the romantically promising one of *City Lights* (1931), where once again he does his utmost to win another distressed girl. Chaplin manages to mix the modern attitude—the individual's quest for dignity and salvation—with the very postmodern one of repetition and hopelessness (even in *City Lights*, most critics believe that Charlie will not be able to get the Girl that he saved).

In a postmodernist sensibility, there is no escape from alienation, only the invitation to the artist to play in the chaos. At the end of *Shadows and Fog*, Irmstedt's magic plays with the audience's suspension of disbelief by making himself and Kleinman disappear. As Peter Bailey notes, the circus in this film is an allegory for art as a "temporary antidote to, then compensation for, human mortality."[25] Trained as we are to reject magical solutions, a postmodernist audience will likely read Kleinman's magical disappearance as wish fulfillment, a fantastical resolution to the ongoing, real problem of anti–Semitism and death.[26] In the practice of one's art (Kleinman's magic) one finds momentary solace from the certainty of death and catastrophe. Such is Allen's personal credo, repeated in several interviews he has given.[27] In *The Circus*, the Tramp walks out of the circus onto the road of life, until such time when he will need to take a new, inevitably challenging job. By contrast, in the sped-up world of postmodern times, Kleinman's escape is only instants long— as we know from his previous momentary magical disappearance. In a postmodern, reflexive cinema, in which art comments upon the conditions of its own making, Kleinman's magical escape is akin to our own ninety-minute immersion in the magic of watching a film. It is no more of an answer to life's persistent questions, yet no less of a delight.

In contrast to *Shadows and Fog*, Chaplin's circus film reflects a moral universe with certain absolutes. The circus is a vertical economic structure in which the Ringmaster/owner presides cruelly over a hierarchy of workers. Elegant tightrope walker Rex is literally on top of the hierarchy; his dress, height, and manners proclaim his provenance from the upper class (we might assume that he joined the circus for kicks). "Professor" Bosco the Magician comes second, the clowns are third, while property men (and Merna, because she is a woman) occupy a decidedly bottom rung. The occupants of each level are treated according to their status: the lower the rung of a worker, the greater the blows, both physical and figurative, s/he absorbs. The Tramp, who strives to be independent of this hierarchy, presents an interesting challenge to the structure because he refuses to believe in its values—a modernist move insofar as it implies that such a narrative choice exists. The film posits that we should value a person according to his goodness of heart instead of the fullness of his pocketbook. Luck, skill, and personal charm are qualities (noticeably opposite to those of the Schlemiel) that enable the Tramp to insert himself into different levels of the structure at different times; his lot is continually changing according to the whims of power and the contingency of events.

In Allen's film, the nightmare world offers not even the comfort of a stable hierarchy, since social categories are blurred by contingency and moral relativity. In postmodern theory, everything is contingent; nothing is fixed. Grand metanarratives that explain the world, such as religion, patriarchy, even purportedly egalitarian systems like Marxism, are suspect. All narratives are subjective; there is no absolute reality, only that which is constructed by various communities. Progress itself is an illusion. Pragmatism replaces moralism as the guide to action.[28] In Allen's film, we see examples of this worldview. Whores enjoy a community of relative safety compared to sword swallowers and Jews. Employment is no marker of safety, compared to ethnicity. Kleinman's employment with a firm is on an insecure basis because of the town's insidious anti–Semitism. Racism cuts across class boundaries, complicating other social hierarchies of patriarchy and capitalism.

Postmodernity does not like a binary. *Shadows and Fog* presents classic binaries of Gentile vs. Jew, male vs. female, commerce vs. art, light vs. dark, only to break them by introducing third or contradicting terms, such as the association of bright light with interrogation (instead of truth), or the cruelty of the Jewish male (instead of his generosity) toward women. This breakage shows binaries to be specious divisions of human experience; it challenges the validity of stereotypes and categories. In the course of the film's complex narrative, these categories are cross-fertilized, their rigidity broken by encounters across their borders, including Irmy's with the prostitutes, and Kleinman's with Irmy. It is this cross-pollination that lightens the mood of *Shadows and Fog* vis-à-vis its source material in Kafka's *Trial* and *Metamorphosis*. Although they disagree on the very nature of the universe—for Kleinman it is dangerous; for Irmy, peaceful—the two protagonists' chance meeting ensures their physical salvation by leading Kleinman to the circus at the precise moment when Irmy faces Death. In the contingent postmodern world, outcomes are based on chance or luck. In saving Irmy's life, Kleinman commits a semi-heroic act, the success of which is minimized by his inability to use weapons. Unlike Charlie's intentional act of self-sacrifice for Merna, Kleinman's bravery is only a momentary impulse ("I can do brave things when I don't think"), succeeded by terrified flight.

As opposed to Kleinman's final dive into the mirror of illusion, Charlie's act of walking alone into the sunrise carries the strong message of heroism, of facing the world versus escaping from it. Like Kleinman's escape, postmodernist solutions are not solutions at all, but accommodations to uncertainty and threat. Kleinman avoids the overwhelming question of mortality (and evil) by escaping into momentary illusion. Contrastingly, at the end of *The Circus*, Charlie turns exactly toward the world, 180 degrees from the direction of the circus. His road to the future is a metaphor for individuation. In typical endings to modernist *bildungsromans*, the hero eschews assimilation or suicide by hitting the road. At the end of Lawrence's *Sons and Lovers*, Paul Morel considers suicide, but then walks "away from the dark, uninhabited country fields and toward the bright city lights."[29] At the end of Joyce's *A Portrait of the Artist as a Young Man*, Stephen Dedalus walks away from Dublin towards Paris, thinking, "Welcome, O life! I go to encounter for the millionth time the reality of experience and to forge in the smithy of my soul the uncreated conscience of my race."[30] In proto-modernist *Huckleberry Finn*, the hero walks toward the western horizon to escape stultifying small-town morality: "I reckon I got to light out for the territory."[31] Modernity is alienating, but individualism is still—in the early twentieth century—a solution of sorts. On the other hand, postmodernity denies the possibility of fixing the indifferent world and scoffs at the idea of one's potential to be indifferent

Different views on the meaning of life. Woody Allen and Mia Farrow as Max Kleinman and Irmy in *Shadows and Fog*, 1991 (Orion/Photofest).

to the world by trying to create one's own path. There simply is no escape. While modernist fiction imagines potentially better places, postmodernist fiction ridicules this fantasy of escape.

Shadows and Fog is also postmodern in its use of a dual narrative with two protagonists and two parallel plots. The subplot amplifies, contrasts, or modifies the theme of the main plot. Dual narrative is a structure that Allen has adopted in nearly all of his films since *Annie Hall* (1977). Using multiple viewpoints is a postmodernist move, insofar as it demonstrates the subjectivity of all narratives and the ways in which one character is inherently able to see only a part of the world or events. When multiple characters relate the same events from different viewpoints, we are reminded of the limitations of a single viewpoint; we face the truth that the Other is as complex and valid as the self. *Shadows and Fog* is divided almost equally into the stories of two fallible, relatable humans (Kleinman and Irmy), who together represent an array of subject positions: male/female, pessimist/optimist, cowardly/brave, alienated/connected, Jew/Gentile, real world/circus. Allen astutely avoids joining these two figures in a romance, perhaps because the main character's existential question (the meaning of life) would be trivialized by focusing on the kind of failed romantic relationship typical of his other films.

Instead of mating, the main characters in *Shadows and Fog* wander through the dark night of the soul. For Kleinman, the trauma is the problem of evil; for Irmy, it is the trauma of heterosexual unions. At the turning point of the film, their paths intersect and they stargaze, after which Kleinman instinctively follows the warm humanity that Irmy exudes, arriving finally at the circus. These questers meet, exchange a brief moment of philosophy, and ultimately turn in separate directions. At the end of the film, Irmy wants to leave the circus just as Kleinman is joining it. In this decision, she may seem more mature than he does, as she is ready to settle down and raise a family, but this comparison obscures the crucial fact that Kleinman is Jewish in a time of holocaust. His struggle is not only about how to earn a living, but also how to keep on living, or—how to survive the Holocaust.

Employing these two different frames of reference, Irmy's and Kleinman's, reflects postmodernist pluralism and skepticism. In particular, the parallel plots encourage us to avoid absolute moral judgment on the characters, since Irmy is both a sensual woman capable of enjoying prostitution and a maternal, generous do-gooder. Kleinman is both an innocent victim of anti–Semitism and a culpable exploiter of women. Watching *Shadows and Fog* and *The Circus* together invites us to contrast Chaplin's modernism—with its heroic individualism and singular viewpoint—to Allen's postmodernism, in which dual plotting and sympathetic rendering of opposites challenge us to suspend moral judgment.

2

Technology and Alienation in *Modern Times* and *Sleeper*

Although *Sleeper* (1973) and *Modern Times* (1936) have hilarious moments, their serious implications are frightening. Comedy outweighs the social message in both films, yet social critiques do emerge, particularly for viewers in later eras. In an interesting crossover relationship, *Sleeper* is mock sci-fi and, as such, doesn't so much intend to send a social message as to send up sci-fi conventions. Yet it does provide a strong visual warning of the ills of the Digital Age. On the other hand, *Modern Times* is an episodic finale to the Tramp's picaresque adventures (Chaplin meant to retire the character when he made his next film, *The Great Dictator*), yet, despite his public denials when the film was criticized for its social content, Chaplin clearly intended to make *Modern Times* a social commentary. Overall, the film fails to deliver a strong, clear message, in part because its comedy is so good, and in part because it lacks narrative cohesion.

Especially in the visuals of its first part, Chaplin's film contains a critique of the Machine Age, that period in the late nineteenth and early twentieth centuries of which the machine was the defining feature. On the other hand, Allen's film is a critique of the Digital Age, the period starting in the 1970s with the introduction of the personal computer, and continuing to the present day, when many of us feel we could not survive without the Internet and our instant access to it. It is interesting to interpret *Sleeper* from our present point of view in the Middle Digital Age (my coinage) instead of from the Early Digital Age when Allen made it. We are now living with many of the digital phenomena that the film predicts. Although the Digital Age can be seen as a continuation and amplification of the Machine Age, there are major shifts in emphasis. Whereas once we feared that machines might take over our bodies, as when Charlie's body becomes machine-like due to his repetitive factory work, now we fear that machines might take over our minds, as when Miles undergoes brain restructuring. The negative social effects of the Machine

Age arise from what Karl Marx called *alienation*: the process by which a worker is made to feel foreign to the products of his labor. Once a worker is alienated from his labor, he also becomes estranged from his life force. Marx wrote, "[T]he external character of labor for the worker appears in the fact that it is not his own but someone else's, that it does not belong to him, that in it he belongs, not to himself, but to another."[1] Becoming a mechanistic part of a social class estranges a person from his own humanity. In *Modern Times*, the iconic image of Charlie caught in the cogs of a machine is a perfect visual example of alienation. He is no longer an autonomous human being, but has become part of the machine that provides him with employment.

The negative social effects of the Digital Age include some of the same symptoms of this alienated mechanistic state, such as loneliness and depression, in addition to a daunting host of new ones, such as loss of privacy, vulnerability to cybertheft, cyberbullying, the pornification of mainstream culture, and a decline in critical thinking. In *Sleeper*, these symptoms are revealed in examples such as Luna's refusal to think, the society's electronic solution to sexual desire, and the threat of brain-reconstruction to anyone who dares think or say anything in contravention of the shallow, hedonistic ethos created and maintained by the police state. To Chaplin's complaint about mechanization, Allen adds the late-twentieth-century understanding that technocracy leads to totalitarianism.

Woody Allen's *Sleeper* is his greatest homage to the auteur he considered the master of physical comedy (Chaplin) and specifically to *Modern Times* as exemplary of good slapstick. In a 2003 interview, Allen told Richard Schickel that most of his acquaintances preferred the "cool brilliance of Keaton," but that he preferred Chaplin because of "that little bit of humanness which sometimes is a weakness of his, and embarrasses all of us."[2] Not surprisingly, such humanness is the quality that makes Allen's persona appealing, too. Both are highly relatable characters. The early Seventies was a time when Woody felt "very taken with the films of Chaplin and Keaton in relation to myself."[3] To explore Chaplin's milieu of silent film, Allen wanted to make a movie with long segments of silent comedy.

His initial concept of a silent setting was a future world dominated by technocrats, in which the workers were forbidden to speak. Fortunately, he changed his mind, because without speech, we would miss the extravagant self-indulgence of Luna (Diane Keaton), shown by her insipid poetry, and her constant demands for instant comfort. Allen allowed the subjects of this society to speak, but he created another class of being, the robot servants, which had only computer-programmed speech. Allen plays one of these robots with a plug in his mouth that prevents him from speaking. Because of his need for anonymity (and the corking device in his mouth), the Allen character (Miles Monroe) must communicate wordlessly to the audience his various anxious and perplexed states caused by perceiving the weirdness of Luna's culture, and the threat of his own extinction as an enemy alien. In Miles's wordless fear and puzzlement, we see a side of Allen that is usually hidden beneath his excessive wordiness. Allen's silent Miles becomes endearing in ways that his speaking nebbish cannot; understanding this process helps to explain the Tramp's appeal as well. The gagging of an actor who is used to talking produces new movement, facial expressions, and gestures that make him more relatable, more of an Everyman, like Charlie's Tramp. This is what happened to thirty-eight-year-old Woody Allen in his most successful comedy up to that point.[4]

It was not as simple for Chaplin to travel in the opposite direction, from silent movies to talkies. After writing a dialog script for *Modern Times* and filming one speaking scene, Chaplin changed his mind and produced a hybrid of silence and sound instead. In *Modern Times*, the human voice is heard indirectly, via the televised and loudspeaker pronouncements of the President of Electro Steel Corporation and the gramophone sales pitch for the feeding machine. Direct speech is reserved for the Tramp's gibberish song as a singing waiter.

The greatest challenge for each auteur was to transition to a new mode of expression: Allen introduced more pantomime, along with a social critique of technocracy; Chaplin added sound, and married a social message to the comedy-and-pathos combination of his earlier films. While Chaplin used a number of diegetic sounds to good effect (burping, banging, crashing, squeaking, auto horns, sirens, cow bells, etc.), the only dialog scene he filmed was the Tramp sitting in digestive agony with the curate's wife. He was "deeply dissatisfied" with the results, and decided to cut all dialog.[5]

His other challenge was that of genre mixing: how to integrate a social message into his fundamentally comic voice. Chaplin and Allen shared this challenge; each would struggle to balance comedy and seriousness for the rest of his life. In many of Allen's films, including *Crimes and Misdemeanors* and *Shadows and Fog*, he approached the problem by creating dual narratives, one serious, the other comical. This method creates a fine balance between the two modes.

This chapter will explore three themes that link *Modern Times* and *Sleeper*—the terrors of the Machine Age versus those of the Digital Age, silent films versus talkies, and the challenges of mixing comedy with a social message. In these thematic comparisons, I will refer to elements of modernism and postmodernism, indicating shifts across the mid-century turning point. The boundaries between modernity and postmodernity are by no means rigid; many elements of each ideology can be found in films from either side of the mid-century. In particular, Chaplin's films can be reflexive about himself and about filmmaking, a characteristically postmodern phenomenon; on the other hand, when Allen's protagonists retreat into their art or their marriages, it can feel like a decidedly modernist strategy.

Two Little Men pariahs, the Tramp and the Schlemiel, are divided chronologically by the Holocaust, which is the defining difference in the ethos of the two ages. The threat of reification—turning human beings into things—intensifies when humanity lives through and beyond the Holocaust. Reification means not only the very literal image that comes to mind, of Jewish skin becoming lampshades, but also a desire to conform to the expectations of various communities, to make oneself an object, so that the capacity for free thinking is lost. Theodor Adorno famously writes, "No lyricism after Auschwitz"; Woody Allen would agree.[6] There is lyricism in his work, of course, but it is consistently undercut by pragmatism, skepticism, and sarcasm. His films are reflexive about the process and purpose of filmmaking: what is the role of art in a godless universe? Computers—the technological innovations that the Allies leveraged to win the just war (such as Alan Turing's code-breaking Bombe, and calculations for making the atomic bomb)—would eventually contribute to people's own reification, when thinking machines are given precedence in the Digital Age. At exactly mid-century (1950), Alan Turing posed the Turing test: if a computer's answers to a human's questions are indistinguishable from a human's answers (as are HAL's, in Kubrick's *2001*), then we can fairly say that machines can think. By the year 2000, according to Turing's prediction, artificial intelligence would be well established in our human civilization.[7] His prediction became all too true.[8]

The two films under discussion have a basic plot similarity. Although neither *Modern Times* nor *Sleeper* is a typical love story, both comedies reach their resolution by the bonding together of a man and a woman in order to fight or flee the machine. Charlie's Tramp finds his best job (as a singer) through his relationship with the Gamin, and together they flee inhuman authority in its various forms, including police and factory owners. Allen's Milo rescues Luna, and in turn is rescued by Luna, from the brainwashing that is the modus operandi of state control. Together, they kill the Leader, though the film ends with no plan for resisting the next iteration of totalitarianism.

Modern Times opens on the statement, "A story of industry, of individual enterprise—humanity crusading in the pursuit of happiness," a satirical comment on the disjunction between the ideal of happiness and the actual conditions of its pursuit—in this case, soul-killing work on an assembly line. The American Dream promises that everyone can succeed through hard work. This film shows just how hard it is to succeed when you are born poor, especially during the Depression. The film's opening shots benefit from Eisenstein's theory of ideological montage. The Russian filmmaker studied the way in which the mind synthesizes successive images to make symbolic meaning.

2. Modern Times *and* Sleeper

The first visual of *Modern Times* is a high-angle shot of a tight-packed herd of sheep moving towards the camera, followed by a similarly framed shot of tight-packed workers climbing up a subway stairway. Cut to long exterior shot of the smoke-belching Electro Steel Corporation factory. Scurrying workers in the foreground dodge traffic in downtown Los Angeles. The analogy is crystal clear: modern factory workers are treated as impersonally as sheep; like sheep, they follow their herd instinct. One black sheep amidst the herd symbolizes the Tramp's difference from the masses. Charlie acts like a black sheep, not so much by design as by sheer ineptitude (as in *The Circus*). He harbors no political intentions to sabotage the factory. But, when his job makes him crazy, he goes on a rampage, destroying the machine that has broken him.

The small task allotted to Charlie is to tighten two nuts on rapidly passing metal plates riding on a conveyor belt, which accelerates according to the whim of the boss (Allan Garcia). This repetitive work turns the worker himself into a machine (just as Marx had said). The stressful demands on mind and body make it impossible for Charlie to turn off at break-time. His body continues to jerk in the motions of his task, and he continues to torque all objects resembling nuts, including buttons on the clothing covering women's buttocks and bosoms. Because we know that the Tramp is crazed at this point, his actions are mechanical rather than erotic. He is not looking for sex, but to fulfill his task. In this way, Chaplin repeatedly evades the Hays Code censors.

The next scene brilliantly critiques Machine Age surveillance of the worker. Charlie is taking a short break in the restroom when a large television screen transmits the image of the factory owner, who barks at him to get back to work. Twelve years before the birth of George Orwell's Big Brother, Chaplin already understands the perils of ubiquitous camera surveillance. During Charlie's lunch break, the boss chooses him to test the new Bellows machine, which is meant to save time by feeding men while they work. This contraption confines the worker and assaults his dignity, conveying a nightmarish sense of trauma. The mouth-cleaning brush repeatedly smacks Charlie in the face; he's fed steel nuts instead of food; and the revolving corn-feeder whirs so fast that flying kernels appear to be his broken teeth. When Charlie is finally released, he swoons, a clear demonstration that our timesaving machinery is killing us. After lunch, Charlie accidentally follows one of the metal plates into the bowels of the machinery. The image of his body threading through the cogs is so striking that it became one of the most famous images of Chaplin's entire oeuvre. Visually and intellectually appealing, it implies that man becomes the very machine that is supposed to help him to pursue happiness. After he is disgorged from the machine, Charlie goes berserk. He first dances a bizarre ballet, then goes on a mad

Indomitable factory worker. Charlie Chaplin in *Modern Times*, 1936 (United Artists/Photofest).

orgy, tightening every nut-like object in view. He pulls random levers until the generators blow up.

After a brief stay in the mental hospital, Charlie is released onto the mean streets of the Depression era. Almost immediately, he picks up a red flag that has dropped off the back of a truck and waves it to signal the driver. Communist demonstrators happen to be marching by, and the police, thinking he is their leader, arrest and put him in jail. High on cocaine that's been concealed in a saltshaker, Charlie attains the superhuman powers to stop a jailbreak orchestrated by convicts much larger than he is. As a reward, he is allowed to decorate his cell with a vase of roses, throw pillows, and a portrait of Abraham Lincoln. These domestic touches remind us of other moments in Chaplin films when he manages to spruce up the starkest of digs (his attic room in *The Kid*, his bunk in *Shoulder Arms*, his cottage in *The Gold Rush*). These flourishes make us feel, for the briefest moment, that the Tramp's life is acceptable, containing the potential for community and coziness, although always in temporary fashion. Walter Kerr believes that *Modern Times* "confronts the issue of 'home' for a man psychologically incapable of integrating himself into society."[9] When he decorates his cell, Charlie is pretending to have a home, yet if he ever found a real home, he would be too afraid to live there. Homelessness is his essential condition. Eventually, Charlie is pardoned for his good deed, but begs to stay, because "I'm so happy here."

Outside on the docks, the teenaged Gamin (Paulette Goddard) steals bananas to feed her family while her father is out of work. At first, the Gamin seems impossibly brave and rebellious. Taking a wide, masculine stance with a knife braced pirate-like between her teeth, the Gamin taunts the police. The Gamin differs from Chaplin's earlier female leads in that she is not the object of Charlie's romantic desire but a comrade on the road of life.[10] Her character equals his in spunk, ingenuity, and dancing ability (Goddard had been a Ziegfeld Follies dancer). Describing their relationship, Chaplin writes: "The only two live spirits in a world of automatons. They really live. Both have an eternal spirit of youth and are absolutely unmoral. There is no romance in the relationship, really two playmates—partners in crime, comrades, babes in the woods."[11] Simply put, to live up to this ideal of autonomy, the two could not be a couple.

Charlie tries to take the heat for the Gamin's stealing a loaf of bread, but a witness identifies the Gamin, and she is carted away in the police wagon.

Comrades. Paulette Goddard and Charlie Chaplin as the Gamin and the Tramp in *Modern Times,* 1936 (United Artists/Photofest).

Fearlessly, she escapes from the moving wagon, and they run away together. Charlie gets a job as a night watchman in a department store. Burglars raid the store, but when one of them recognizes Charlie as a former coworker, they end up celebrating with a keg of the store's rum. Charlie is rearrested, and, while he serves his term, the Gamin spruces up a dilapidated wooden shack for them to call home. In a reversal of traditional gender roles, the woman is good at carpentry, while Charlie is inept. Charlie gets fired from a shipbuilding job when he accidentally removes a block and the ship slides out to sea.

Charlie briefly works at another factory until the workers go on strike and he is re-arrested. In the first factory scene, Charlie was at the mercy of the boss; now, he enjoys a brief advantage over his foreman (Chester Conklin), who gets stuck in a machine. Charlie feeds Chester roughly, treating his mouth as though it were another machine. Charlie may be getting revenge on a mean boss, or maybe he is just indelicate and incapable of nurturing. In its bizarre use of the Foreman's mouth as a passive receptacle of food, the sequence suggests the strange orality of Bakhtinian grotesque. Ignoring the Foreman's need to chew, Charlie stuffs a whole hardboiled egg down his gullet, and uses a dirty oil funnel to pour coffee in too. When the Foreman protests, Charlie switches to the device of a chicken carcass. Feeding an entrapped man via the dead body of an animal is so far removed from the natural mode of eating that it signifies something else. The whole sequence dramatizes Marxist alienation.

Meanwhile, the Gamin finds a job dancing in a café. She convinces its manager (Henry Bergman) to hire Charlie as a singing waiter, though he says he can't sing. Under pressure, Charlie ad-libs, having lost the copy of lyrics that he had jotted on his detachable shirt cuffs. He improvises a gibberish song that the crowd adores, probably because his burlesque is mischievously sexual. Marking the first time that he uses his own voice on film, the scene became justly famous for his ability to convey narrative and emotion through mime and gibberish. Gibberish is an exaggeration of the sensual qualities of language, of its sound rather than its sense, whereas mime is an exaggeration of the sensual qualities of movement, a stress on the articulations between poses to accentuate the essence that they are meant to describe. Mime and gibberish humorously emphasize the ways in which speech and movement can be broken down into their component parts. This made-up language might be viewed as Chaplin's protest against the talkies.

The Gamin has been fleeing the Welfare patrol that wants to incarcerate her in an orphanage. When they find her at the café, Charlie helps her escape. The next morning, sick of running, the Gamin breaks into tears, wailing, "What's the use of trying?" Charlie snaps her out of it: "Buck up—never say die. We'll get along!" Charlie and the Gamin link arms and walk down the middle of a paved road towards the California hills. The End.

2. Modern Times *and* Sleeper

Sleeper inhabits a very different universe from the Depression-era California of *Modern Times*. Place: the middle of the country formerly known as the U.S.A., now a technocratic police state. Year: 2173. The film opens on two leather-jacketed toughs discussing the discovery of a frozen alien in a rusty capsule. Although aliens pose a threat to the social order, a couple of rebellious doctors decide to revive Miles Monroe (Woody Allen). A health food store owner in 1973, Miles was killed in a botched surgery and cryogenically frozen. Once awakened, he is groggy and speechless, giving Allen a chance to emulate the physical skills he so admired in Chaplin's silent acting. While trying to regain his motor skills, Miles staggers like a happy drunk, with a smile for all. Unlike the usual Woody persona, Miles is very pliable. When security thugs arrive in the lab to question the overuse of electricity, the doctors have to pretend that punch-drunk Miles is one of their own, knowing that aliens would be either killed or reprogrammed if discovered. Just before their arrest, the kind doctors plead with Miles to save their civilization from its totalitarian regime: "Find out what the Aries Project is, in the Western District."[12]

Partying in 2173. Woody Allen (center) as Miles Monroe in *Sleeper*, 1973 (United Artists/Photofest).

Miles constructs a robot disguise and gets a job as a servant in the home of Luna Schlosser (Diane Keaton). There he overhears that the Aries Project is a government strategy to destroy the Underground Movement, a revolutionary group that plans to kill the Great Leader and take over. The citizens are completely hedonistic, using high-tech devices like the Orgasmatron (a sex booth)[13] and the Orb to achieve orgasms without sex and intoxication without drugs. In this society, intellectualism is evil, but lowbrow poetry à la Rod McKuen[14] and sad-eyed waif paintings are considered "keen" (a pun on artist Margaret Keane's name).[15] As soon as they exhibit signs of freethinking or dissatisfaction, people are either liquidated or have their brains restructured.

The next day, Luna takes Miles to the robot factory to get his head replaced "with something more aesthetic." There follows a scene in which Allen echoes *Modern Times*, with higher stakes: whereas the Tramp lost his mind in the steel factory, Miles stands to lose his head. While he is passing in the factory as a robot, no one seems to notice that he wears glasses over his plastic face, and often takes the metal microphone out of his mouth, mak-

In line for a new head. Woody Allen as Miles Monroe in *Sleeper*, 1973 (United Artists/Photofest).

ing him obviously different from all the other robots. Allen does a very good imitation of the other robots' movements. Fearful of losing his head, Miles starts a high-speed chase around the operating table of the robot factory, using many slapstick devices, and specifically emulating the *Modern Times* scene in which Charlie runs circles around the conveyor belt, taunting his co-workers with an oilcan.

Having escaped immediate danger, Miles kidnaps Luna, begging her to help him locate the Aries Project headquarters. Luna is completely hostile to the alien, and adamantly opposed to any political project for the betterment of her civilization. While they are stranded in a Colorado evergreen forest, Miles promises to feed her if she will help him, and goes foraging for some futuristic food. He comes upon a garden of produce enlarged to gargantuan size. When intercepted by a gardener, Miles repeatedly slips on a banana. Allen uses sped-up action to allude to slapstick, but his speed is faster; the Digital Age is even more of a rat race than the Machine Age. Miles lugs a celery stalk and a banana back to his sardonic damsel in distress. Nearby, a man leads a giant chicken home for the slaughter, a Chaplinesque echo of the giant chicken hallucinated by Big Jim in *The Gold Rush*. The scene vividly portrays technology getting out of hand. The absurdly gigantic food expresses our human sense of smallness and impotence in a world run by computers.

When they stop at a residence to borrow a vehicle, Luna betrays Miles by calling the police on a Skype-like device. Their homosexual hosts employ a campy robot that provides Miles with a Hydrovac suit for emergencies.[16] The security thugs ambush Miles and Luna, but capture Luna instead of Miles because she has been contaminated by spending time with the alien. In the Hydrovac suit (a giant rubberized man-shaped balloon), Miles defends Luna against the cops, conking them with a rubber arm and jumping on top of them. Miles and Luna hydroplane across a pond, powered by the gradually deflating Hydrovac, which has been punctured by security men's bullets.

Enjoying a brief romantic idyll in the kind doctors' ransacked home, Luna and Miles talk about sex. Luna explains that her society has solved the problem of sex by making people frigid, but invites him into the Orgasmatron to "perform sex" with her. The coldness of it turns Miles off. When security forces burst in, Luna escapes, but gets lost in the forest. Erno, the handsome leader of the Marxist Underground ("tall, blond, Prussian, Nordic, Aryan Nazi type"), comes to Luna's rescue. Miles is captured and receives a total brainwash when the brainwaves of beauty contestants are wired into Miles' brain to make him stupid.[17] Reprogrammed Miles is happy with his new job: threading spools on a wall. He has sex (using the machine) with his vacuous blonde coworker.

Luna and Erno kidnap Miles to work in the Underground Movement. But first, they must reprogram him back to his 1973 personality. By reenacting major traumas of his life, they believe they can shatter his Miss America persona. Luna and Erno reenact the Sunday family dinner of 1962 during which Miles had told his irate parents he was divorcing his wife, Harlene (the name of Allen's first wife and a scene from his real life). Recalling this trauma gives his psyche a jolt that restores his identity.

Disguised as doctors, Luna and Miles break into the Delta Laboratory, where the Aries Project is located. At a top-secret meeting, they learn that the Underground had bombed the Leader's house ten months ago, but his nose was found in the rubble and kept alive. Mistaking Miles and Luna for ENT specialists, the scientists expect them to clone the nose. A HAL-like talking computer tries to guide them through the surgery, while a dozen doctors watch from a balcony overlooking the operating theatre. Miles steals the nose and throws it under a steamroller. When they pause among the sunflowers to congratulate themselves, Luna tells Miles that she thinks he loves her, and he concurs. Luna asks if he believes in anything at all, and he replies, "Sex and death, two things that come once in a lifetime ... but at least after death, you're not nauseous." They kiss. The End.

In *Modern Times*, Chaplin weds physical comedy to a new dimension, the social message. *City Lights*, *The Kid*, and many of his short films had criticized social norms and class prejudice. With *Modern Times*, however, Chaplin took on a topical political issue. *City Lights* made fun of the unhappy millionaire, and *The Kid* lambasted child welfare institutions, but *Modern Times* takes on the ills of capitalism itself, such as its tendency to reify the worker and to periodically break down into recession or depression. The film illustrates graphically that our worship of the machine, and its dominance in our world, are depriving us of our individualism and human values. In the Machine Age, the economy is bureaucratized and mechanized. People are secondary to production.

In the future world of *Sleeper*, Allen's message is similar, but by 2173, technology has advanced to such a point that our individual humanity is gone. Citizens of the Central Parallel of the American Federation are as dehumanized as the robots that they use for servants. If they aren't satisfied by the pleasures afforded by technology, the government will restructure their brains. The citizens are so homogenous that we see little difference between the robots and the humans.

In the police state, there are three classes of humans: hedonists (Luna and friends), police, and rebels (doctors and revolutionaries). Like the hedonists and the police, the underground rebels are one-dimensional; their isms are pat and formulaic—a satire on Marxist ideology. The humans are either programmed by computers or socially conditioned to do, think, and feel as instructed. The image of the Leader (Timothy Leary) is accessible 24/7 on their home telescreens. They turn on the TV to enjoy his calming effect, as when Luna gets upset over a minor linguistic mistake. The Leader fashions himself as more of a guru than a politician; it is the security police who enact the brutality of the regime rather than the "benign" Leader. The kind doctors who revive Miles are an exception to the incurious nature of the subjects, as they are interested in the phenomenon of an alien being. With Luna as the epitome of the technically constructed human being, we see the costs of technological progress in the Digital Age: a loss of humanity, individualism, sexual intimacy, and critical thinking. Allen's future world consists of a brainwashed and thought-controlled populace, a reiteration of the dystopias in Orwell's *1984* and Huxley's *Brave New World*.

Though set in the future, science fiction concerns the ills of the time in which it is written. By the time *Sleeper* came out in 1973, the Watergate scandal had engulfed America, its revelations gravely damaging Americans' trust in their leaders. On a more personal level, Alvin Toffler expressed an early consciousness of the perils of Digital Age technology in his bestselling *Future Shock* (1970), which described a widespread psychological condition of anxiety due to the perception that too much change was occurring so rapidly that it overwhelmed the capacity of the human mind to process—a definition shockingly close to that of trauma. Indeed, some trauma theorists contend that even just to live in a patriarchy is to be traumatized.[18] The OPEC oil crisis of 1973 negatively affected Americans' sense of global superiority, as their economic supremacy was severely threatened by OPEC's embargo which caused inflation, recession, and apocalyptic thinking among the American public.

These events produced in some Americans a bunker mentality of fending for oneself, with the family as the only remaining social unit. In Allen's *mise-en-scène*, human isolation is typified by the doctors' stand-alone futuristic home. Although the pine-treed mesa is beautiful, it lacks infrastructure: no neighbors, shops, or communities. Larger institutions do exist in *Sleeper*, but they are strictly regulated by top-down management and ideologically controlled by the one Leader and his program of enforced catatonia. The laboratory where Miles is resuscitated, the robot lab that decapitates its workers, and the Delta Laboratory where medicine is used to prolong the Leader's life after death—all are institutions with a decidedly sinister, totalitarian feeling. Allen's vision of the future is saturated with early 1970s phenomena—not only *Future Shock*, the OPEC crisis, and the tightening noose around President Richard Nixon, but cryogenics and the seamy side of the sexual revolution. As such, Allen's dystopia is different from the future worlds of later science fiction, such as the virtual reality of *The Matrix* (1999) or the robot-as-human-companion/betrayer in the more recent *Eva* (2011), *Her* (2013), and *Ex Machina* (2015). Whereas these later films capitalize on our fear of artificial intelligence taking over human lives, Allen's satire focuses on the human tyranny that administers the technocracy.

Besides economic and political upsets, Americans of the early 1970s confronted the negative repercussions of the sexual revolution. After the initial euphoria and sense of liberation from age-old social constrictions, so-called free love had revealed its seamy side. A great loss of intimacy accompanies what Erica Jong named the "zipless fuck" as a model for human sexual intercourse (*Fear of Flying*, 1973). Because the Woody Allen persona so often expresses an interest in unusual sexual configurations such as three-ways, sex with sisters, and adulteries, it is noticeable that Allen actually condemns free love in this movie. Luna says: "I thought we should have had sex, but there weren't enough people." Perhaps the premise that a machine could bring people to climax better than people could was enough to shock Allen into reevaluating the meaning of sexual relations.

Against these dehumanizing settings, Chaplin and Allen's heroes seek to preserve their own humanity. Miles is more resistant to technology than Charlie, who does not fight it directly. Although the factory machinery causes Charlie to go nuts, he does not take up arms against the system; the incriminating red flag ends up in his hand by pure chance. This episode emphasizes the Tramp's apolitical nature, disavowing any involvement with Communism. Given that Chaplin was hounded for his supposed Communist tendencies during the Cold War, this scene takes on new significance, as though Charlie and Chaplin were both framed as Reds.

The social message that *Modern Times* promises in the first factory scene is one that the film as a whole does not deliver. Lawrence Howe has argued that Chaplin is ambivalent about the message (mechanization is bad) because of the fact that Chaplin is the beneficiary of the technology of filmmaking, and of the capitalist economic structure that has made him rich from making movies. Furthermore, Chaplin presents the American Dream (the house with white picket fence) as an un-nuanced, positive goal, without reference to the fact that home ownership is possible only as the result of mass production, mechanization, capitalism, and dehumanizing employment in factories.[19] On a similar note, Eric Flom believes that Chaplin walks a middle road between business and labor. At least three sequences demonstrate that workers are as misguided as their business managers: when a worker's riot results in the death of the Gamin's father, when the Jetson Mill workers go on strike just a few hours after they had earned the opportunity to work, and when Charlie reads the headlines "Strikes and Riots" and "Breadlines Broken By Unruly Mob" and throws aside the paper, shaking his head with a sigh. The film, Flom concludes, "does not overly sympathize with either side."[20]

Complicating further the idea that *Modern Times* is a social message film, Dan Kamin argues for total reflexivity. Rather than being a film about the Depression, the Machine Age, unemployment, and poverty, *Modern Times* is a film about Chaplin's prolonged resistance to, and eventual conformity with, the industry standard of sound film. Kamin sees the black sheep at the beginning of the film as a metaphor for Chaplin persisting in using predominantly silent modes long after his colleagues had adapted to sound. In this reading, Charlie's body being fed through the cogs of a machine is an allusion to film moving through a movie camera. As Charlie is sucked into the machine, so Chaplin is being sucked into Hollywood industry standards.[21]

The differences between Miles Monroe and Charlie the Tramp reflect important distinctions between modernist and postmodernist attitudes. The Little Tramp rebels against the machine in several personal ways that are emblematic of his Tramp character: unintentional sabotage (going berserk), polite torture of the supervisor (the rough feeding of Conklin), and setting a boat adrift in the shipbuilding sequence. But these incidents hardly constitute a blanket indictment of the inhuman working conditions in a machine society. Charlie's small acts of rebellion are consonant with a modernist belief in the individual as the repository of authenticity.

By contrast, in postmodernity, the necessity for communal action (often achieved by online communities, as in the Arab Spring or #MeToo movements) is fully recognized as being the only possible mode for social change. Economic, ecological, and political problems are seen as global; a rudimentary understanding that institutions (patriarchy, capitalism, racism) and nationalist, economic hegemonies are root causes of these problems is widespread among citizens of the industrialized world. Miles demonstrates this knowledge when he bashes various ideological approaches to the problem of human destructiveness. The God solution doesn't exist, the revolution solution lasts only six months ("it doesn't matter who's up there, they're all terrible"), and the science solution is basically narcissism disguised by tweed jackets and foundation grants. Unlike the Tramp and the Gamin, Miles is not alone; he joins the Underground struggle against the Leader. If he doesn't exactly embrace their ideology of Marxism and primitivism (they believe in free love and raw meat), he understands the dire necessity of changing the politics of the new state where he is now stuck. He won't tolerate a future in which he will be made as dumb as Miss America.

True to postmodern narrative strategy, the ending of *Sleeper* is open and unresolved. This narrative incompletion shifts the viewer's focus away from the flimsy love story ("Heterosexual romances don't last because of a chemical in our brains that makes us sick of each other," says Luna) to the broader parody of the future. The big picture is not the sexual problems of two little people but the question of how to govern ourselves. *Sleeper* may not be a film to make us think about how to resist the computerization of our lives (or to have made a 1973 audience think the same), but, in its highly aestheticized, fully realized big-canvas picture of an inhumane future, it does leave us with this paradox: If we keep developing our technologies, particularly that of artificial intelligence, we will lose touch with our humanity.

Another contrast between Allen's post–Holocaust world and Chaplin's prewar world is *Sleeper*'s message that industrialization and nationalism lead to war and totalitarianism. Almost all science fiction about the future posits a world in which a technocratic totalitarian government spells the loss of individual freedom. Of course, science fiction is not a late-twentieth-century creation; it goes back to the very first time that ancient storytellers ever speculated about the future. In the 1920s, German Expressionists depicted a dark, machine-dominated future; Fritz Lang's *Metropolis* (1927) depicts a world in which inhumane bosses controlled monstrous machines and the hordes of miserable workers who operated them, an allegory for the fascism that was already rising in the Weimar Republic. On the other hand, Allen, with his awareness of both the Holocaust (emblematic of humans' capacity for atrocity) and the social upheavals of the 1960s, instinctively links his satire of mechanization to a sociopolitical commentary. *Sleeper* links technocracy to totalitarianism, but pre–World War II Chaplin does not yet make that connection.

This difference does not in itself make *Sleeper* a better film than *Modern Times*, but it reflects the modernist valorization of the individual versus the postmodernist understanding of our interdependency and contingency. In *Modern Times* and other films, Charlie's redemption consists in preserving his personal dignity by leaving behind all employment that bores, demeans, or humiliates him. But in postmodern *Sleeper*, it is not possible to talk about redemption. In postmodern narrative, redemption is a suspect state: in a godless universe, how can one be saved? The postmodernist mode cannot offer serious romantic solutions. Instead, it parodies the words and conventions of romantic and quest narratives.[22] Rather than a traditional romantic hero who takes the lead, saying, "I love you," Miles is the recipient of Luna's overture. Smiling broadly, she says, "I think you really love me." With some embarrassment, Miles exclaims, "Of course I love you, that's what this is all about." The word *this* is a vague referent, capable of referring to many things—perhaps to their constant hostility and bickering, to his jealousy of Erno, or to their failure to overturn the government—but, curiously, not to affection, which they don't exhibit. Another Allen character (Alvy Singer of *Annie Hall*) famously disliked the word *love*: "I don't love you. Love is too weak a word for what I feel—I luuurve you, you know, I loave you, I luff you, two F's, yes I have to invent."[23] Allen's protagonists have to reinvent the verbal expression of love because, first and foremost, they are insecure about the potential for abandonment; and second, they are postmodernists whose self-reflexive irony causes them to abhor sentimentality and clichéd expressions, even to distrust the very feelings that these words express. After Miles' admission of "love," he immediately changes the focus back to himself: "And you love me, I know that, and I don't blame you, honey." In this radical departure from traditional romantic dialog, Allen adeptly parodies the romantic conventions.

Modern Times and *Sleeper* mark turning points in the careers of their creators. Nine years after the first talkie (*The Jazz Singer*, 1927) wowed world audiences it was time for Chaplin to face his demon: he needed to incorporate sound and dialog in order to remain in the game. Chaplin was resistant to the talkies because he believed that a silent Tramp was more relatable: "A good silent picture had universal appeal both to the intellectual and the rank and file. ... I was determined to continue making silent films, for I believed there was room for all types of entertainment. Besides, I was a pantomimist, and in that medium I was unique and without false modesty, a master."[24] Chaplin's other innovation in *Modern Times* was to address the pressing issues of the day as he saw them. After witnessing the effects of the Great Depression during his world tour and at home, he felt the need to acknowledge the economic struggle of millions of people, while at the same time using his art to give them at least momentary release from their suffering.

Allen's film career is filled with homages to auteurs and genres he admires. In the early seventies, he particularly admired Buster Keaton and Charlie Chaplin. *Sleeper* is his most direct homage to both. *Sleeper* also represents a new dimension in Allen's genre experimentation. Although his previous films had been genre-parodies, *Sleeper* marks a move away from the episodic structure of earlier films, one which make us feel we are watching an act in a nightclub that happens to take place on sets (*Take the Money and Run, Bananas, Everything You Always Wanted to Know about Sex* But Were Afraid to Ask*). *Sleeper* is a tightly structured drama, complete with rising action, climax, and resolution. Drama like this needed more likable characters. Building on the *bildungsroman* quality of the character Allan Felix from his 1972 movie *Play It Again, Sam* (who learns to stop posturing and act natural in front of women), Allen creates Miles Monroe, whose likability is greatly enhanced by his nonspeaking, childlike persona when he first comes out of the deep freeze. Once he regains his mental and motor control, Miles moves fairly quickly from the complaining, neurotic New Yorker who is in denial of the world he's been reborn into, to a somewhat heroic, action-oriented alien detective who solves the mystery of the Aries Project and goes on to kill the bad guy (or, at least, his nose). In *Sleeper*, Allen's technical mastery shows significant advances beyond that of *Everything You Wanted to Know about Sex*; his cameraman experiments with low and high angles, master shots, and close-ups.[25] The bright, saturated color of both interiors and exteriors creates an ambience of surrealism. The various props of the technological society are fully realized, be they giant celeries, completely white-walled homes with lighted floors (like the spaceship interiors in *2001*), a futuristic pod-house raised on a stem, or the driverless bubble cars that emit an uncanny robotic hum.

After wrapping *City Lights* in 1931, Chaplin found inspiration to write a somewhat more serious script. To publicize *City Lights*, Chaplin embarked upon an eighteen-month tour of Europe and the Far East, hobnobbing with famous people as diverse as Winston Churchill and Mahatma Gandhi. The success of *City Lights* had bolstered his self-confidence. Now it was time to rectify a gap in his development, his almost complete lack of a formal education. From now on, he would aspire to make seriocomic films with social messages. Biographer Richard Carr went so far as to say that, for Chaplin, comedy was only a means to an end, which was his desire to be taken seriously. Carr called Chaplin "a man who was, at his core, always making up for the impoverishment of his childhood."[26] Freud would agree with that assessment. In Freud's opinion, "He is undoubtedly a great artist; certainly he always portrays one and the same figure; only the weakly, poor, helpless, clumsy youngster for whom, however, things turn out well in the end. ... He cannot get away from those impressions and to this day he obtains for himself the compensation for the frustrations and humiliations of that past period of his life."[27]

Education was his attempt to heal that impoverishment. In his autobiography, Chaplin states, "I wanted to know, not for the love of knowledge but as a defense against the world's contempt for the ignorant."[28] This core ambition links him closely with Woody Allen, who had a similar sense of deficiency (he repeatedly dropped out or was kicked out of college) and a compensatory drive to attain high seriousness in his art.

Despite his desire to be taken seriously, Chaplin read only lightly. More often, he tried to acquire knowledge through conversation. Thomas Burke, whose melodramatic East End stories about poverty Chaplin admired, gives this description of his friend's intellect:

> His mind is extraordinarily quick and receptive; retentive, too. He reads very little, but with a few elementary facts on a highly technical subject, his mind can so work upon them that he can talk with an expert on that subject in such a way as to make the expert think. He thus appears a very well-read and cultivated man when, in fact, his acquaintance with books is slight. ... He takes no concern in the historical past; his spiritual home is his own period.[29]

During his world tour, Chaplin's ability to pose as an intellectual (as well as his celebrity) gained him a place among London's political and social elite. Invitations to visit Winston Churchill, Albert Einstein, Lloyd George, Labor P.M. Ramsay MacDonald, Lady Astor, George Bernard Shaw, and H.G. Wells proved that Chaplin had beaten the notoriously hide-bound British caste system, rising from his poverty-stricken childhood to become *de facto* royalty.

Among these social and political leaders, the economic crisis was a frequent topic of conversation. Applying his quick-study technical ability, Chaplin wrote a paper called "The Economic Solution," in which he proposed a plan for social credit. He advocated shortening the workday and guaranteeing a minimum wage in order to boost the economy and protect the rights of the workingman. Discussing these ideas, Einstein complimented him by saying, "You're not a comedian; you're an economist."[30] Although convinced that Machine Age mentality was destroying human dignity, Chaplin argued in favor of industrialization when discussing India's poverty with Gandhi. But Gandhi informed him that, in the long view, eschewing industrialization would help India to throw off the yoke of their British colonizer.

However stimulating these meetings with the world's political, artistic, and intellectual elite may have been, it was Chaplin's encounters with the cheering masses in foreign cities that contributed most directly to the feeling of *Modern Times*. Although he appreciated their admiration, the crowd's adulation made him feel "sick spiritually because I know what's behind it. Such drabness, such ugliness, such utter misery, that simply because someone makes 'em laugh and helps 'em to forget, they ask God to bless him."[31] His awareness of the reality of their daily lives made Chaplin want to give back some of the love. Also fruitful for his artistic conception of the Machine Age was an interview with a reporter who had witnessed conveyor belt workers at Henry Ford's automobile plants: "a harrowing story of big industry luring healthy young men off the farms who, after four or five years at the belt system, became nervous wrecks. It was that conversation that gave me the idea for *Modern Times*."[32]

At the end of the technocratic movement, the historical moment was just right for his audience to appreciate this movie. Lawrence Howe describes the short-lived rise and fall of the technocratic movement in American history: "Confidence in technology peaked in the mid-1920s, and then waned just as quickly before bottoming out by the early 1930s, when technological unemployment was seen as its consequence."[33] A 1932 *Fortune* magazine article coined the phrase "obsolete men" to denote workers who had been superannuated by machines. By 1936, anti-machine sentiment was widespread enough for audiences to heartily appreciate the machines running amok in *Modern Times*.

Behind every piece of dehumanizing technology are the weak people who make and use it (a concept that is vividly demonstrated when Toto pulls the curtain to reveal the Wizard of Oz blowing smoke and fog across his outsized image in the 1939 film). The challenge to the filmmaker is how to represent these technocrats satirically without necessarily demonizing them and thereby reducing a complex social critique to pure melodrama. Chaplin succeeds in making his authority figures vulnerable. In his portraits of industrial management, including the big boss, the visiting engineer, and the foreman, Chaplin focuses not only on their obvious flaw—inhumanity toward workers—but on the ways in which their mastery of technology is incomplete. Like the workers, they too get stuck in their machines. The Bellows Feeding Machine demonstrates its engineer's incompetence when it breaks down and goes berserk. The foreman falls into the machine he operates and gets stuck there during lunch. The workers go on strike, thereby shutting down the works. Charlie is able to blow up the machinery with a few random pulls of levers.

At midcareer, both directors wanted to stretch—in opposite directions—into areas in which they felt least comfortable. For Allen, it was silent physicality; for Chaplin, spoken dialog. Allen's attraction to the silent form is a validation of Chaplin's oeuvre, more than three-quarters of which consists of silent films. Chaplin's "humanness," which Allen admired, was fully realized in *Sleeper*'s silent sequences. But when Miles opens his mouth, he loses the kind of universal appeal that only a silent Little Man can have. Allen is well aware of this fact. In an interview with Richard Schickel, he said:

> I had the idea that it was easier working in a silent era. Most people think that silent comedies were harder, 'cause you didn't have a voice, you couldn't speak. But silent films were easier. When you added the voice it became much more complicated; it's really the difference between checkers and chess. Consequently both Chaplin and Keaton were killed when the voices were added—it becomes much less abstract and much more real.[34]

Abstract—meaning theoretical, conceptual, and intellectual—is an interesting choice of words in this context. Slapstick is hitting and chasing people, throwing pies in their faces, and slipping on banana peels: in a word, anti-intellectual. Yet the form is abstract in the sense that the audience of a silent film has to supply meaning with their own interior language, be it the sensual, pre-linguistic form,[35] or worded in an interior monologue. The Tramp is effective because the audience recognizes themselves in his predicaments. Gerald Mast describes the difference between silents and talkies by contrasting language's specificity with movement's generality:

> Chaplin had avoided speech in the two earlier sound films [*Modern Times* and *City Lights*] because he knew that Charlie the tramp was an Everyman figure, his universality a product of mime, gesture, and facial expression, which are also generalizations. Words, however, are highly specific—not only in translating general feelings into specific terms, but also in immediately identifying the speaker's education, class, level of vocabulary, and precise habits of thought.[36]

For Allen, talkies are more difficult than silents because he knows that his speaking persona outs him as a smart, Jewish Manhattanite, thereby reducing his audience appeal by the measure of those demographics. But when he is Miles-the-Robot, speechless in both senses (cork crammed in his mouth, and bewildered by the New World), he becomes an Everyman. Miles' robot represents a universal fear of a dystopian future in which there's only a slight difference between the robots and the humans. In this role, Allen's scared, mournful eyes speak for all humans in the face of a bewildering, cruel, and unredeemable world, whereas if he spoke, it would denote a particular kind of New York Jewish angst. Amplifying the pathos of his gaze is the white greasepaint of his robot mask, which alludes to the clown makeup of the great silent comedians.

Allen rarely gets credit for his skill at physical comedy. This is the film in which he takes the greatest physical risks in order to emulate Chaplin and the silent comedians, including dangling from a high window on computer tape (like Harold Lloyd), slipping on a banana peel, and balancing on a ladder that is not tethered to anything.[37] In *Sleeper* and his next film, *Love and Death*, Allen reaches the height of his physical powers. Instead of his hilarious physicality, however, Allen's enduring popularity is built on the intellectual persona created in films from *Annie Hall* (1977) onwards. From his dance with Death at the end of *Love and Death* to his robotic sexual attack on a tall, slender African American model in *Sleeper*, Allen demonstrates a unique skill in klutzy physical comedy. Even though Allen is actually athletic and fit, he couldn't be described as graceful. Graham McCann describes Allen's unique way of moving thus: "His whole body when in motion seems to fragment into a cluster of exclamation marks, reacting in amazement to the shock of city life."[38] Change "city life" to "future life," and the description fits Allen's way of darting about *Sleeper*'s Colorado landscape. Allen's absurd nebbish look—the slight build, short stature, stringy long red hair, oversized black-rimmed glasses, big nose, and out-turned feet—link him more with Groucho Marx (another man who consistently crouches forward) than with other, bigger physical comedians like Jerry Lewis or Allen's idol, Bob Hope. Even in his youth, Allen's posture was slightly forward-leaning, a meaningful somatization of the anxiety his characters feel. This stance is opposite to the upright, space-taking, assertive posture of the typical red-blooded American male—which may be Allen's point.

To illustrate the shift that occurs when Miles goes from silence to talking, I'll describe the scene when he has been carried to the kind doctors' house while still in the last phases of thawing from the deep freeze. In an interesting long shot, from the point of view of the male doctor in a second floor window, we see the kind female doctor and Miles about thirty feet away in the garden. Miles is still walking in a dazed manner, alternating between exaggerated marching steps with raised knees, and stiff, unbending legs like a zombie or tin soldier. The lady doctor stops to face him, and we know that she is revealing to him where they are (the Federation), and in what year (2173). In a gradually intensifying manner, Miles dramatizes the phases of receiving traumatic news: denial (he treats the revelation as a joke and pushes her gently on the shoulder); shock (he bends double and rocks back and forth from the waist with laughter); realization (he opens his mouth wide, then falls down in a dead faint, legs akimbo). Cut to the interior of the doctors' living room, where a speaking Miles is now reacting to the news verbally. The difference in his persona is so great that it is jarring. Is this really the same cute defrosting man who has been cutting capers? "I can't believe this. My doctor said I'd be up and on my feet in five days. He was off by a hundred and ninety nine years," he whines, with emphatic vocal inflection and handwringing. No longer the grinning alien calmly accepting the assistance of his caretakers, Allen enters into full kvetching mode.

In contrast, the Tramp in *Modern Times* does not make such a drastic modal shift between silence and talking. Chaplin carefully curates the introduction of the spoken word for the Tramp, managing to enhance the character's likability with the singing of his song, rather than to detract from it. The fact that the Tramp chooses to ad lib the forgotten lines in gibberish, rather than clear lyrics, further postpones the death of the Tramp by language, for Chaplin was certain that such would be the effect of his character speaking. In 1936, he wrote:

> Occasionally I mused over the possibility of making a sound film, but the thought sickened me, for I realized I could never achieve the excellence of my silent pictures. It would mean giving up my tramp character entirely. Some people suggested that the tramp might talk. This was unthinkable, for the first word he ever uttered would transform him into another person. Besides, the matrix out of which he was born was as mute as the rags he wore.[39]

Matrix is an interesting word choice. Chaplin's eloquent last sentence refers to the matrix of the silent film world. But he is also talking about the Tramp's birth, which wouldn't have occurred had Chaplin himself not been born. Thus the last sentence also points to Chaplin's mother, Hannah, and the miserable conditions under which he and his brother, Sydney, had lived with her: their poverty, their father's alcoholism, Hannah's mental illness, and their incarceration in various state institutions. The memory of such pain was ineffable.

The Tramp's face was famous for expressing a mute melancholy that, along with the raggedy clothes, spelled out the inconsolable pain of his creator's childhood. To express this pain in words was impossible. As trauma theory expresses this idea, trauma is an event or sequence of events that surpasses the capacity of the mind to process (and therefore the event is revisited upon the psyche repeatedly in the form of dreams, flashbacks, and *déjà vu*).[40] Freud said of Chaplin, "[H]e always plays only himself as he was in his early dismal youth. He cannot get away from those impressions and to this day he obtains for himself the compensation for the frustrations and humiliations of that past period of his life."[41] As Chaplin worked through the trauma of his childhood in his silent films, he did not yet have the verbal language to express it (and wouldn't until making *Limelight* in 1952).

In addition to being the directors' turning points between silent and sound film (Chaplin) and verbal to visual gags (Allen), *Modern Times* and *Sleeper* represent new levels of sophistication in their creators' understanding of genre. Blending comedy with a social message, they each hoped to make a statement about contemporary society. In *Sleeper*, Allen smoothly integrates comedy and narrative. The plot is interesting, the setting is creative and pretty, and our delight at seeing Allen engage in dangerous slapstick is great. These factors outweigh the occasional unevenness of the throwaway one-liners. Throwaways are the gags that Allen could have used in a stand-up act; they weren't tailored to the precise setting and plot of *Sleeper*. For instance, he tells a social scientist, curious about some 1970s artifacts, "This is [a picture of] some girls burning a brassiere; you notice it's a very small fire."

Contemporary reviews of *Sleeper* were complimentary. Richard Schickel wrote, "The simplest measure of *Sleeper*'s success is perhaps the fact that one recalls it not by quoting Allen's one-liners but by trying to describe—inadequately—his beautifully built visual gags." This ineffability in the face of Allen's spot-on cleverness proves the point that actions speak louder than words. Even Pauline Kael, who often panned Allen's work, liked this one: "He's turning into that rarity, a verbal comedian who also knows how to use his body. And his acting has developed: he can register more emotions now." Paul Zimmerman duly recognized Allen's Chaplin imitation: "He strives consciously for Chaplinesque poignancy, sacrificing the funny line of the writer for the funnier mime of the actor."[42] The plot isn't perfect, and it lacks a satisfying ending, but *Sleeper* is far better in that regard than *Bananas* (1971) and *Everything You Always Wanted to Know About Sex* But Were Afraid to Ask* (1972). Much of the credit goes to good writing, set design, direction, and the acting of Allen, Keaton, and the supporting cast. While Miles identifies a set of joke-store teeth and a Howard Cosell TV appearance from the 1970s, Dr. Tryon (Don Keefer) treats such icons of popular culture in amazed reverence, as though they were fossils from a prehistoric age. Diane Keaton and John Beck (as Erno) mimic terrible Yiddish accents with straight faces, in order to bring Miles back through trauma (though the outtakes show Allen needing to cut and retake many times, due to his own uncontrollable laughing fits).[43] The well-made narrative, the appeal of the futurist setting, the strong supporting acting, good jokes, and Allen's own physical virtuosity make *Sleeper* a successful film.

But does *Sleeper* succeed in sending a social message? It is possible that *Sleeper* reveals more of a message to a later, twenty-first-century audience than Allen may have intended at the time of its making, particularly since many of the futurist jokes that Allen created in 1973 have become realities today. Allen and his contemporaries may have joked about these potentialities because they didn't believe they would come true—to name just a few: driverless cars, domestic robots, a cloned mammal, genetic gardening, impotence due to pornography addiction, and telescreens everywhere, mostly for our looking into, but also for surveillance by businesses, government, police, and other institutions. Today, cryonics is a legitimate business that invites people with fatal diseases to be frozen, their hope being that, when they are revived in the future, there will be cures for their diseases and they will live again.[44] Because Allen's jokes are realities in today's world, it is educational to watch this film forty-five years after its making. We may now take its implications a little more seriously than Allen intended.

Parody is a mode that seeks to make gentle fun of a genre by repeating it with a difference. The social message that parodies are meant to convey can range in tone from light (merely jesting at the genre conventions) to serious (making an intervention against reprehensible social practices). *Sleeper* seems like light mockery of science fiction, but, considered in its historic moment, it may have more relevance to Watergate, Vietnam, the Cold War, and other early seventies traumas than we realize when we are merely enjoying its gags. This would be especially true for viewers familiar with Stanley Kubrick's *2001: A Space Odyssey* (1968). In addition to being the first auteurist science fiction, which raised the genre above its usual kitschiness, *2001* was an intense critique about where the space race could take us, politically and spiritually.

Given *2001*'s high status in the sci-fi world, *Sleeper* makes many allusions to that movie. Miles's cryogenic freezing parallels the situation of the three astronauts sleeping in suspended animation for several years before HAL is programmed to awaken them. HAL-9000 himself reappears as the similar-looking Biocentral Computer 2100 Series G and is voiced by the same actor, Douglas Rain. *2001*'s social messages carry over, too. If screenwriter Arthur C. Clarke's cosmology is confusing and esoteric (one of the most common criticisms of the movie), one thing at least is perfectly clear: *2001* points a figure at human greed and competition. The will to win the Cold War space race effectively aborts a space mission of discovery, killing the astronauts onboard, and destroying their chance to meet the higher intelligence behind the monolith. HAL has been programmed to perform two mutually exclusive missions: conduct a safe journey of the Discovery spaceship, and hide its real mission from its captains due to NASA's fear that the Soviets will make contact with the monolith before Americans do. Because HAL cannot fulfill two contradictory objectives, he suffers a nervous breakdown, and kills to prevent being killed. In *Sleeper*, Allen pits the Underground and the Technocracy against each other in a hostile, paranoid way that mirrors that of the Russians and Americans in *2001*. Similarly, Discovery's astronauts, Dave Bowman and Frank Poole, have become so technically sophisticated that they have lost most of their human qualities. They talk like automatons, they refer to their families in a detached way, and, although they eat dinner side by side, they watch programs on their iPad-like tablets rather than looking at each other. There is no chitchat aboard Discovery. So too have the people of Allen's Federation lost touch with each other. Scientists proved that romantic relationships don't last because of the chemical that makes people get on each other's nerves, so the citizens have stopped trying to relate, and just pop into the Orgasmatron for instant stimulation. In both films, the directors have devised imaginary future worlds in which intimacy has vanished. This constitutes a social message: we should be careful how much we allow machines to take care of us, or we risk giving away our humanity to the machine.

Allen's conversation with Eric Lax about the making of *Sleeper* does not refer to any intended social message; it focuses instead on the logistics of outdoor filming, preparing stunts, and building expensive props. Yet one segment of the interview reveals Allen's awareness that part of his work comes from an unconscious place. In a Barthesian sense,[45] the film can be said to write itself; through a process of looking through lenses, being on location, and collaborating with a crew, the director's vision is constantly in flux. Allen told Lax:

> I was thinking about *Sleeper* today in terms of how I hate machines in real life. I have no patience with them. I break them. ... And I noticed in *Sleeper* one of the recurrent themes is that advanced technology doesn't work: a guy shoots a future gun and it blows up; I go into a futuristic kitchen and that malfunctions. ... You would think that I'm doing that on purpose, that I'm trying to create a character that doesn't get along with machines. But it's always involuntary. I don't consciously try to put in those things.[46]

To see *Sleeper* as a condemnation of the primacy of computers in the Digital Age is a possible reading, though not the only reading. If, on the other hand, a viewer believes that *2001* sends such a message, then Allen's movie evokes a series of associations with that film that may lead the viewer to take seriously the threat of artificial intelligence taking over human lives. Whether you read a social message into *Sleeper*'s parody or not, you are equally entertained by a plot, jokes, and production values that weave together a cohesive, playful parody of science fiction.

Modern Times lacks that integration of its various parts into a congruous whole that *Sleeper* achieved. The promise of the first factory section is not delivered as Charlie continues on his adventure. After his first bout with the machine, his enemy shifts into the more abstract forms of poverty, unemployment, and the welfare officials who are chasing the Gamin. This film is the rare one in which Chaplin creates a secondary plot to parallel the Tramp's (a device that Allen constantly uses with excellent effect). The story of the Gamin's efforts to feed her family, and then to evade the orphanage officials once her father is killed, is an interesting story in its own right, and it weaves smoothly into the Tramp's when they join up to picture their Dream House about halfway through the film. She also provides an encouraging, warm presence in the Tramp's life: the person who is waiting for him when he gets out of jail, who finds him work and a home. But, until the café scene, the two protagonists don't face their antagonists together. Out of chivalry or double standards, Chaplin may have hesitated to place a female on the road as a fellow tramp. Evidence of this hesitation can be seen in the alternate ending he had planned. In this ending, the Tramp's breakdown would occur near the end of the film instead of the beginning. Upon his discharge, the Gamin would be waiting for him in the hospital lobby, dressed in a nun's habit and accompanied by a Mother Superior. When he says goodbye and begins to walk away down the long, dusty road, the Gamin feels conflicted about following. Chaplin's scenario draft reads:

> There is something inscrutable in her expression, something of resignation and regret. She stands as though lost in a dream, watching after him and her spirit goes with him, for out of herself the ghost of the Gamin appears and runs rampant down the hospital steps, dancing and bounding after him, calling and beckoning as she runs toward him. Along that lonely road she catches up to him, dancing and circling around him, but he does not see her, he walks alone. ... She is awakened from her revelry [reverie?] by a light touch, the hand of the Mother Superior. She starts, then turns and smiles wistfully at the kindly old face and together they depart into the portals of the hospital again. FADE OUT[47]

Possibly Chaplin believed that a cloistered life was a better choice for a destitute woman than the roustabout life of a tramp. The ending he ultimately chose, that of the two tramps leaving town together, was somewhat risqué. Given the climate of suspicion regarding Chaplin's morals, the image of the older man linking arms with the girl to travel *à deux* was suggestive. To make it clear that the Tramp and the Gamin were innocent of sexual activity, Chaplin's Tramp slept in a shed attached to the dilapidated shack on the one night that he and the Gamin spent together.

Chaplin's problem with the film's ending reflects the disconnected and episodic character of the whole film. Otis Ferguson complained that *Modern Times* was "really a collection of two-reelers which might have been called The Shop, The Jailbird, The Watchman and The Singing Waiter."[48] Lawrence Howe went further, claiming that the unevenness of the picture was due to the internal conflict of the director, who was both critical of mechanization of the culture and a prime benefactor of that mechanization. I agree that Chaplin's ideological uncertainties contributed to the structural problems of the film. In Chaplin's attempt to blend a social critique of anti-industrialization with a sentimental plot, he failed precisely by not joining up the comrades to fight against the authorities. But that would be a different film altogether.

George Potter notes that Chaplin enjoys the privilege of a positively disposed world audience, which gives him a platform for his message about human suffering, but suggests that Chaplin lacks the narrative skills to realize the task, and "tries to force the social critique into the genre of farce and reconciliation that marked his artistic expression."[49] The social message of *Modern Times*, that industrialization was leeching humanity of its freedom and joy, comes across strongly in the first two-reeler, The Shop, but is more or less abandoned after the first quarter of the film. The second factory scene doesn't make the same point as the first; it is a set piece about the Tramp's inability to nurture another human being in need. Charlie's energetic movements, and his forcing of large amounts of food down Conklin's gullet, replicate the abuse that the Bellows feeder wreaked on him in the first scene. The thread that links the four set pieces (factories, jail, café, store)—and those side bits about the Gamin's life on the docks—is a thin one. Although he desired to leverage his status as the world's best known actor/director in order to produce a sociopolitical critique-as-artwork, Chaplin did not achieve this goal.

Modern Times nonetheless holds an important place in film history. The strong image of a crazed Charlie caught in the cogs of the machine he serves has outlasted the Machine Age in the American imagination. Among science fiction films, *Sleeper* is not the first example that comes to mind as a condemnation of the Digital Age. Yet, considering it as a reflection of several traumatic events that took place during its cultural moment, we find that *Sleeper*'s conditions of artificial intelligence and dictatorship are eerily prescient of our own time.

3

Master/Slave Dialectic in *The Great Dictator* and *Zelig*

"My one regret in life is that I am not someone else," wrote Woody Allen in the preface to his autobiographical play, *The Floating Light Bulb* (1982). It is one of Allen's great-sounding lines; it makes you laugh at the same time that you feel the pathos of a man who has everything and cannot be happy. This line was written while he was working on his most creative screenplay in which a man actually does become someone else every time he gets near other men. The ultimate conformist, Zelig wants to be liked and to be safe, and achieves this by physically resembling anyone with whom he interacts. Allen's one-liner reveals that he thinks there is something Zelig-like in himself, increasing the intrigue that this human chameleon offers.

"Something about ... Chaplin suggests not that he is a victim but rather, menacingly, that he would seek victims, pounce on them, tear them apart," wrote Theodor Adorno after meeting the filmmaker.[1] In contrast to Allen and Zelig's, the resemblance of Chaplin to his characters, the Jewish Barber and Hynkel in *The Great Dictator*, is obvious. Likable, dignified, and innocent, the Jewish Barber is a more settled version of The Tramp. Imperious, vain, cruel, and histrionic, Dictator Hynkel is a parodic version of Chaplin as director and partner, according to traits described by family members, lovers, and friends in their numerous memoirs and interviews.[2] Both *Zelig* and *The Great Dictator* explore the psychological phenomena of mirroring, doubling, and projecting. They propose the question, what motivates cruel tyrants? And, what makes people follow such leaders?

The Great Dictator and *Zelig* are set in the interwar years, when conformity became a cultural phenomenon, and fascism gained power in several European nations.[3] Chaplin and Allen were fascinated with the late twenties and thirties. During that era, Chaplin gained a political consciousness. He began to be listened to, even though he hubristically overshot the mark, repeatedly claiming he'd be able to single-handedly "avert the world crisis," according to one girlfriend, May Reeves.[4] Allen selects this era for the setting of several films (*Zelig, Shadows and Fog, Radio Days, Bullets Over Broadway, Midnight in Paris, Purple Rose of Cairo, Sweet and Lowdown, Magic in the Moonlight*). He is gripped by nostalgia for the twenties, possibly because he believes that people were more innocent in the pre–Holocaust era when the economy and liberalism were at a peak.

Allen is also clearly gripped by fear of anti–Semitism, which culminated in Hitler's death camps during World War II. Trying to understand how this could have happened, Allen explores anti–Semitism and fascism in films such as *Shadows and Fog* and *Zelig*. With typical deflecting cynicism, he denies the idea that brutality is difficult to understand. In "Random Reflections of a Second-Rate Mind" (1990), he stated that he was not mystified by the occurrence of the Holocaust, because "inside every heart lived the worm of self-preservation, of fear, greed, and an animal will to power ... that the Holocaust could occur was not all so strange. History had been filled with unending examples of equal bestiality, differing only cosmetically."[5] Despite denying its impenetrability as a subject, he demonstrates a fascination for it as he returns to anti–Semitism and the Holocaust again and again, sometimes humorously, as in Alvy Singer's paranoia (in *Annie Hall*) that he hears anti–Semitic remarks all around him, and sometimes more seriously, as in *Shadows and Fog* (1991) and *Anything Else* (2003), where David Dobel buys a gun in case the Nazis come to get him.

The Great Dictator opens on a war between the Allied Forces and the Central Powers in the year 1918. A Jewish soldier (Chaplin) from the nation of Tomainia saves a wounded pilot, Commander Schultz (Reginald Gardiner), but during a plane crash, he gets a concussion and suffers amnesia. Twenty years later, the private leaves the hospital where he has convalesced, unaware of the rise of a dictatorship under the ruthless Adenoid

"My world!" Charlie Chaplin as Adenoid Hynkel in *The Great Dictator*, 1940 (Charles Chaplin/Photofest).

Hynkel (also Chaplin). He reopens his barbershop in what is now a Jewish ghetto surveilled by Hynkel's stormtroopers. The Barber falls in love with his neighbor, Hannah (Paulette Goddard) and together they try to resist the stormtroopers. Meanwhile Commander Schultz, now working for Hynkel, recognizes the Barber as the man who saved his life. He orders the stormtroopers to leave him alone and cease traumatizing the ghetto. But Hynkel orders a total purge of the ghetto when he learns that a Jew won't lend him money for a military attack on neighboring Osterlich. Hynkel fires Schultz for insubordination (having a different opinion about military strategy). Excited by the prospect of conquering the world, Hynkel dances a *pas de deux* with his balloon-like globe. Schultz flees to the Barber's neighborhood to hide, but the stormtroopers discover him and take both the Commander and the Barber to a concentration camp. Hannah and the neighbors escape to Osterlich while it is still a free country. Hynkel argues with Napaloni, dictator of Bacteria, over who should invade Osterlich. Hynkel invades Osterlich and his stormtroopers attack Hannah at her friends' vineyard. The Barber and Schultz escape the camp dressed in Tomainian military uniforms. Because of the Barber's strong resemblance to Hynkel, the stormtroopers think he is the dictator. They lead him to a podium in front of thousands of soldiers and civilians to announce the takeover of Osterlich. Instead of lauding their victory, the Barber pretends, as Hynkel, to have a change of heart. He tells the soldiers to lay down arms and stand up for peace and brotherhood. Hannah hears the speech over a radio. The Barber speaks directly to her, exhorting her not to give up hope. She is buoyed by a radiant vision of the new world he proposes. The End.

Zelig begins in the late 1920s in New York City, when a strange human chameleon comes to the attention of reporters and doctors. Leonard Zelig (Woody Allen) wants so much to be liked that he physically morphs into an appearance resembling whomever he happens to be speaking with. The media, doctors, and professors grab the opportunity to explain, publicize, and psychoanalyze him. Even Dr. Eudora Fletcher (Mia Farrow) initially pursues the case in order to raise her own status and become famous. She is the psychiatrist assigned to Zelig's case at New York Hospital. Under hypnosis, Zelig reveals the horrible abuse he suffered as a child from his parents, siblings, and neighbors. He decided it was safest to blend in, thus developing his chameleon condition. Fletcher cures him by pretending to be him, which fosters his recognition of his own pattern. She also falls in love with him. Just as Zelig is regaining a normal personality, a series of lawsuits are brought by disgruntled past spouses, employers, and even surgical patients of Zelig. He apparently had adopted many disguises and played several professional and intimate roles when he was a chameleon. The stress of publicity and courtroom trials causes his relapse, and he disappears. Fletcher looks the world over for him, eventually spotting him on the podium at Hitler's Nuremburg rally. Fletcher brings a small plane to the rescue; however, unnerved by the Nazis' pursuit, she is unable to continue flying. Zelig takes over the wheel, apparently gleaning Fletcher's piloting skills with his chameleonic osmotic method. Landing in New York, they establish a new world record of upside-down transatlantic flight. Now cured, forgiven, and newly lionized by the public, Zelig is able to settle down and marry Fletcher. The End.

Both films explore fascism and use Hitler as a symbol for human megalomaniac tendencies; both are equally engaged in trying to understand how the little man can either stand up to or go along with such a sinister force. The form of comedy most adept to treat such serious phenomena is absurdism—or, existentialism played for laughs.[6] Hence, Hynkel falls in love with his floating globe, emblem of limitless power. And Allen imagines fascism's draw for hollow men like Zelig. For centuries, philosophers and psychologists have attempted to understand the cause and nature of evil, a force often expressed by the assumption of power over others, an infliction of harm upon others, and an attitude of indifference to one's common humanity with the other. For the purpose of this study, Hegel's theory of Master/Slave dialectic and Nietzsche's theory of Master/Slave morality provide frameworks for ways in which to examine the phenomena of dominance and submission in *Zelig* and *The Great Dictator*. Hynkel is a great dominator and Zelig an equally impressive submitter, yet analysis proves that each one contains elements of the opposite quality. Chaplin demonstrates this phenomenon by psychological doubling, while Allen chooses to heal Zelig through being mirrored by a woman analyst.

Philosopher Georg Wilhelm Friedrich Hegel had an answer to the question of the etiology of evil, which he posed in terms of Master and Slave (in German, also Lord and Bondsman). In 1807, Hegel wrote *Phenomenology of Spirit* to describe his theory of historical and personal development, a process that moves people from consciousness to self-consciousness and ultimately to absolute knowledge. Although these terms confuse most commentators (especially postmodernists, who deny the existence of absolutes), the Hegelian Master/Slave narrative is a fairly simple allegory about both collective (historical) and individual psychological development. It goes like this: Two consciousnesses meet, and they can either treat each other like objects, ignoring the other, or they "become mesmerized by the mirror-like other" and attempt to assert their will in a "life-and-death" struggle:

> Self-consciousness is faced by another self-consciousness; it has come out of itself. This has a twofold significance: first, it has lost itself, for it finds itself as an other being; secondly, in doing so it has superseded the other, for it does not see the other as an essential being, but in the other sees its own self.... First, it must proceed to supersede the other independent being in order to become certain of itself as the

essential being; secondly, in so doing it proceeds to supersede its own self, for this other is itself.[7]

In their "struggle to the death," one masters the other, who concedes to being enslaved. The victor emerges because he does not fear death; he does not see his identity as being dependent on life. The slave consents to slavery out of fear for his life. The Master is not content in his dominance, however, since the recognition that he seeks from the other is only partial when the Master sees the other only partially. The dominant one fails to see his self-reflection in the subservient one: "Adequate recognition requires a mirroring of the self through the other, which means that to be successful it must be mutual."[8] The Master is dependent on the Slave for recognition. Through his dependence on the Slave, he weakens his own relationship with nature and the material world, since the Slave does his work for him, crafting products and performing services for the Master.

As the Slave creates more products for the Master, he begins to see himself reflected in the products he creates and to take pride in his creativity (Marx develops this idea in his theory of dialectical materialism). Consequently, the Slave is no longer alienated from his labor and begins to develop self-consciousness, while the Master is dependent on the Slave for labor, and becomes enslaved to him.

Here the concept of sublation comes in. The essence of dialectical movement is that the first term (thesis) is contradicted by the second (antithesis), and their collision makes a new third term (synthesis) by the process of sublation. In the dialectical movement, sublation occurs when the old terms are both preserved and changed in the new hybrid. Similarly, the characters in a narrative are changed by their relationships through recognizing the self in the other. The most dramatic moment of this recognition occurs when Dr. Eudora Fletcher analyzes Leonard Zelig by mirroring his confusion. Fletcher becomes more gentle and self-accepting when Zelig recognizes these qualities in her. Zelig, in turn, becomes less confused by seeing himself in Fletcher's love for him. In *The Great Dictator*, recognition occurs in a less direct manner when Hannah unknowingly prepares the Barber to give his later speech about liberation. Hannah models the qualities of hope and optimism for the Barber to assimilate. This sublation occurs not through Hannah and the Barber standing in a Master/Slave relationship to each other, but by virtue of Hannah, the Barber, and their neighbors finding pride enough to fight the stormtroopers in particular, and Hynkel's ideology in general.

I have quoted and described Hegel's theory at length because these concepts of mirroring are fundamental to my understanding of what is happening in both films. By supplementing Hegel with Friedrich Nietzsche and Jacques Lacan, we get a fuller reflection of possibilities for self-development in Zelig, Eudora Fletcher, Hynkel, and the Jewish Barber. In *Beyond Good and Evil*

(1886), Nietzsche argued that the fundamental human instinct is a will to power. Obviously, not everyone can have power in every sphere, so morality emerges to justify and challenge power imbalance. According to Nietzsche, there are two fundamental types of morality: Master and Slave. The ruling group (whom Nietzsche calls "noble") determines what is good for others based on what is good for itself:

> The noble human being separates from himself those in whom the opposite of exalted, proud states finds expression: he despises them.... The opposition of good and bad means approximately the same as noble and contemptible. One feels contempt for the cowardly, the anxious, the petty, those intent on narrow utility.... The noble type experiences itself as determining values.[9]

Master morality values such traits as pride, strength, confidence, and activity. What makes Chaplin's dictator Hynkel so comical is that his public persona projects these traits, but his inner self is craven; it requires the constant assistance of his yes-men Garbitsch and Herring, his servants, secretaries, and Dictator Napaloni to shore it up. Similarly, the fascist propaganda that Hynkel and his henchmen spout is based on their sense of racial superiority, as in the Nietzsche passage above. *Die Juden* (the Jews), in Hynkel's first speech, are so reprehensible to him that his genitals steam when he speaks of them. His microphone bends in the heat of his scorn.

In contrast to the Master's view of himself as noble and therefore good, the Slave regards the ruler's vaunted virtues with suspicion. He envies the Master's power, but he does not benefit by the Master's value system. Instead, he values the qualities that serve to ease his own discomfort. Nietzsche describes the values of Slave morality: "pity, the complaisant and obliging hand, the warm heart, patience, industry, humility, and friendliness are honored—for here these are the most useful qualities and almost the only means for enduring the pressure of existence."[10] These are the qualities that Chaplin's Jewish Barber praises in his famous speech at the end of the film. He believes that most humans uphold this type of morality, rather than Master morality. He orates from the high dais: "We all want to help each other. Human beings are like that. We want to live by each other's happiness—not by each other's misery. We don't want to hate and despise one another. In this world there is room for everyone."[11] Slave morality assesses actions according to their good or evil intentions, whereas Master morality assesses actions according to their good or bad consequences for the ruler. To achieve any power in a historical dialectic, the slaves must "corrupt the strong" into believing that the will to power is evil. Distrustful of the many European populist movements and revolutions of the eighteenth and nineteenth centuries, Nietzsche called democracy a "herd animal morality," a "lower" morality based on fear, and an "heir to the Christian movement."[12]

Psychoanalyst Jacques Lacan (1901–1981) extends Hegel's and Nietzsche's formulations of power dynamics among humans. The French thinker posited the formation of ego during the Mirror Stage of childhood development. At the age of six to eighteen months, the toddler recognizes itself in a mirror. The image of wholeness he sees in the mirror contrasts with his sense of fragmentariness due to his lack of motor coordination. This creates a sense of rivalry with his image. To resolve this tension, the child identifies with the image, giving rise to the ego. The subject becomes alienated from the self, creating the Imaginary Order: "The I is thus fixed in a fictive format: our conception of ourselves is necessarily a fiction which we are then put to defend from the onset of the Real."[13] The onset of the Real refers to "that which exists outside symbolization, and outside the analytic experience."[14] The Real is that which we cannot know. Hynkel's frustrations with himself, his staff, and outside threats to his power depict a subject much alienated from self, one that is absolutely dependent on mirrors to maintain its image. Hynkel surrounds himself with human mirrors (henchmen and sycophants). Herring abjectly fawns on his commander, while suave Garbitsch diplomatically massages Hynkel's histrionic executive orders to minimize the damage

Mirrors enhance his ego. Charlie Chaplin as Adenoid Hynkel in *The Great Dictator*, 1940 (Charles Chaplin).

that his boss causes. The Double Cross mission to kill all the Jews and create an Aryan world is Garbitsch's pet project, but he lets it appear that Hynkel is in charge, while simultaneously reflecting and magnifying the dimensions of Hynkel's own ambition and racism.

Hynkel also uses literal mirrors to magnify his sense of control. Directly behind Hynkel's desk stands a tall bureau of filing drawers (like a card catalog) whose facade gives the impression that the dictator is in control of his empire. Such a large file suggests that he reads many political and historical documents and performs his duties with efficiency. When he opens the faux file cabinet, however, there are no files but instead a triptych of full-length mirrors before which he preens. In Lacanian fashion, he finds the strength to declare war on Osterlich only while mugging before the mirror. The ego image is far more powerful than the real man. When Garbitsch regards Hynkel's image in the mirror, he sees the ego image with which Hynkel identifies, rather than the weak, fragmented self that he knows his commander to possess.

In contrast, the Jewish Barber is humble, down-to-earth, and practical. The only mirror the Barber uses to regard himself is the shiny bald pate of one of his barbershop customers, a surface which cannot actually reflect him. This knowledge allows us to laugh *with* the Barber, instead of the response that his alter-ego Hynkel provokes, which is to laugh *at* him for his vanity. The Barber suffers no such disconnection between his self and ego. The dictator's "rivalry with his image" requires him to seek his reflection in every possible object, including humans. Since he can never reflect back the consciousness of the other, he is neither satisfied nor at ease.

Hegelian Master/Slave dialectic occurs in both films, with Zelig and Hynkel playing the symbolic roles. Zelig occupies the position of Slave—he is bound to his psychological condition, to doctors, to his sister and Martin Geist, to the media, to the plaintiffs who sue him. In contrast, Hynkel is Master of the empire. As in Hegel, Zelig's Masters are dependent on his recognition of them, but he cannot provide it since in his diseased state he can only parrot them, rather than providing a thinking reflection of them. Consequently, the doctors project their own illnesses (cancer) and theories (faulty alignment, hormone imbalance) upon him without success because they have not "seen" him. One doctor literally twists his patient to fit his theory: chiropractors "realign" Zelig, leaving him with his feet facing backward. The fact that the doctor would allow reporters to take a picture of this egregious error is astounding, but it demonstrates his blindness to his actual skills in favor of his ego's heightened view of them. During his illness, Zelig's encounter with any other Hegelian self-consciousness is one of utter and immediate capitulation to the Slave position. He does not recognize himself in the other, and he fears destruction if he does not imitate the other: "I do it [change appearance] to feel safe," he tells his analyst, Dr. Fletcher.

However universal Zelig's tendencies to conform may be, they are also particularized by his experience of being Jewish in the 1930s. Zelig's capitulation to the perceived needs of others is a Jew's fear of not fitting in, a fear of dying by the machinations of anti–Semites. The Hegelian dialectic applies to groups as well as individuals. For Nietzsche, Jews are the epitome of slave morality, because they know how to survive under the worst conditions.[15] Iris Bruce considers Zelig's illness akin to that of Gregor Samsa in *The Metamorphosis*. Nineteenth- and twentieth-century rhetoric often described Jews as "vermin." Like Gregor, Zelig climbs the walls and walks on the ceiling while undergoing a dangerous drug treatment. By giving their protagonists mysterious conditions, Allen and Kafka "make visible the dehumanizing commodification of life in twentieth-century society."[16] Similarly, Ruth Johnston sees Zelig's chameleonism as a metaphor for ethnic assimilation. *Zelig* is set in the 1920s and '30s when American melting pot ideology and "100 percent Americanism" were at their peak. Because Jews did not have a homeland of their own, they became "a free floating ethnic signifier of otherness."[17]

In contrast, Ruth Perlmutter believes that in *Zelig*, Allen is ridiculing shallowness in all types of people: "Allen is reviling Americans and Jews for their bad taste and capitulation to the superficial." She states that Allen wants to speak against anti–Semitism, but for some reason cannot do so directly. Sending Zelig to the Nazis for a last-ditch effort to belong is humorous because it is "such an unthinkable role for an American Jew." She believes Allen uses such humor "to camouflage his messianic impulse."[18] Allen is known neither for messianism, nor the desire to ameliorate the evils of the world; in fact, his style is quite the opposite. In speaking about his idea for the film, Allen did not mention Jews or anti–Semitism per se, only that Zelig's personality is "the kind that leads to fascism."[19] In other words, the Zelig condition could happen to Jews and non–Jews alike. For this reason, it is productive to view Zelig's condition and his eventual recovery as an individual (psychological) as well as collective (historical) phenomenon. On the one hand, Zelig's recovery gives the film a pleasing resolution through the humanistic message that love cures illness. On the other hand, the resolution is somewhat artificial and incomplete, because, as Ruth Johnston points out, Zelig recovers by embracing the WASP lifestyle of the Gentile Dr. Fletcher, adopting her style and values instead of embracing his own heritage.

Zelig assimilates instead of resolving the fundamental childhood issue to which he confessed under hypnosis: his Jewish parents "joined the anti–Semites" in baiting young Leonard, creating a self-hating Jew. Leonard's noxious family environment closely parallels Allen's own. In Zelig's case, the parents' constant violent fighting and their failure to nurture their children resulted in the illness of all three offspring: Ruth became a thief, an alcoholic, and a cruel exploiter of her brother Zelig's condition. Their brother committed suicide, and Leonard developed the chameleon condition in order to "be liked and be safe." In Allen's case, the parents' constant fighting and failure to nurture also resulted in illness: Allen's self-admitted lifelong depression, anxiety, and obsessive compulsions. Describing the relationship of their parents, Allen's sister Letty Aronson says, "there was a period of years when they never even spoke, when I was growing up.... They either argued, or didn't speak."[20] Allen thought they were "on the verge of breaking up every single night for the first thirty of those years [of their marriage]. So when I went to school in the morning, I never knew if I was coming home to both parents."[21] Allen had a contentious relationship with his mother; he said that she slapped him every day, a practice that she admits to the camera in Robert Weide's documentary, *Woody Allen* (2011).[22]

Another documentary, *Wild Man Blues* (1997), covers Woody, Letty, and Soon-Yi's tour of France with Allen's jazz band. This film contains a poignant and telling scene with his aged parents. Perhaps because he knew they would demonstrate their indifference, thereby explaining his lifelong depression, Allen decided to film a scene in which he shows his parents the numerous medals and awards that he received while on tour. His parents callously disregard this proof of their son's success. His father comments on the skill of the engravers rather than the meaning of the awards. Biographer David Evanier reacts to this scene: "The parents' behavior is joyless as they behold their son, a star beloved by half the world, who has been good to them and to his sister Letty. Their attitude toward Allen seems almost pathological in its complaint and bitterness. There is no acknowledgment, no recognition of what Allen has accomplished."[23] The quality that Evanier describes is so pathological that at first the scene seems staged, as though it were part of a Woody Allen feature film. Yet it is real: its tone is consistent with the critical attitude shown by his mother in the 2011 documentary by Robert Weide and with numerous statements by Allen about his depression and its link to his parents' ongoing indifferent or critical responses to him. Sometimes he expresses their hostility in jokes, such as, "I was kidnapped. My parents snapped into action. They rented my room."[24]

I have described at length these attributes of Allen's family psychodrama because they shed light on Zelig's fundamental problem, an internalization of his undesirability as a member of his family and as a Jew. Allen has responded to the label, "self-hating Jew," with characteristic ironic deflection: "it's true I am Jewish and I don't like myself very much ... it's not because of my persuasion."[25] Yet he does many things that belie the statement: he frequently parodies Jewish stereotypes, he chooses non–Jewish lovers, and he dreads various recollections of his upbringing. His problem of accepting himself is inseparable from his reaction to his childhood Brooklyn Jewish milieu. This does not in itself add up to a self-hating Jew, but his background, which was Jewish, created his view of the world as a dangerous place filled with untrustworthy human beings. He writes, "It's very important to realize that we're up against an evil, insidious, hostile universe. It'll make you ill and age you and kill you. And there's somebody—or something—out there who for some irrational, unexplainable reason is killing us."[26] His thoughts on the Holocaust, which I'll address shortly, attest to that view.

Linked to Zelig's failure to resolve his Jewish identity issue is the fact that, although the recovered Zelig gives the "occasional lecture about his experience," he never mentions any explanation or analysis of his having become a Nazi. The film closes around 1938, the time of Hitler's mass rallies, which Zelig attended. Even more disturbingly, Zelig seems to have been working closely with the Nazis. When Dr. Fletcher spots Zelig at Hitler's speech, he is in the second row on the podium, just behind and to the right of Hitler. These seats would have been granted only to those in the innermost circle, raising questions about just how far Zelig had gone into his Nazi personality before being saved. Instead of using his experience of becoming a Nazi to alert Americans about the very real and imminent dangers of fascism, Zelig only gives "occasional" lectures about himself, but not about the Nazis. The film, then, is less about how the human desire for conformism leads to fascism and more about how one individual recovered from psychosis through love and a good analyst. Stephen Papson describes this lack of political content as a "retreat into idealism without material grounding." Allen "desires an authentic autonomous individual without being able to recognize any social formations which might support it."[27] In short, Allen doesn't believe that any social structure is adequate to curtail that "worm of self-preservation, greed, fear and animal will to power" that he finds in the heart of all humans.[28]

Despite its lack of social commitment, the film creates a compelling story of healing through relationship, which happens to be a cornerstone of contemporary therapy and psychoanalysis. In one of the most compelling analysis sessions ever seen on film (and an illustration of Hegelian sublation), Dr. Fletcher breaks through Zelig's resistance by mirroring his condition. This causes him to have to mirror himself, since imitating others is all that his psyche knows how to do. Remember, Zelig always "becomes" a doctor when around real doctors. When Fletcher says she wanted so badly to be liked that she has been pretending to be a doctor in order to fit in with her friends, Zelig is powerfully affected. He feels physically and mentally ill. When Fletcher insists that he should diagnose her illness, Zelig drops the disguise and says, "How should I know? I'm not a doctor." With his guard lowered, she puts him under hypnosis to probe his unconscious. What she finds is very interesting for both his cure and her future. His family and neighborhood environments were so violent that Zelig felt alienated from life and from himself. Everybody beat each other, just as Allen's mother had

Zelig playing doctor. Woody Allen (center) as Zelig in *Zelig,* 1983 (Orion/Photofest).

beat him. At twelve, Zelig asked a rabbi the meaning of life, but the rabbi would only tell him in Hebrew, and then wanted to profit from Zelig's ignorance by charging him for Hebrew lessons. The result was that religion seemed just another game to Zelig, another way to ostracize the poor, the unlucky, the Jewish.

On the positive side, during his hypnosis, Fletcher learns that Zelig is in love with her. Along with this welcome revelation, however, she also has to hear unmediated criticism rising from his unconscious. After telling her he hates her country house because of the mosquitos, the grass, and her cooking, he continues:

"And the jokes you try and tell, when you ... when you think you're amusing, they're ... long and pointless ... there's no end to them."

"You're very sweet ... 'Cause you're ... you're not as clever as you think you are. You're all mixed up ... and nervous ... and you're the worst cook."[29]

Mary Nichols reads this passage as a reflection on Zelig himself, that it is he who is mixed up and nervous.[30] I disagree, because the rest of the sentence is clearly about the doctor: her bad jokes, her faulty self-estimation, and her bad cooking. Instead, I think Zelig is finally finding his critical voice, for it is just after this session that he begins to express negative opinions about Brahms and Mussolini, and positive ones about baseball and the Democratic Party.

Furthermore, where Nichols reads Zelig's desire to "take care of" Fletcher as his healing moment, I see his critique of her as an assumption of mastery. It is his will to power coming through as his "unconscious speaks." In order to gain a personality and command over his own ego, it appears that Zelig needs to put her down. In Hegelian, Nietzschean, and Lacanian terms, this is how the psyche functions.

Zelig is wrong about Eudora Fletcher. Far from coming across as ignorant, confused, or nervous, Dr. Fletcher appears remarkably calm, despite the consistent humiliation of working with doctors who distrust her authority because she is a woman. Her persistence in seeking a new modality of curing a unique disease is remarkable, given the length of time it takes, and the constant need to placate her supervisors as she asks for more time. It is noteworthy that the only intellectual who recognizes Fletcher's skill is another female professional, Susan Sontag, who describes Fletcher's cure as a "triumph of aesthetic instincts." Sontag goes on to say, "her techniques didn't owe anything to then current schools of therapy. But she sensed what was needed and she provided it, and that was, in its way, a remarkable creative accomplishment" (97). Of course, viewers cannot judge the quality of Fletcher's jokes (which Zelig calls horrible), since she makes none onscreen, but we can safely say that Eudora is intelligent, probably more so than she thinks, rather than less. Zelig may be criticizing his doctor's intelligence because he is threatened by the power she has over him. He has good reason to be afraid, since the narrator describes Fletcher's method as an attack: "in the trance state, the personality will be deeply probed, and then restructured" (78). Restructuring the brain is an ongoing concern of Allen's; what frightened *Sleeper*'s Miles Monroe most about the totalitarian government was the prospect of having his personality "restructured" by computers and state doctors. Letting someone restructure one's brain puts one in the ultimate vulnerable position, even (or especially) when that person is a psychiatrist.

In addition to fear of mental takeover by a doctor, there is another reason for a man to feel threatened by a woman's analysis of his psyche. In patriarchy, men fill the Master role, while women fill the Slave role. As Virginia Woolf said, women's role is to mirror their men with magnification (and certainly not to restructure them according to the women's own intelligent theories): "Women have served all these centuries as looking glasses possessing the magic and delicious power of reflecting the figure of man at twice its natural size."[31] Zelig may be a victim of anti-Semitism, but he is still considered superior to at least one class of beings—women. Notably, Zelig would undergo metamorphosis with all comers *except for women* (until he met Fletcher, whose status was higher because she was a doctor). Prior to analysis, Zelig refuses to change himself into a woman. Becoming a woman would mean giving up the only shred of power and dignity he possessed, his manhood.

Zelig as Gentile. Woody Allen in *Zelig*, 1983 (Orion/Photofest).

Femininity and femaleness are devalued in patriarchy, whereas masculinity wins status, security, power, and love.

In the magic moment of his self-recognition in the other, Zelig does "become" a woman, since he mirrors Dr. Fletcher. This transgendering leap may be the very experience that saves him. Post-cure, Zelig adopts more characteristically feminine traits than any other Allen persona possesses. He smiles frequently, touches people affectionately, mugs for the camera, making every effort to please others. Mary Nichols extols Zelig's cure by means of his and Fletcher's mutual recognition of the other's strengths and weaknesses. Yet, I find this essential difference between them: Zelig undervalues Fletcher's intelligence, while Zelig's lack of intelligence and taste never affects Fletcher's estimation of his value.

In my reading of *The Great Dictator*, on the other hand, normative gender attributes and roles are reversed. Hannah is the strong one, the Barber weaker and more timid. This imbalance is due in part to the fact that Chaplin, still nervous about letting the Tramp speak, chose to have the Barber speak as little as possible. His silence allowed Hannah to dominate conversations that were more like monologues, while the Barber made only the briefest of interjections. The strangeness of this mode of relating is particularly noticeable during the scene in which Hannah tells the Barber the dream of owning her own business. In this desire, Hannah eschews the traditionally feminine way of getting ahead, which is by marrying the male business owner. While the Barber absent-mindedly lathers and begins to shave her face, Hannah carries on in an animated manner. The fact that he "mistakes" her for a man with whiskers is in itself a reflection of the gender role reversal that is going on, and of Hannah's androgynous traits. Hannah also shows physical courage when she shouts back to the stormtroopers who have just bullied a grocer, "Why, I wish I was a man; I'd show ya!" Their response is to throw tomatoes at her, whereupon she calls them pigs. Before he knows about the regime, the Barber stands up to the stormtroopers with a paintbrush and a can of paint as weapons, but he loses his aplomb as soon as he understands the regime's systemic discrimination against Jews. Later scenes show him hiding in barrels and chests, and surreptitiously passing along the coin-in-a-pudding that would mark him as the elected martyr for the cause.

Nowhere do the imbalance and role reversal between Hannah and the Barber come across as meaningfully as the scene on the rooftop. They are watching the barbershop burn down after being firebombed by the stormtroopers. This scene powerfully conveys Hannah and the Barber's relationship. It is the pivotal moment of the film, just as the moment when Fletcher mirrors Zelig is the turning point in that film. If there is any moment when the Barber gains the courage to make his final speech, it must be this one (even though we see no signs of his receiving her urgent message), because when we next meet him, he is transformed. On the roof, Hannah is in profile to the camera, while the Barber sits with his back to us, against a backdrop of high flames consuming his barbershop. Sensing his depression, Hannah tries to encourage him: "Never mind, we can start again. We can go to Osterlich, that's still a free country.... Mr. Jaeckel's brother's got a vineyard in Osterlich. You could come, too. If we work hard and don't eat much, we can save money. We can buy a chicken farm. There's nice money to be made in chickens." A beat of silence before Hannah begins to cry. In my reading, she cries because he is so unresponsive.[32] For all intents and purposes, she has asked him to marry her and run away together. These many months, she has been able to retain hope despite the persecution of the Jews. It rests on her shoulders to save their lives by planning for their escape. In contrast, the Barber is paralyzed, an epitome of depression. Faceless to the viewer, he might as well be a statue or a silhouette rather than a man.

The final scene at Osterlich reverses these gender roles, making the Barber so impossibly brave that he defies death and becomes the harbinger of hope, just as Hegel's Master wins his battle with the Other because he does not fear death. Immediately after his speech, the authorities will most likely call the Barber's bluff, and arrest, torture, and kill him for treason. At Jaeckel's vineyard, Hannah lies unconscious in front of their cottage until miraculously she "hears" the Barber's impassioned speech from the distant city. We do not

3. The Great Dictator *and* Zelig

see a radio, and so this transmission seems telepathic. This mental telepathy echoes the way in which Rochester's voice wafts across a hundred miles of Yorkshire moors to bring Jane Eyre back to him. Chaplin likely watched the 1921 and 1934 *Jane Eyre* adaptations, and may have been inspired by the romantic device. The Barber's voice admonishes Hannah to look forward to a future when people will be free and kind. His words rouse her from the ground where she had lain, knocked down by soldiers. She gazes intently at the breaking clouds, symbolic of the brighter future ahead. The Barber's words produce a revelation, and the film ends on her radiant smile at the vision. The hope that she had poured into the Barber on the ghetto rooftop is transmitted back to her magically on the air. The Barber now becomes the agent of change, while Hannah is the willing vessel.

But Hannah does not relinquish her own power to the Barber or to patriarchy. Rather, she appears to serve as his model and muse. For it is she who enables him to rise to the occasion of his great speech by virtue of one idea, "hope." Before his speech, the Barber blanches at the prospect of speaking Double Cross gibberish to millions. Schultz exhorts him to "Speak; it is our only hope." "Hope," repeats the Barber, mantra-like, as he approaches the dais. Hannah has always stood for hope: when she encourages the Barber on the ghetto rooftop, when she speaks directly to the camera about a future world where the tormentors will "stop hating and leave us alone," and finally, in her wordless appreciation of the Barber's speech, as she sees a bright future through the parting clouds. As the Barber acquires speech, Hannah goes silent: a clear reversal of the rooftop scene and their previous relationship.

Both *The Great Dictator* and *Zelig* represent romantic interaction as a potentially transformative element. By reflecting the Other, Zelig and Dr. Fletcher attain a higher degree of self-consciousness (in a positive, Hegelian sense). Hannah and the Barber attain their own mutual enlightenment through camaraderie, being fellow Jews against the Double Cross party. But Hegelian sublation does not occur in this film on the collective level (beyond the romantic subplot). Zelig, the Barber, and Hynkel do not manage to sublate into a third term by the Hegelian process of colliding with the other, fighting to the death, and finding a synthesis. In fact, the films avoid direct confrontation between the political Master and Slave. The Barber never even meets Hynkel, and Zelig never confronts his allegiance to Hitler that constituted the nadir of his disease.

The Barber's speech is meant to fulfill this role of sublation by contradicting the thesis of Garbitsch's speech. The Double Cross Minister of Propaganda declares, "Democracy, Liberty, and Equality are words to fool the people. No nation can progress with such ideas. They stand in the way of action." The Barber provides the antithesis: "We want to live by each other's happiness—not by each other's misery."[33] The Barber points out to his soldier audience that they have kindness inside of them (Hegelian consciousness of the other). But the third term of the dialectic—synthesis of the two preceding arguments—is missing. Because Chaplin cannot realistically create a meeting of minds between Double Crossers and Jews in this plot, the speech becomes an addendum to the action rather than its natural conclusion. The character of the Barber morphs into that of the filmmaker, and Charlie Chaplin himself makes a speech for which the Barber had no skills. In doing so, the director grants the vulnerable character on the dais a moment of safety. He causes the soldiers to appreciate the Barber's Slave Morality speech. They cheer and wave instead of the more likely result of revolting against him. Filmed footage of the soldiers laying down arms does exist, but was not used, perhaps because Chaplin realized it was too unrealistic. Even if some of the soldiers believed the Barber's disguise, and thought he was Hynkel, others would not. News of the real Hynkel, who'd been mistaken for the Barber and incarcerated, would soon be heard. The henchmen on the dais would come to their senses and arrest the Barber. Only in a magical world could the Barber's speech create an immediate reversion of power to the Slaves. It would be the first successful bloodless revolution ever to occur based on a three-and-a-half minute speech. Maybe Chaplin really did think this was possible by the power of his own rhetoric; after all, he had boasted in 1931 that he could "avert the world crisis single-handedly."[34]

More than megalomania, however, the problematic ending can be described in terms of genre mixing, or contract-breaking, as Charles Maland calls it. Maland explains that *The Great Dictator* breaks an implied aesthetic contract between director and audience in three senses[35]: (1) Ideologically, Chaplin violates the convention of political neutrality by defending a controversial political message (that the Nazis were evil and the United States should stop them), which is not an acceptable component in a classic Golden Age film. (2) Narratively, he violates the expectation of a closed ending in which the hero is rewarded, the antagonist punished, and the romantic couple rides into the sunset. Instead, Chaplin leaves us with an open question: whatever is going to happen to the beloved Barber who has just risked his life to denounce fascism? One thing is certain: he will not be free to rejoin Hannah on the idyllic Osterlich vineyard. Either he will be freed to form the new government, or more likely he will be executed for his troubles. (3) Stylistically, Chaplin violates the convention of continuity editing by filming the speech as a long, uncut scene. The camera focuses on Chaplin's face and torso for a full three and a half minutes, without cutting to the crowds, Schultz, or the henchmen to show their reactions. Considering that the standard length between cuts during this period of moviemaking was seven seconds, Chaplin's violation is extreme. This aberration underscores the fact that he is ending the film in a different genre than the one in which he started. This new genre might be called the public service announcement, propaganda, or sermon, something very different from the political satire with which he began.

The genre that best describes *The Great Dictator* as a whole is satire. Character development and realism are secondary to exposing dictators' distorted worldviews and self-perceptions. Chaplin adds romance to the satirical plot for several reasons: because sex sells, because his feisty wife Paulette is apt for the role, because Hannah and the Barber's involvement enlivens the ghetto scenes. Once he adds politics to the mix, however, Chaplin's perennial problem with genre blending reemerges. As discussed in the previous chapter, blending the social-problem element into his comic and sentimental modes always presents an insurmountable challenge. To deliver his message of hope, Chaplin felt he had to separate message from action. By the time he had written the identity-switching portion of the film, giving the Barber a chance to play Hynkel in a different tune, he had painted himself into a narrative corner. How could the Barber speak truth to power without committing suicide? The only imaginable rescue from the dais where he is surrounded by the Double Cross upper echelon is skywards. Yet a successful rescue from the air, such as that which saved Zelig from the Nazis, is unrealistic. The eyes of thousands are upon the Barber. Once the Barber is on the platform, there is no *deus ex machina* that could save him, nor does Chaplin fabricate one.

The unreality of the ending is related to the failure of sublation, the finding of a third term with which to resolve conflict. Using characters as symbols often creates this dilemma. Because Hynkel and the Barber-morphed-into-Chaplin are more symbolic than real, the precarious interaction that the Hegelian dialectic prescribes, and which is illustrated by Zelig and Fletcher's magic moment, is impossible. The Barber cannot achieve Hegelian self-consciousness because he disappears, morphing from a lighthearted amnesiac into another entity altogether, Charlie Chaplin. Nor does Hynkel achieve Hegelian self-consciousness, because he is a symbol of dictatorship, not meant to represent a real person. He is a joke about Hitler, but not a historical representation of the man. Moreover, dictators don't, by definition, incorporate aspects of the enemy into themselves, unless it is strategically fruitful to do so. Although Hynkel physically resembles Adolf Hitler, the fact that his essence of dictator-ness is replicated in Napaloni implies that the actual butt of satire is the propensity of some humans to act on their will-to-power as though there were no limits to their conquests. Eric Flom speaks to this characteristic of the film when he argues that *The Great Dictator* is flawed by focusing its criticism on Hitler: "unless we extend Chaplin's satire of the German leader as a commentary on Fascism as a whole, he falls flat in aiming ridicule at that system of government. His obvious fascination with Hitler and attempt to expose him as a buffoon so dominates the film that the broader theme is muddled, despite our awareness of his satiric intentions."[36]

If *The Great Dictator* could have been improved by allowing the Barber to detour around the dangerous gathering, transmit his speech from a safe distance, and rejoin with the Jaeckels and Hannah in the vineyard, *Zelig*'s problem is the reverse. By removing Zelig and Fletcher from the political arena at the end of the film, Allen misses the opportunity to give them a social commitment in the form of a fight against Nazi ideology. It is 1938; anyone who has penetrated the inner circle could be valuable as a spokesman against the regime. Zelig might have used his experience with the Nazis to speak to people about the phenomenon of fascism, instead of just his individual experience of disease. Throughout the film, Allen is at pains to show how Zelig's disease is related to America's celebrity craze, its media dishonesty, and the intellectuals' solipsistic imposition of theory upon persons, making their interpretations of Zelig as variable as they are. If Chaplin's satiric genre weakens the force of his affirmative political message, Allen's reflexive style grabs the focus of his story and detracts from the force of his psychological insight: that our desire to conform is so powerful that, if not checked, it leads to fascism. Allen himself said he was disappointed that "the content of the picture didn't resonate as deeply as the technique did at first."[37]

Perhaps that is because the pastiche mode of the film (talking-head interviews from the past and present, doctored historic newsreels with Zelig superimposed, scratchy black-and-white footage of Zelig's life, newspaper headings, and voiceover narration throughout) removes our focus from the narrative as it directs our attention to the means of narrating. In so doing, it makes Zelig and Fletcher less real; in fact, it makes us wonder whether they really exist, even within the make-believe world of the film. At one point, two *New York Daily Mirror* reporters look into the camera and say, "to get a story, you'd jazz it up a little, you'd exaggerate; you'd even maybe play with the truth a little bit, but ... here was a story. You just told the truth and it sold papers" (34). This confession leaves the viewer wondering whether even Zelig himself is merely a fad, a fake, a phenomenon constructed for the profit of storytellers and souvenir makers. The ending, meant to be a resolution, actually feels open-ended and vague. The end titles tell us that "Leonard Zelig and Eudora Fletcher lived full and happy years together." At this point, our habituation to the propaganda-making quality of the narrator causes us to distrust this representation. We read, "She continued practicing psychoanalysis while he gave occasional lectures about his experiences." This statement raises the question whether Fletcher learned anything about the profession of psychoanalysis from her experience with the doctors at New York Hospital, proven to be charlatans in the course of their work with Zelig. The last line feels unsettling, describing a life unfinished: "On his deathbed he told doctors that he had had a good life and the only annoying thing about dying was that he had just begun reading *Moby Dick* and wanted to see how it came out"

(129). Clearly, Allen means to provide both a frame (his failure to read *Moby Dick* is what precipitated his illness in the first place) and a joke about the difficulty of reading certain works of serious literature. As a dying line, however, its relative triviality underscores the incompleteness of the film itself. It fails to answer the question, how do we become our own person if we lack a Dr. Fletcher who cares so deeply about us becoming one? If we are not lucky enough to find true love like Zelig did, how can we be cured of our own insecurities?

In the case of Chaplin's film, the problem is the reverse. In the ending, Chaplin singlehandedly tries to solve the problem of fascism by means of a rousing speech. The impossibility of doing so in the course of a single oration underscores the weakness of the ending. While Chaplin aimed too high in having the Little Man fix the world, Allen perhaps aimed too low, losing his character and situation in the complexity and satiric elements of his form. Such limitations reflect the pitfalls of modernist and postmodernist modes themselves. Modernism posits fragmented consciousness; its heroes are confused and changeable, unsure of the security or reality of any of the traditional institutions. Yet modernist narratives nevertheless tell the story of an individual's struggle against the system. Chaplin's Barber tries to fulfill this mandate, single-handedly hoping to change the world by speaking to thousands of Double Cross soldiers and millions of world radio listeners. In contrast, postmodernism denies the existence of absolutes, focuses on chance rather than human agency as the explanation for events, and delights in mixing high and low registers to tell a story. Postmodernist narrative is told from multiple points of view. Allen's *Zelig* is a tale told by tabloids, doctors, philosophers, historians, men-on-the-street who want to be Zelig, women-with-babies who want to harm Zelig, but notably, never by Zelig himself. In playing the two lead roles himself, Chaplin errs on the side of narcissism. But Allen loses the center of his film when he focuses more on the stories of Zelig than on Zelig himself.

In *Zelig* and *The Great Dictator*, Allen and Chaplin both explore the problem of fascism, but Chaplin appears to think it was solvable by exhorting Slaves to refuse to serve their Masters, while Allen does not try to solve it, but only to jokingly satirize the conformist personality. Fascism requires Slaves to reflect back the dominance of the Master. But fascist regimes never last, and Hegel's explanation for this good phenomenon is that Masters fail to recognize the Otherness of their Slaves. The heroes of these films address fascism in very different ways. The Barber breaks the fourth wall to address the audience, indicating that the medium of narrative film is not sufficient to address such a large problem. What Chaplin cannot resolve within the world of the film, he seeks to resolve by directly addressing the audience. Zelig, on the other hand, does resolve his slavishness to other people, or more precisely, to the psychological condition that causes him to conform to others by imitating them. But Zelig does not resolve or participate in the political Master/Slave dialectic that enables fascist regimes to thrive, but also, by eventual confrontation with the other, enables a third term to emerge. After direct experience with Hitler and his strategies, Jewish Zelig retreats into a bourgeois lifestyle with his Gentile wife, left with the small personal ambition of finishing *Moby Dick*.

4

Getting Away with Murder in *Monsieur Verdoux* and *Crimes and Misdemeanors*

"Getting away with murder" is a metaphorical expression meaning to do something wrong without being criticized or punished. But what happens to a person when they actually commit murder? Are remorse and punishment necessary for rehabilitation, or are some people able to forgive themselves and live well without these rituals of social expiation? Is murder ever justified? And does having a conscience depend on believing in God?

These questions may seem too profound to be answered through the medium of film, yet that challenge is in itself sufficient reason for a brave auteur to attempt it. Both Allen and Chaplin do so, with different degrees of success. *Crimes and Misdemeanors* (1989) investigates whether a man can get away with murder in his own conscience if he chooses not to believe in God. Due to Allen's double-plot structure, realistic dialog, effective flashbacks, subjective camera, and dramatic musical score, the film creates, if not sympathy (commiseration), then at least empathy (standing in his shoes) for the murderer, and a plausible psychological explanation of why he commits the crime.

Monsieur Verdoux (1947) takes a very different tack, asserting that capitalism's business model can foster the conviction that murder is the only viable way of avoiding poverty, thereby justifying this most heinous of crimes. This absurd notion is the product of Chaplin's hostility toward American puritanism and anti-communism. During the years in which he made the film, he was publicly reviled for his affair with aspiring actress Joan Barry and his marriages to young women.[1] With the negative publicity from the Barry trial, the most famous entertainer in the world was made infamous. At the same time, the FBI, along with members of the House Un-American Activities Committee and conservative organizations such as the American

Legion and Catholic War Veterans turned public opinion against Chaplin by accusing him of having Communist sympathies.[2] Due to the disconnection between the comical Verdoux and the serious critique of war and capitalism tacked on in the final ten minutes, the film lacks artistic coherence and a convincing social statement. Although James Agee, André Bazin, and Chaplin himself have called this his best film, most reviewers find it a sharp comedown from the daring brilliance of *The Great Dictator*. *Monsieur Verdoux* is daring in a different way, the way of one who doesn't care for reputation, who in fact wants to destroy it (more on this later).

Monsieur Verdoux (1947) is set in France between 1930 and 1937. The protagonist (Chaplin) is a serial murderer of middle-class widows, a contemporary Bluebeard based on two actual lady-killers. Henri Désiré Landru was swindled by his employer, and subsequently swindled and killed eleven war widows. Thomas Griffiths Wainewright was a cultured, elegant English gentleman who wore a ring filled with strychnine and secretly murdered his relatives to get their money. Dismissed during the Depression from his job as bank clerk, Verdoux (Chaplin) decided that marrying and killing widows was the best way to earn enough money to keep his wife and child according to his high standards. Verdoux's appeal to women lies in his unctuous charm. With his foppish dress and manners, and especially his love of roses, he breaks down the resistance of even the stoutest of dowagers. Two of the victims are unremarkable stereotypes of a shrew and a bourgeois, respectively, but the third—vivacious and vulgar Annabella Bonheur (Martha Raye)—provides comic relief. Like a cartoon character who bounces back after innumerable instances of mayhem, she is invulnerable to Verdoux's several murder attempts. Finally, Verdoux meets a different kind of woman, called simply the Girl (Marilyn Nash), whom he respects because she "would kill to protect her husband"—exactly what Verdoux thinks *he* is doing, killing to protect his wife and child. When her war-wounded husband dies, the Girl capitulates to economic pressure and marries a munitions manufacturer. A few years later, Verdoux loses his savings in another crash (Chaplin confusingly stages stock market crashes in both 1929 and 1932). He also loses wife and son by unspecified means. When Verdoux learns of the Girl's marriage, he interprets it as the death of her idealism, and it is the last straw. He decides to turn himself in, calling the act his "destiny." At his trial he proclaims that by murdering women for profit, he was only doing on a small scale what the government does on a grand one. War and business are ruthless; he was merely copying government and corporate business models. "One murder makes a villain; millions a hero," he philosophizes.[3] To the priest who administers last rites, he does not deny that God exists, only that, in a world so corrupt, he does not know what sin is. His executioners lead him to the guillotine.

"You are murder-proof!" Martha Raye and Charlie Chaplin as Annabella Bonheur and Henri Verdoux in *Monsieur Verdoux*, 1947 (Charles Chaplin/Photofest).

Crimes and Misdemeanors (1989) features two protagonists in parallel plots that represent the crime (main plot) and the misdemeanor (subplot) of the title. In the main story, Judah Rosenthal (Martin Landau) is a successful married ophthalmologist, philanthropist, and father, who has been having an affair with flight attendant Dolores (Anjelica Huston) for the past two years. Judah is afraid of detection, whereas Dolores believes he will soon leave his wife, Miriam (Claire Bloom). When Judah tries to end the affair, Dolores complains that she has given up other romantic opportunities based on Judah's promise to leave his wife. If Judah refuses, Dolores threatens not only to reveal the affair to Miriam but to expose Judah's shady financial dealings. Desperate, Judah takes the advice of his brother Jack (Jerry Orbach) to hire an assassin to kill Dolores. Immediately after the deed, Judah is consumed by guilt. When Judah tells his brother that he wants to turn himself in, Jack threatens to kill Judah to protect himself.

In the subplot, Cliff Stern (Woody Allen) is experiencing marital difficulties of his own. His English professor wife, Wendy (Joanna Gleason), doesn't respect Cliff because of his low-paying job (making documentaries about social issues) and his save-the-world complex. Cliff's current documentary is about a Holocaust-survivor psychology professor, Louis Levy (Martin Bergmann). Despite losing his family in the death camps, Levy believes that life in a hostile universe is nonetheless worth living if you can find love and beauty in your personal life. Wendy persuades her brother, Lester (Alan Alda), a successful sitcom producer, to hire Cliff to make a PBS documentary about Lester's "creative mind." Cliff hates Lester, who is a pompous, smug, womanizing buffoon, a true narcissist. Cliff's documentary about Lester exposes all these qualities, so Lester quashes the project in production. When Louis Levy kills himself, Cliff feels adrift and gives up his documentary. Cliff is in love with the associate producer of the PBS documentary, Halley (Mia Farrow), but Lester is the more successful beau. He plies Halley with roses and caviar, finally winning her hand in marriage. The wedding of Lester's niece brings the two plots together. Cliff and Judah coincidentally meet in an unoccupied room at the banquet hall. Pretending it is an idea for a screenplay, Judah tells this stranger the story of his murder, remorse, and unexpected recovery from guilt. In order to make a successful movie, Cliff recommends that the "character" confess his crime and atone for his sin. As Judah's rabbi brother, Ben (Sam Waterston), dances with his daughter, a voice-over by Louis Levy (from Cliff's interviews) concludes the film with the message that love solves the problem of an indifferent universe.

Both films express cynical views of humans' capacity for moral action, questioning what motive we might have to act justly if there is no God to punish us (Allen), or when our whole socioeconomic system fosters and rewards inhumanity (Chaplin). Allen's film posits alternative ways of thinking about morality. Three of its characters (Levy, Ben, and Cliff) exemplify morally responsible thinking, though they are also flawed individuals. In contrast, Chaplin's film posits no resolution to the filmmaker's sense of an unjust world. In both films, the main spokesperson for truth demonstrates entertaining, rebellious behavior and witty commentary, but his own immaturity (Cliff) or psychopathology (Verdoux) belies his message of deep truth and his satire of society. Cliff Stern's vaunted act of goodness in refusing to glorify a bad man (Lester) in order to become successful is a dubious claim to righteousness: just because he cannot be bought does not make Cliff a good person. In comparison, Monsieur Verdoux's claim to be no worse than American capitalism is not a self-compliment, in addition to being the faulty logic of a sociopath. In rhetoric, Verdoux's argument is called the *tu quoque* ("you too") fallacy, also known as the appeal to hypocrisy, which asserts that if someone else also does the wrong action, they cannot accuse one of the same. *Tu quoque* is a childish refusal of responsibility by attempting to distract the accuser.

Both films end in a dialectical void, finding no adequate reason for individual morality in a godless universe. Professor Levy says love is the answer, but given love's fickleness, and Levy's suicide, it isn't foolproof. Rather than theology or philosophy, I claim that it is psychology that provides grounds for the existence of morality in all people. The possession of a conscience is not dependent on a belief in God, religion, or other patriarchal institutions. Using recent psychoanalytic theory regarding the mother/infant dyad as the grounding for conscience, this chapter will describe reasons for which Judah Rosenthal failed to develop a strong enough conscience to resist killing his mistress. His superego was overdeveloped in aspects of negative morality. In the case of Monsieur Verdoux, this phenomenon is magnified to the level of psychopathology. Chaplin's protagonist is a logical extension of Judah, his rationalization of murder taken to the *nth* degree.

In order to understand the psychology of one who murders and considers it just, it is helpful to know the different functions of superego and conscience according to psychoanalytic theory. In the early twentieth century, Sigmund Freud used the terms *conscience*, *ego ideal*, and *superego* interchangeably, though he maintained that the superego was the container of the other two functions (*The Ego and the Id*, 1923). The superego is composed of internalized ideals acquired from our parents and society. Its primary function is to repress desire and make the ego act morally. Freud theorized that the superego is a relatively late-blooming component of the psyche, one which suddenly appears when the Oedipal-stage child (four to five years old) "shatters" its Oedipal longings out of fear of castration. The superego is not the source of goodness, but is always partly corrupt insofar as it reflects the values of the unfair world we live in ("might makes right" is an example of a poor value that the culture holds). Freud's greatest insight into the superego was the role it plays in sexual repression.

Late twentieth-century psychology has considerably modified Freud's model by acknowledging that the superego, like the society it reflects, is sexist, racist, heterosexist, classist, and childist (childism is believing that one's child is one's property).[4] These prejudices are the values that the child internalizes. Their negativity creates conflict with the child's conscience. The severe ideologies that surround us contribute to the harsh and punishing Freudian superego that causes the ego and conscience to suffer. In *Freud, Women, and Morality* (1988), Eli Sagan remarks that far more violence is done in our society by the ideologically driven superego (for example, terrorists) than the so-called beastly drives of the id (such as sex and substance addicts).

Monsieur Verdoux exemplifies this ideologically driven superego. He internalizes the competitive, heartless world of business, with its corrupt, me-first morality. Verdoux's failure to respect the demands of his conscience (reciprocity, caring, compassion, identification with the victim) against those of the superego causes him to identify with the aggressor. On an individual basis, he copies what he sees as the murderous economy of the Depression and the slaughter of innocents by the atom bomb. Although the movie is set in the interwar period, the years of its production were after the war, in 1946 and '47. The animus that Verdoux feels against the world derives from Chaplin's repulsion at the use of atomic weaponry, as well as the negative publicity generated by the Joan Barry trials and the HUAC witch hunt. In his statement to the court, Verdoux refers specifically to the A-bomb: "Is [the world] not building weapons of destruction for the sole purpose of mass killing? Has it not blown unsuspecting women and children to pieces and done it very scientifically?" He is referring to the tens of thousands of civilians killed and maimed by the 1945 U.S. bombing of Hiroshima and Nagasaki. Chaplin expressed his hatred of the atom bomb in several interviews: "the scientists are more irresponsible even than the politicians"; he "could never forgive mankind for the Nazi atrocities and for the atom bomb"; "nations will never solve [the problems that threaten peace] in an atmosphere of hate and suspicion, nor will the threat of hydrogen bombs solve them."[5] The atom bomb epitomizes civilization's moral decay.

A better version of Verdoux would have pitted the values of conscience against his sick superego's reflection of the business values of his culture. The film begs the question of what had happened in childhood to a person who could rationalize such killings. We now know that the roots of one's conscience begin in the infant's first year.[6] Over the past forty years, psychoanalytic theory has emphasized the importance of mothering for the formation of superego and conscience, rejecting the Freudian belief that identification with the father at the time of resolving the Oedipal complex is the origin of superego. The conscience, which Eli Sagan considers a separate, fourth dimension of the psyche rather than a component of the superego, is the desire to do good to other people. It arises from the infant's nurturance by and identification with the mother in the pre–Oedipal phase, from birth to four years of age.[7] Theorists describe this formation of conscience in various ways: "sweetness," and "receptivity to cherishment" (Young-Bruehl); "the fundamental principle of reciprocity, the need to give back what one has been given" (Carveth) and "identification with the nurturer" (Sagan).[8] As formulated by Sagan, conscience is a fourth structure of the psyche (after ego, superego, and id) which needs to be differentiated from superego insofar as it is the source of *all* people's good nature toward others. (Even psychopaths, argues Sagan, don't get away with murder without severe self-harm done to the psyche, however unconscious.)

On the other hand, Freudian superego is "born of the Oedipal struggle between a boy and his father, harsh and punishing in its stance toward misconduct, making use of the threat of castration as its principal mode of police power."[9] Freudian superego develops late, between ages four and five, long after what psychologists now consider the most important years of mental development—from birth to two years old. Freud's theory ignores the role of the nurturing mother in producing conscience in infants. With its negative, punitive function, the Freudian superego cannot also contain conscience, the caring, compassionate function of the psyche. Conscience, born of the experience of nurture by the primary caretaker, is the instinct to care for others and, by extension, to avoid harming them.

Conscience is an important concept for understanding Woody Allen's antidote to existential angst, a feeling that many of his characters suffer from. As a little boy, Alvy Singer describes his sense of meaninglessness: "The universe is expanding and ... someday it will break apart and that would be the end of everything" [so it's not worth doing homework] (*Annie Hall*). "If nothing lasts, why am I bothering to make films, or do anything, for that matter? ... [T]he human condition is so discouraging" (Sandy Bates in *Stardust Memories*). "One day about a month ago, I really hit bottom. You know, I just felt that in a Godless universe, I didn't want to go on living" (Mickey in *Hannah and Her Sisters*). "Is there anything more terrifying than the destruction of the world? Yes. The knowledge that it doesn't matter one way or the other. It's all random, resonating aimlessly out of nothing and eventually vanishing forever" (Lloyd in *September*). In an interview with Eric Lax, Allen explains that the crisis of a Judah Rosenthal or Cliff Stern is the crisis of meaninglessness in a godless universe. The answer is not getting away with murder, but leading a decent, moral life: "To me it's a damn shame that the universe doesn't have any God or meaning, and yet only when you can accept that can you then go on to lead what these people call a Christian life—that is, a decent, moral life. You can only lead it if you acknowledge what you're up against to begin with and shuck off all the fairy tales that lead you to make choices in life that you're making not really for moral reasons but for taking down a big score in the afterlife."[10]

Professor Levy and Rabbi Ben share this view with Allen. Although Levy lost his family in Auschwitz, he can still see the basis for morality in the world. He holds the existentialist position that it is up to the individual to take moral responsibility in order to lead a satisfying life. He says, "We are in fact the sum total of the choices we have made." Even choosing well does not mean we will be happy: "We then unfold so unpredictably, so unfairly; human happiness does not seem to be included in the design of creation." For Levy, love is the answer: "It is only we with our capacity to love that give meaning to the indifferent universe."[11] Given his suicide, however, we can only surmise that Levy didn't find enough love, whether because he was single or because the love of his students and colleagues was not the right kind to save him. Perhaps the trauma of the Holocaust destroyed his ability to love, even though he theorized that humans should be capable of recovering. As Halley says, even the best philosophy can go only so far. Levy's verbal affirmation did not go so far as to save his life.[12] Sometimes our thoughts and beliefs don't gibe with our acts.

Rabbi Ben is a better example of a successful lived philosophy. His byword is forgiveness. When Judah confides in Ben about his dilemma over his affair and Dolores's threats, Ben advises him to confess and ask Miriam's forgiveness. Judah cannot do this because he thinks that the knowledge would be too overwhelming for Miriam to handle: "She worships me." If this is true, then part of this marriage's dysfunction is that Miriam has an unrealistic imago of her husband.[13] If partners cannot see and understand the negative aspects of each other, they have built their relationship on a shaky foundation. True love entails an acceptance of the other's faults; this is the knowledge that Ben passes along to Judah, who is unable or unwilling to grasp it. Judah cares more for his status and appearance than for the inner harmony that he might attain by truth telling. Although critics have complained that the blinding of Ben is a crudely metaphorical device to suggest that he cannot see the darkness of the world, his handicap could also be read in the opposite way.[14] In spite of the vicissitudes in life (which he believes God has sent him), Ben is still able to love God. He accepts the fact that we cannot control all aspects of our lives. We still must have faith in order to live well: "I couldn't go on if I didn't feel with all my heart a moral structure with real meaning and forgiveness and some kind of higher power. Otherwise, there's no basis to know how to live," says Ben. The rabbi forgives God for blinding him, and in compensation for this forgiving nature, he enjoys a loving family. We see his daughter's admiration as they dance in the final moments of the film.

While Ben derives his goodness from a profound belief in God, Levy grounds his in the instinctive mechanisms of early childhood development. One of Levy's speeches in Cliff's film both echoes my discussion of the origins of conscience and foreshadows Levy's suicide. Levy says, "We must always remember that when we are born, we need a great deal of love in order to persuade us to stay in life. Once we get that love it usually lasts us, but the universe is a pretty cold place. It's we who invest it with our feelings, and under certain conditions we feel that the thing isn't worth it anymore." Levy and Judah both decide "the thing isn't worth it anymore," but Levy chooses death, while Judah chooses a kind of living suicide, the numbing of his conscience so that he can remain in his marriage and profession.

Judah's strange moral choice can be understood by examining his childhood. One scene is pivotal to his development (the only childhood sequence that Allen provides)—the Seder held at his father's house when Judah is thirteen, to which the adult Judah returns in memory. This scene is skillfully written, suspenseful, and intellectually stimulating. Like Plato's dialogues, it gives us antithetical views of morality that are argued by two charismatic characters: Judah's father, Sol, and Judah's Aunt May. In "The Ring of Gyges,"

4. Monsieur Verdoux *and* Crimes and Misdemeanors

Plato describes a magic ring that makes its possessor invisible. The philosophical question that arises from this magic power is whether the person will use it to do good or evil. Will he silently aid others, or will he get away with murder? Glaucon says that man is basically selfish; he obeys laws only in order to achieve selfish ends. He believes that man will do evil if he is given a magic power. Socrates disagrees, saying that people obey laws because they want that which is good for self and others. Virtue is its own reward. The invisible man will use his power to do good. John Pappas applies the Gyges parable to *Crimes and Misdemeanors*.[15] Gyges's invisibility in the parable is equivalent in the film to the murderer's crime going undetected.

At the Seder, Sol argues with Aunt May about the existence of God. Brief interjections by other Seder members pepper the conversation, mitigating the tension between the two antithetical positions. Sol's position is that an omniscient God sees and punishes all sins, while his sister May believes there is no God, citing the Holocaust as proof. How could a loving God allow a Holocaust to happen? There is no moral structure to the universe, nor does she believe that people construct one in the absence of God. Allen employs his signature mix of high and low registers to make the dialogue both funny and meaningful at the same time (May wants to get over the "mumbo jumbo" of Sol's reading the Haggadah so they can eat dinner). Unlike the skilled writing, the camerawork is too limited in this scene. Rather than giving a picture of the whole table, the camera finds only the speakers May and Sol. If instead Allen had used a master shot, wide-angle shots, or a slow pan, this would have allowed us to see the reactions on each Seder member's face. The limited camera focus contributes to the scene's overall neglect of Seder's traditional purpose, which is to teach children about the exodus of the Jews from Egypt so that they can appreciate their tradition and the blessing of not being enslaved like their forebears.

During this scene, Judah and Jack are seated together at the corner of the table furthest from their father. We see them only once. When Man-in-Yarmulke says he doesn't believe in Seder, but only goes through the motions from force of habit, Judah smirks at his older brother Jack. One is tempted to think that this smirk signifies Judah's agreement that religious ceremonies hold no power for him and thus forecasts the eventual murder that he will commit. In reality, it is only a quite appropriate expression of an adolescent questioning authority. What does forecast the murder is his aunt's moral position and Judah's eventual adoption of it as rationalization for his crime. Adult Judah stands in the doorway wearing a terrified look as he discovers the origin of his sin. He asks his aunt and his father what would happen if someone committed murder. May replies, "I say if he can do it, and he gets away with it, and he's not bothered by the ethics, then he's home free." To May, there's "no moral structure," and "human impulses toward goodness are basically nothing." Like Glaucon (and Hobbes, Machiavelli, and Nietzsche), May doesn't believe in the basic goodness of human beings. She may be an intellectual, as Sol says, but she is not the most articulate of aunts: she doesn't explain her position carefully for the benefit of the children present at the Seder. On the other hand, the conviction with which she tells all present that there is no God, no morality, and no consequence to crime is enough to make her an extremely effective character at the Seder—and in Judah's moral formation.

If we compare Sol's leadership of the Seder to what is prescribed in the literature on the subject, we discover that he does not do a very good job. Seder is intended as a reminder to adults, and a teaching to children, of the story of the Jews' liberation from slavery. Seder leaders are supposed to interrupt the reading of the Haggadah to discuss different points with the children present and to offer a Torah insight into the meaning of the words. Children are meant to ask questions. The leader's role is not strictly informational but also moral: "not knowledge, primarily, but empathy is required."[16] Sol lacks empathy for May's position, and for the children's need to find mediating positions between the two extremes. Instead of leading a discussion that incorporates multiple viewpoints, Sol gets angry and demands control over his Seder ("I don't like talk like this at my Seder"), thereby ignoring the purpose of the ceremony, which is to elicit questions from the children. Although there is one young boy who is listening attentively and twice interjects that he finds this debate "interesting," Sol never responds to the child. The difference between this child's upbringing and the Rosenthal brothers' is noticeable. We are not sure whether Jack and Judah even have a mother, whereas the child is obviously cherished: the proof is in the attention of his mother and the confidence with which, despite his youth, he asserts his opinion. The woman seated between Man-with-Fedora and Man-with-Yarmulke *might* be Judah's mother, since she praises Sol as a wife might do: "Sol's kind of faith is a gift. It's like an ear for music or the talent to draw. He believes, and you can use logic on him all day long, and he still believes." But she does not address her attention to the two teenage boys. The Rosenthal brothers have two opposing role models to choose from on this important question of morality. Should they admire their father, as his (apparent) wife does, or should they argue against his faith and his rigidity, as his sister does? The tension in the room seems to be more about personality than religion.

At this event, and in Judah's life, Sol plays the Hebrew patriarch. He is more interested in establishing authority over his unruly sister than in passing on Jewish tradition to his sons, whom he ignores. "Back to Russia!" he rudely remarks, to put May in her place. His is a punishing God who offers no assistance to confused or troubled people. Sol tries to dismiss May's stance by saying she's had a "very unhappy life," at which she laughs heartily. It is difficult to judge whether Sol's opinion about May is true, though her philosophical position and her smoking addiction would support such a reading. In psychoanalytic terms, Sol represents the superego: harsh, punitive, rigid, and judgmental. Like most children, Judah internalizes his father's commands sufficiently to provoke much guilt over his decision to do murder. After the act, his own religious pronouncements acquire the angry intensity of his father's: "I believe in God. I know it! Because without God, the world would be a cesspool." On the other hand, Judah also internalized enough of his aunt's skepticism to say this about his situation, before the murder: "What good is the law if it prevents me from receiving justice? Is what [Dolores] is doing to me just? Is this what I deserve?" This is his superego talking; it posits an alternative view of morality in which he is the victim, Dolores the perpetrator—and this gives him the right to retaliate with murder.

To mediate the harsh voice of his father and the embittered nihilism of his aunt, Judah needs a nurturing mother figure to help him form a conscience. The only time we see Judah involved in a nurturing relationship is during flashbacks of his good times with Dolores, two in particular. Once, he lies on the couch with his head in her lap as she smiles down at him and strokes his hair. They are comfortable together, clearly cherishing one another. The other time is when they run together on the beach, and Dolores with

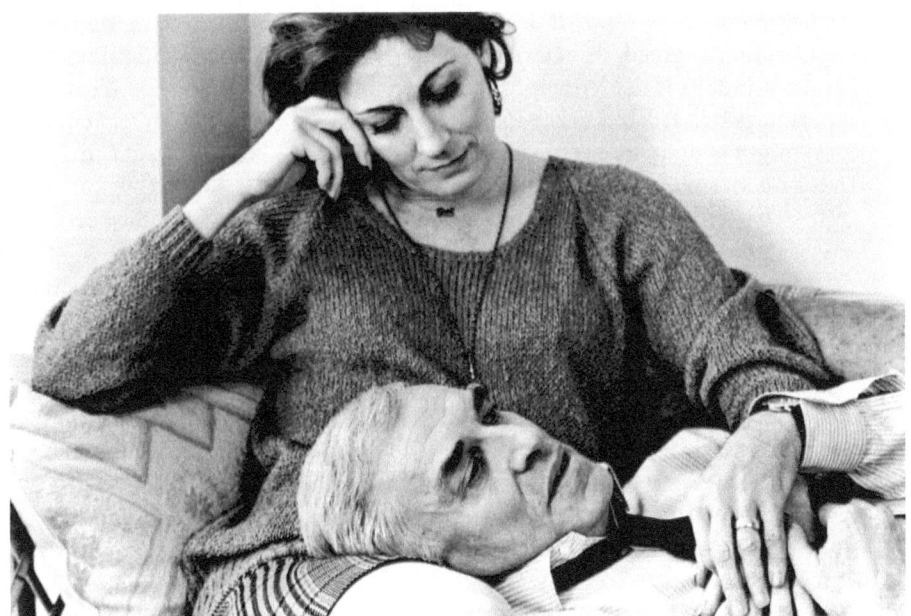

Cherishment. Anjelica Huston and Martin Landau as Dolores Paley and Judah Rosenthal in *Crimes and Misdemeanors,* 1989 (Orion/Photofest).

true vulnerability tells him she wants to learn everything from him. This evidence of receptivity and respect is another form of cherishing. Although Judah quickly objectifies Dolores once she becomes a threat to his status, the love he experienced with her may have been his only escape from the critical superego and its ego ideal that drive him to achieve professional excellence (Judah strove for the status of excellent eye doctor and famed philanthropist). In an argument Dolores tells him, "You're always relaxed when you're away from home. Your whole face changes." She acts as a mother-substitute for Judah, and is not only nurturing, but admonishing. Like a good mother, she activates his conscience, provoking his guilt by telling him she cannot live without him. Killing her causes his conscience (which says, "she's not an insect; you don't just step on her") to argue fiercely with his superego, which demands "justice," and freedom from "that neurotic woman."

In addition to the righteousness of his father, Judah has internalized the American business ethic of ruthless competition. In this way, he resembles Chaplin's murderer, Verdoux. After all, it is not only his marriage that Dolores's murder is intended to save, it is his license to practice medicine, since she threatens to expose his financial misdemeanors. Weighing the value of a free conscience versus the value of keeping his financial and professional standing, Judah chooses the latter, using deadly means to do so. In Mark Roche's words, "Though Judah stands as an isolated individual, he symbolizes a more overarching sense of decay. He has internalized much of modernity, its consumerist greed, its external standards of success, and its moral bankruptcy."[17] Judah's is the "corrupt superego" of late capitalism; his justification for crime is self-serving, and could appear rational only to those who believe that "might is right," the very words of his Aunt May. Like *The Great Gatsby*'s Daisy Buchanan, Judah is able to "smash up things and creatures," and then "retreat back into his money," finding protection and value within the cocoon of class privilege.[18]

Part of the appeal of *Crimes and Misdemeanors* is the moral ambiguity in each of its leading characters, and the sheer variety of them. This ubiquity of criminality suggests that we are, as the speaker of T. S. Eliot's *The Wasteland* says, hypocritical readers. We are each implicated in the small and large acts of negligence and evil that these characters commit. We are not always right-thinking or right-acting, although we readily judge others for doing the same misdeeds that we regularly commit. The film's title hints that there is more than one crime and more than one misdemeanor in this film. It is interesting to read critics' various answers to the conundrum of who is the committer of the misdemeanor. To many, it is Lester who plays the lead role in the subplot, paralleling Judah in his selfishness.[19] His misdemeanors include firing a writer because he had cancer and was no longer funny, the seduction of young interns, and his undeserved winning of Halley. Sander Lee believes that Halley is the malfeasant because she gives herself in marriage so that she can bolster her own career. Her crime is "different from Judah's crimes only in degree, not in kind."[20] This judgment is another fine example of ways in which male and female viewers inevitably evaluate characters differently. If Lee's opinion is true, then marriages undertaken with any degree of self-interest are criminal, and resemble murders in their *mens rea*, or criminal intent. Countering Lee, we should notice that Halley gives Cliff perfectly plausible reasons why she likes Lester, and it is not necessary to substitute Cliff's judgment of Lester for Halley's. Differences in male and female readings of films will be discussed further in Chapter 5.

The most interesting candidate for the misdemeanor committer is Cliff, since he is the one to whom the audience is invited to relate. Vis-à-vis the other characters, Cliff inhabits a philosophical middle ground. He admires Levy and aspires to become life-affirming like the philosopher. In his moral outlook, Cliff belongs to neither the idealist camp with Ben, nor the nihilist camp of May and Judah, nor the traditionalist camp of Sol.[21] Rolling his eyes at Lester's narcissism, Cliff gives expression to our distaste for the executive blowhard. Also admirable is Cliff's love for his ten-year-old niece, Jenny. On her father's deathbed, Cliff had promised that he would educate the child.

True love or self-interest? Alan Alda and Mia Farrow as Lester and Halley Reed in *Crimes and Misdemeanors,* 1989 (Orion/Photofest).

He tells his sister that he adores his niece, and proves this by taking her to restaurants and matinees and bringing her presents.

However positive, this relationship is also the source of Cliff's most serious failing. He overindulges his affection for the child, discusses inappropriate matters with her, and depends on her good estimation of him. One can no longer watch Allen's films without being aware that he was accused of molesting Mia Farrow's seven-year-old daughter, and this may color our reading of the Jenny-Cliff relationship. More disturbing than kissing his niece on the mouth, guiding her down the street with his hand on the nape of her neck, and sharing his plans to commit adultery with Halley, is another detail that might easily go undetected. When Cliff visits his sister Barbara in their apartment, Barbara tells Jenny to go away and do her homework. Jenny disappears into a doorway only fifteen or twenty feet away from the living room while Barbara breaks down. Between sobs, she loudly tells Cliff about her date rape by a sexual pervert. Meanwhile, we neither hear nor see Jenny's door close, which suggests that she is privy to her mother's story of sexual degradation by a casual acquaintance who tied her up and defecated on her face. The mother should have closed the door or spoken to Cliff outside, but Cliff was also responsible because he is an adult. Whatever can be said for Cliff's positive regard for his niece has to be balanced by his failure to draw a stronger boundary between adult and child.[22]

The scene of Barbara's confession is disturbing in another way as well. When Barbara tells Cliff everything about her bizarre encounter with a sadist, expecting solace from her brother, he replies, "Barbara! You idiot! This guy could have cut your throat, he coulda murdered you. You're such a dope. I wish I could have sympathy for this." For Cliff, it is more disturbing that Barbara "stupidly" uses the personal ads as a way to meet men than the fact that she was humiliated by a pervert she picked up through these ads. The brother fails to sympathize with his sister. Cliff does, however, get his just deserts immediately after this failure of compassion. When he returns home to tell his wife about Barbara's experience, he receives a shockingly cold treatment from her. She doesn't care about Barbara or anything to do with her husband.

In addition to his insensitivity and weak boundaries, critics have enumerated Cliff's other flaws: pride, laziness, and unearned moral superiority. Peter Bailey finds Cliff just as egotistical as Judah: "One of the film's most striking achievements is that the Cliff subplot seems less like comic relief than like a minimalist version of Judah's."[23] Sam Girgus identifies Cliff's "unearned moral superiority" and "enhanced artistic sensibility," as well as "misplaced pride in failure, self-servingly imagining a degree of heroism in his recalcitrance to popular values and success."[24] When Halley asks Cliff to give her a little credit for liking Lester, Cliff replies that he cannot do so. Cliff

4. Monsieur Verdoux *and* Crimes and Misdemeanors

is unable to accept that people whom one likes and respects may judge others differently, even creatures as apparently despicable as Lester. This moment of rejection and judgment echoes the earlier moment in his sister's apartment when Cliff refused to give Barbara the kindness she needed.

On the other hand, some critics grant Cliff a quality of nobility. They see his refusal to aggrandize Lester in his documentary as a brave act. Sander Lee and John Pappas describe Cliff's decision to sabotage his "Creative Minds" documentary as an existential moral choice that elevates him above the common man. If we agree with Plato's Glaucon, then we will be surprised that a man would relinquish this chance to make other well-paid films. If we are more like Socrates, however, we don't question the fact that Cliff, the voice of truth, would obviously want to expose Lester for the manipulator he really is. Invited to make a documentary about Lester's creative mind, Cliff films at inopportune times, such as when Lester bribes women to sleep with him in return for roles or excessively chastises writers for not being funny. Sometimes, just letting the camera run while the supposedly brilliant mind is talking is enough to expose Lester's inanity. Lester's aphorism, "If it bends, it's funny; if it breaks, it's not funny," delivered in braying tones, reminds Cliff of an ass, so in the film, he puts Lester's words in a real donkey's mouth.

Though he frequently gives himself away as morally confused at best and narcissistic at worst, our final impression of Cliff is colored by the positive role he plays towards Judah in the penultimate scene, when Judah tells his story to Cliff, thinly disguised as "an idea for a film." Cliff judges Judah's narrative from the point of view of an artist; this reflexive move buys Allen some moral leeway. Cliff describes what moviegoers would want for a good ending: "If the character turns himself in, you will have tragedy." Without that conventional, morally satisfying ending, what are we left with? The tension between what Allen-playing-Cliff says and what Allen-the-director does in letting Judah go scot-free, makes us wonder why Allen lets Judah get away with murder. Perhaps Judah's resistance to the law reflects Allen's desire to subvert the conventional structure of movies, where good is rewarded and evil punished. Gregg Bachman reads the whole film as a commentary on the filmmaker's resistance to conventional Hollywood narratives. Reflexive filmmakers like Allen "are always in search of ways to subvert this intended order."[25] Every character is involved in this subversion. In this reading, Allen makes Rabbi Ben blind because, traditionally, the exceptionally perceptive rabbi would enjoy keen vision. Judah subverts the Hollywood plot that would require his confession and seeking of forgiveness. Cliff subverts the conventional tone of documentaries about "great" individuals by likening Judah to a jackass and to Mussolini (179). Although thoughtful, Bachman's critique doesn't satisfy those who look for moral guidance in their stories.

Some critics have written about the reflexive nature of *Crimes and Misdemeanors* (its being a film about making a film), but most focus on the main thematic point: whether Judah truly got away with murder.[26] The preponderance of critical opinion is that he did not: assertions of director and character to the contrary, our need for justice means we simply cannot accept that a protagonist whom we have "felt with" throughout the film turns out to be immoral and to lose his conscience. Even Allen isn't content with *Crimes and Misdemeanors* as his final pronouncement, but has had to return repeatedly, like Freud's return of the repressed, to the psychological question: Does the conscience have the capacity to forgive the self for committing heinous crimes without the intervention of the legal system, and the murderer's serving time to pay for them?

Since *Crimes and Misdemeanors* (1989), Allen has made three other films that reiterate this perturbing question.[27] In 2005, *Match Point* offers a similar plot, but uses a cutthroat tone. Like Judah, the protagonist, Chris, murders to protect a marriage and a family business. Unlike Judah, Chris hails from the lower class. His lucky entrée into a higher class via marriage provides justification, in his mind, for doing whatever is necessary to keep that status. Chris and Judah both murder mistresses who pester them about leaving their wives. Unlike Judah, the only problem Chris has with his conscience is one dream in which he confronts the ghosts of his murder victims. During this dream, his defense that his crimes were "necessary" seems to satisfy his conscience, and he goes scot-free. In place of the Jewish religious heritage of characters in *Crimes and Misdemeanors* which frames the ways in which Judah's conscience talks to him, *Match Point*'s theme is the determinative role of chance in our lives. Since his luck rewarded him with a good job, a kind wife, and no criminal prosecution, Chris accepts luck as the presiding law of the universe. For Chris, as for Aunt May, there is no moral structure. As screenwriter, Allen rewards Chris for his misdeeds, if getting away with murder is indeed a reward. Another difference between Judah and Chris is ethnic. Elliot Shapiro perceptively points out that after *Crimes and Misdemeanors*, Allen's leading men who murder are not Jewish. He concludes that, throughout his oeuvre, Allen usually connects ethical behavior with Jewishness.[28] This premise is borne out by the next murder film, in which again it is a Gentile who lacks conscience.

In just two years' time, Allen revisits the murder-and-conscience theme, giving it an opposite and more satisfying resolution. In *Cassandra's Dream* (2007), working-class brothers Ian and Terry Blaine struggle with money issues. Their passive, unambitious father is no role model, whereas their uncle is a successful surgeon who has repeatedly bailed them out of financial crises. This time, before financing their business plans, Uncle Howard wants a favor in return. He offers to pay his nephews to kill his former business partner who is threatening to testify against him. Ian is willing, Terry more reluctant. Once the murder is done, Ian manages to put it behind him, while Terry is so upset that he decides to confess to the police. Ian plans to kill Terry, but they get into a fight during which Terry pushes Ian, causing a fatal fall. Terry drowns himself over guilt for the two deaths he has now caused. Several parallels to Judah's situation occur in this film: there are two brothers, one hardened, the other sensitive; a doctor is willing to kill to protect his reputation; both guilt and indifference are experienced after the murder, but in this case the reactions are split between two brothers instead of one person. The most significant difference between *Cassandra's Dream* and *Crimes and Misdemeanors* is the ending: in *Cassandra's Dream*, both murderers are punished. Marat Grinberg has compared this film to Greek tragedy for "its perfect Aristotelian dimensions," and to Hebrew scripture, in its sense that justice will be done ("murder will out," in the words of Sol Rosenthal).[29] Nobody gets away with murder. Terry's conscience is riotous, while Ian dies for his crime. In this sense, Ian's death is not actually an accident, but a punishment contrived by God or the gods.

Unlike Allen's previous murder film, in which Chris Wilton's family background is only lightly alluded to, *Cassandra's Dream* returns to the theme of the family drama as the incubator for the protagonists' capacity to commit bad deeds. Between an ineffective father and a rich, powerful uncle, the Blaine brothers choose the murderous uncle as role model. Between an authoritarian father, who held status in the Jewish synagogue, and an "unhappy aunt," who powerfully resisted their father's authority, the Rosenthal brothers chose Aunt May. Both sets of brothers make the Oedipal choice to reject the father's authority and align with the more attractive, law-defying alternative. Punishment for their crime is the ending that Cliff Stern would approve. With *Cassandra's Dream*, Allen seems to be returning to wholesome moral grounds.

In 2015, he returns once again to the murder-and-conscience issue. *Irrational Man* gives us a more abstract murderer than any of the previous ones—Judah, the Blaine brothers, or Chris Wilton. (In comparison to these, Chaplin's Verdoux has the most abstract motivation of all.) The irrational man of the title, Abe Lucas (Joaquin Phoenix), chooses Raskolnikov from Dostoyevsky's *Crime and Punishment* (1866) as his role model. Both Raskolnikov and Abe Lucas murder because they believe their victim is a bad person. Abe kills a judge whom he does not know in order to protect a woman, whom he also does not know, from the predicted bad outcome of a child custody hearing. As scholars of philosophy, Abe and Raskolnikov are lost in theoretical abstractions. They decide to put to the test Utilitarian Theory, which holds that ridding the world of a bad person will increase the sum total of world happiness. Both philosophers want to see if it really works. Utilitarianism did not work for Raskolnikov, whose guilt drove him to confession followed by years in prison, but it does work for psychopath Abe Lucas. His feeling of accomplishment after the murder gives him back his libido and zest for life. Before the murder, Lucas is a depressed philosophy professor who has run out of philosophy. In a godless universe, how do we find meaning? It's a question that Abe answers by playing God, deciding who should die in this unjust universe. Abe's girlfriend, Jill (Emma Stone), discovers the murder but is willing to protect Abe—up to the point when an innocent man is being tried for Abe's crime. Knowing that she is planning to turn him in, Abe tries to murder Jill. Much like Ian's in *Cassandra's Dream*, Abe's attempt backfires. Abe dies by falling down an elevator shaft that he had tampered with in order to kill Jill. Along with the question of getting away with murder, this film also explores a compelling secondary question: how can an intimate of a killer accept the fact that they have loved a murderer? The film ends with Jill's attempt to heal herself from trauma.

At the present time, the ratio of Allen's murderers who get away with it and those who do not is two (Judah and Chris) to three (Ian, Terry and Abe). The issue of conscience remains unresolved, however, and I expect we will see yet another Allen film that investigates the question. Neither *Cassandra's Dream* nor *Irrational Man* answers the question because Allen used a *deus ex machina* to punish the cavalier murderers Ian and Abe instead of having them punish themselves with conscience. Each was getting away with murder in his conscience but was accidentally killed in trying to murder the witness. If, in these last two films, Allen is shifting away from his moral unconventionality by punishing the perpetrator, it may be for literary purposes; as Cliff Stern would say, the audience wants to see justice fulfilled. But the questions of depth psychology remain unanswered. Allen is still fascinated with a character like Judah, Chris, Ian, or Abe, who claims to have gotten away with murder. He is still asking the questions, how does that person's mind function, and what kind of background and circumstances could form such a mind? Surprisingly, for a man who has undergone psychoanalysis for at least thirty years, Allen is less focused on the family background of the murderer than on the circumstances of the murder and the ways in which the murderer's conscience reacts to his crime. He tends to refer to unhappy childhoods, if at all, in concise family scenes meant to convey discontent in broad outlines. Except for *Crimes and Misdemeanors*, Allen's murder films characteristically evade the subject of the perpetrator's childhood, focusing more on the philosophical condition of adult existential angst than on the psychological conditions of childhood development that give rise to it.[30]

This lack of psychological interest is even more pronounced in the murder film from Charlie Chaplin. Verdoux first appears *in medias res* as a successful Bluebeard; the film never looks back for psychological causes of his disease. The character Verdoux is an enigma. We don't want to laugh at a murderer, yet we can't help but recognize the comedian, Charlie the Tramp, in this new and elegant iteration. Whereas Charlie the Tramp was frequently aggressive (kicking people in the rear or boxing men of vastly superior size), he became violent only when necessary to protect his dignity or to defend himself or a pretty girl. Verdoux, on the other hand, kills for a living. As André Bazin points out, Verdoux is the opposite of the Tramp in many ways: elegant where the Tramp is shabby, eloquent where the Tramp is silent, an investor where the Tramp lives hand to mouth. Most importantly, Monsieur Verdoux is a successful, efficient seducer of wealthy ladies, whereas the Tramp could charm women but not marry them, being without money or prospects.[31]

Naming the genre of this odd film might help dismantle the enigma of its message, for genre formulations can sometimes explain how to understand bizarre heroes. Why do we still like the Charlie persona when he is a serial killer? The genres that suggest themselves are allegory, farce, and the social problem film. An allegory is a story that has a secondary meaning outside the literal story, a genre often used for political or religious critiques. *Verdoux* is no *Animal Farm*, however, for the capitalism that Monsieur Verdoux condemns is too abstract for a clear message to emerge (whereas in *Animal Farm*, the players and the plot had one-to-one correspondences with actual Communist leaders and their actions). The film also fits most of the characteristics of farce—light tone, highly improbable plot situations, exaggerated characters, and slapstick. Yet it doesn't feel farcical; its dénouement is anything but light. Nor does *Monsieur Verdoux* fit the genre of the social problem film, for two reasons. First, it does not put the social problems of a whole group on display, only Verdoux's. Second, the teaching moment that occurs at the end of the film is a farce because the teacher is an unrepentant murderer. According to Donna Kornhaber, *Verdoux* "is not easily reducible to a *film à thèse*," because the closing comments are "the words of a serial killer delivered in his own defense." They may be an explanation for modern morality, but "they may also be only so much self-serving sophistry."[32]

As a staunch admirer of Chaplin and of this film in particular, André Bazin identifies a genre—myth—that he believes can resolve its inconsistencies.[33] Charlie is a mythical figure who has been living in the public imagination for thirty years prior to this film. *Monsieur Verdoux* kills the mythical hero, giving rise to a public revolt. The Verdoux character is the chief avatar of all of the iterations of Charlie. The Tramp has never been loved because he was good, but rather because he is naughty in an appealing way. The myth of "Charlot" (the French term for Charlie) transcends the individual films in which he appears and enters into "the consciousness of mankind" (19). Some of the attributes of this mythological hero, according to Bazin, are "exceptional depth, special credibility, consistency of behavior, a magical radiance in his glance" (19). Regarding morality: "faults do not detract from our interest in the character or from our sympathy. ... Being on the side of the hero of a myth, the fact that we are both for and with him, fortunately is not uniquely dependent on the moral categories of which he may be the embodiment" (30). This statement initially strains credibility, but when tested on classical and medieval heroes, it rings true. Odysseus was an egotist and a womanizer, Beowulf a blood-hungry avenger. The next step in Bazin's argument makes better sense. He says that, because the public loved their mythical Charlot, they hated the entity that killed him at the end of *Verdoux*. Chaplin knew he was the ultimate victor, because "the spectator condemns the condemnation of a man 'justly' condemned by society" (31). Society becomes the murderer of Charlie.

Bazin's theory works well to explain why today's Chaplin fans enjoy the film, and why French spectators of the 1940s and 50s weren't turned off by its immorality. But American viewers of the late 1940s and 50s were a different story. Their moral sensitivity to Chaplin was intensified by the false rumor that he was a Communist and by gossip about his sexual proclivities generated by the 1944 Joan Barry trials. The distrust worked both ways. With this film, Chaplin set out to express his resentment of this gossip and persecution. Charles Maland points out the bad timing: "Having committed himself to progressive politics in *The Great Dictator* and his Second Front speeches, feeling himself a victim of fascist forces in the way he was treated during the Barry trials, Chaplin set out to make a film that expressed a progressive critique of capitalist society just as the Cold War was setting in with a vengeance."[34] Either his timing was off, or Chaplin was willing to risk the public's inevitable disapproval of this project. He was also courting trouble with the INS (Immigration and Naturalization Services) and the FBI. Working so intentionally against the grain, his bold move is reminiscent of his United Artists partner, D. W. Griffiths, who made *Intolerance* (1916) in order to vindicate himself against charges of racism in his previous film, *The Birth of a Nation* (1915). The "intolerance" of the title was meant to describe the attitude of critics who condemned the film. Similarly, Chaplin tried to vindicate his public reputation as a lady killer by showing them what an actual lady killer was like.

Despite Bazin's insistence that the film reads as myth, I will proceed to read it psychologically, as most audiences do. We go to films in order to identify with characters, and through catharsis to release some of our own feelings of isolation and suffering. Monsieur Verdoux is a man without a conscience. We have defined conscience as the source of good feelings and actions towards others, a feeling of sweetness toward family and friends, and an aversion to assaulting, murdering, and otherwise harming others. Although Verdoux has a wife and son whom he claims to love, there is little evidence of this love in the two short scenes when he is at home. On the contrary, he neither listens to nor watches them carefully. Mona tells him that he is stressed and desperate, and, if his job is going to make him ill, she wishes they were living in one room. They had been happier when they were poor. As Ignatiy Vishnevetsky points out, "Mona and little Peter are important to Verdoux only because they offer him a false sense of normalcy and a justification for his crimes. He doesn't kill to make them happy; he kills to assuage his own unhappiness."[35] As for Peter, Verdoux doesn't show any particular kindness or attention to his young son. Instead, he projects his own violence onto an innocent. Peter is stroking the cat's back and tail when his father looks up from his paper and cries, "Peter, don't pull the cat's tail. You have a cruel streak in you; I don't know where you get it. ... You play too rough. Remember, violence begets violence." This statement is more than an opportunity for dramatic irony. It is an example of Verdoux's punitive superego. He passes along aphoristic prohibitions that he must have learned in his own childhood and ignored. Rules that Father preaches but doesn't practice hold no authority for a child.

Verdoux's superego is far stronger than his somnolent conscience. At the murder trial, his closing speech is full of faulty overgeneralized judgments. As Kornhaber points out, Verdoux's speech is characterized by reductive aphorisms that minimize the complexity of all situations and suggest a mind that has checked out. In her chapter "Substituting Speech for Style," she describes his manner of philosophizing: "It is not just that such statements depend on a radical degree of certainty to mean anything at all and leave no room for skepticism and doubt. It is also that they consign grand ideas to a single typology, reducing meaning to one property and excluding all other possibilities" (257). This passage could also be describing the voice of the corrupt superego, one that knows rules without understanding their meanings, that preaches values without feeling their substance. To the Girl, Verdoux says, "This is a ruthless world, and one must be ruthless to cope with it." Not only does this formula come without explanation, it directly contradicts Christian, Buddhist, and other moral teachings that recommend we walk away from provocations rather than copying them to escalate hostilities.

At the end of the trial, Verdoux makes a strange speech. It isn't easy to know whether he intends this argument as justification for his crimes, or whether he is using the witness stand as a soapbox, giving his last message to the world before he dies. "As for being a mass killer, does not the world encourage it? Is it not building weapons of destruction for the sole purpose of mass killing? Has it not blown unsuspecting women and children to pieces and done it very scientifically? Huh! As a mass killer, I'm an amateur by comparison."

A faulty analogy is one that assumes because two things are alike in some respects (I am a French citizen and my government consists of Frenchmen), they are necessarily alike in some other respect (we both have the authority to kill people). Besides the faulty analogy in Verdoux's argument, he also uses the *tu quoque* (you too) argument, as mentioned above. Because the government sponsors war and capitalism, which kill people directly and indirectly, he thinks that he, too, can kill people with impunity.

Superego does not foster logical morality. As Freud noted, it is a morality based on fear of repercussion. In this sense, it does not constitute an affirmative duty to care for others, but a caution against being caught for misdeeds or ugly thoughts (originally, the Oedipal child's death wish against his father). Verdoux's superego tells him that he is right to murder because he has been wronged: "For thirty-five years, I used my brains honestly, then nobody wanted them." His murders are vindication for his unemployment, just as Chaplin's creation of Verdoux vindicates his ill-treatment at the hands of women (Joan Barry, ex-wives Mildred Harris and Lita Grey, journalist Hedda Hopper, his abandoning mother) and representatives of law and government (prosecuting attorneys in his divorce trials, J. Edgar Hoover, and members of HUAC). In the film, Chaplin reserves the killing blow for the Church, which Verdoux casts as just another business. When the priest asks him whether he has remorse for his sins, Verdoux replies, "Who knows what sin is, borne as it was from Heaven from God's fallen angel. Who knows the ultimate destiny it serves. After all, what would you be doing without sin?" His equivocation over the meaning of the word "sin" conveys a sense of the speaker's amorality, his inability to know right from wrong. This would seem to provide an explanation, except for the fact that Verdoux is not insane. Psychopaths know the difference between right and wrong but do not care about committing wrong. Verdoux enjoys the game of argumentation right up to the last; he wants to die with dignity, if only that of a well-dressed sophist.

Verdoux is a striking fictional example of a person whose superego has squelched the "still small voice" of conscience.[36] Only once does he show stirrings of fellow feeling. Eager to try out a new poison, Verdoux picks up the Girl on the street and brings her home. As he waits for her to drink the poisoned wine, they chat about the meaning of life. When the Girl describes her love for her deceased husband, Verdoux changes his mind about killing her, because her feelings mirror his own. The Girl says, "He was wounded in the war, a hopeless invalid. That's why I loved him. He needed me, depended on me, like a child. But he was more than a child; he was a religion, my very breath. I'd have killed for him." Verdoux's modus operandi is justified by just such a love for the wife and child he killed for. The Girl becomes his alter ego; she offers a better version of his own twisted love for his wife and child. Being a part of him, she is not a candidate for extinction. Because she is so young and uncorrupted (this is her first night of prostitution; she hasn't yet turned a trick), Verdoux can project his own younger self onto the Girl, the person he was before he had started his "business."

4. Monsieur Verdoux *and* Crimes and Misdemeanors

Verdoux's alter ego. Charlie Chaplin and Marilyn Nash as Henri Verdoux and the Girl in *Monsieur Verdoux*, 1947 (Charles Chaplin/Photofest).

More than wanting to save her, Verdoux can't seem to differentiate himself from the Girl. With his own son, Verdoux had too little identification: unable to see that Peter was only stroking the cat, whereas Verdoux was killing his victims, Verdoux couldn't identify with Peter's innocence. With the Girl, he identifies so strongly that, when she gives up her struggle to maintain integrity (by marrying a munitions manufacturer), he immediately gives up his own struggle to maintain the business of killing, a tiresome job requiring many impersonations. He gives in to what he calls his destiny, which is apparently to use the courtroom witness stand to teach the world a lesson about evil capitalism. Verdoux's conversations with the girl are not sympathetic but didactic. Most of his reductive philosophizing takes place for her benefit. His alternating attraction to and repulsion by the Girl (he is disgusted when he thinks she wants money instead of friendship) is only a reaction to the idea of moral purity, not to any actual kindness he feels towards her. Conscience is non-existent in his character, and without conscience, he can get away with murder.

Unlike Allen, Chaplin is not fascinated by the philosophical or psychological complexity of the murderer. After Verdoux, he does not revisit the question of the conscience-free man; his last three movies are about aging (*Limelight*), anti–Communism (*A King in New York*), and love (*A Countess from Hong Kong*). Verdoux is the epitome of a flat character: he does not grow or change, but is one-dimensional. The serial killer is an odd mouthpiece for Chaplin's statement about the ills of capitalism and his mistreatment by American institutions and individuals. Yet he could not have made the film without thinking about the meaning of conscience, the product of identifying with and wanting to reciprocate the mother's nurturance.

Chaplin's relationship with his mother was an ambivalent one, as established clearly in Stephen Weissman's and David Robinson's biographies.[37] He was grateful for her sweetness and her support of his acting aspirations, but he was also afraid of the insanity gene that she might pass on, and traumatized by her abandonment each time she checked into Cane Hill asylum. Once she moved to Los Angeles, he visited infrequently because it made him sad to witness her condition. Abandoned by his father when Chaplin was two, Hannah had to stitch together a living for herself and her two sons by singing and sewing. Due to her inability to pay the rent, they moved house frequently. Often, there were only tea and bread for meals. Yet Hannah electrified their environment with her dramatic games and her undeniable sweetness. From her he learned how to mimic people's movements, which became his greatest asset as a silent actor: "I learned from her everything I know. She was the most astounding mimic I ever saw. ... It was in watching and observing her that I learned not only to translate motions with my hands and features, but also to study mankind."[38] Hannah also supported both sons' aspirations for theater careers and made them feel special: "in spite of the squalor in which we were forced to live, she ... kept Sydney and me off the streets and made us feel we were not the ordinary product of poverty, but unique and distinguished."[39] This is no small gift from an ill woman living below the poverty line.

Psychobiographer Weissman believes that young Chaplin felt powerless in his inability to help his mother and that he compensated by playing onscreen heroes: "[H]is alter-ego screen character's rescue of physically stricken or socially fallen or oppressed women would become the recurrent theme, echoed and re-echoed in his films" (110). Chaplin appears to have had a good foundation for a healthy conscience, but the indignity of his early poverty was something that continued to sadden him even when he became rich and famous. The persistence of this pain resulted in a marked rigidity, temper tantrums, and manipulation of the actors, women, and children close to him.[40] If Verdoux resembles his maker at all, it is in his strong outsider's conviction that he must live by his wits, create his own rules, and constantly keep up appearances.

4. Monsieur Verdoux *and* Crimes and Misdemeanors

We examined Allen's childhood in the Introduction and Chapter 1, with an emphasis on the coldness of both parents, his mother's hurtful criticisms, and her daily beatings of young Woody. Aspects of Allen's psychic life reappear in Judah Rosenthal. His mother was a regular temple-goer, yet Allen did not perceive her as deeply religious. One of his best one-liners is that his parents' values are God and carpeting. This line suggests that their class aspirations are equivalent to or dominant over their religion, with carpeting representing both aspirational home décor (a status symbol), and something they are as anxious about as the state of their souls. Certainly Martin and Nettie Konigsberg did not reflect such ethical extremes as Sol and May. On the other hand, they failed to provide a sense of existential safety for Allen, who has repeatedly stated that the world is a cold, indifferent place, and that no amount of success can make up for his sense of dread and depression. Strangely, given his relative material comfort, Allen received less nurturance as an infant than Chaplin did. Allen remembers being threatened by a babysitter/relative who said that she could easily suffocate him in his crib, and began to demonstrate.[41] Perhaps the horrors of an indifferent universe gave rise to Allen's creation of Judah Rosenthal. Allen is very aware that such people exist and remains intellectually curious about their lack of conscience. While Chaplin's serial killer is a product of historical legends Henri Landru and Thomas Wainewright, and of the director's need of a mouthpiece for his personal frustrations, Allen's high-class citizen/murderer is a contemporary dramatization of Raskolnikov's dark night of the soul and a heightened expression of Allen's own angst.

5

What Is Love in *Limelight* and *Manhattan*?

Thereza "Terry" Ambrose of *Limelight* (1952) and Tracy of *Manhattan* (1979) both love older men who love them back but refuse to commit to them. In both cases, age difference is the man's excuse. Forty-one years separate Terry and Calvero; Tracy and Isaac Davis are twenty-five years apart. Each man's guilt about being older than the female is not the true reason for his failure of love, however, but a rationalization for his resistance. Both Chaplin and Allen were in relationships that entailed the same age span as that of their characters, but age was not a barrier to either director's choice of love object. While the films may dramatize a latent or unconscious guilt in their creators, it is also true that the age objection is specious and hides another motive. Why do two directors who are married or in a relationship with a woman exactly as young as those in their films refuse to grant characters the same satisfactions?

This chapter will focus on possible psychological reasons for the male characters' resistance to love, aesthetic reasons for the directors' narrative choices, and the gender politics of critics who have written about these films. The relative innocence of each female lead threatens the self-image of her male lover, causing him to reject her for being too clear a mirror of his own deficiencies. In addition to her nobler character, the female lead in each film is an artist who shows great promise in her field. In contrast, Calvero, the clown of *Limelight*, is washed up, and Isaac, the writer in *Manhattan*, is insecure about his fledgling writing talent. His girlfriend, Tracy, demonstrates the authenticity in their relationship that he lacks in both his love life and his work. This lack is impeding his ability to write his novel. In their lovers' opinions, Terry has become a "great artist," and Tracy is already a "wonderful actress." In patriarchy, a more successful female partner is a threat to a man. A nobler partner might be a threat to either man or woman.

Of corresponding interest to the films' failed relationships is the response of many male critics to them: the majority deny the existence of the female leads' love for their partners. Because of their dominant patriarchal gender role, male critics are unwilling to grant human complexity to Terry and Tracy and tend to objectify or fetishize them instead of affording them credibility equal to that of their male counterparts. They find it unsettling or impossible that young women love their older, feebler boyfriends. Reception theory and feminist film theory explain why male and female spectators may interpret characters differently. We tend to identify with the character of the same gender as ourselves, or with the one who exhibits characteristics stereotypically associated with the gender with which we identify. Most males identify with male characters. Allen's work complicates easy generalizations, however, because his female characters offer intelligent criticisms of their male partners. Although his vision is androcentric, his male leads are sympathetic enough to foster identification by female viewers.

The chapter title suggests I will answer an ambitious question: what is love? I have chosen Plato's *Symposium* (370 BC) to shed light on the question, as it is the most famous literary treatment of the subject. Even in the twenty-first century, its insights remain valid. I am not the first to think of the classics when interpreting Allen films. *Woody Allen and Philosophy* (2004) is a collection of essays that approach Allen's films through classical philosophy because, as Tom Morris writes, "Woody Allen fills his films with the most important philosophical questions and ideas."[1] These ideas invite comparison with the ancient texts upon which they are founded; hence, I look to Plato's *Symposium* for a discourse on love that has sufficient *gravitas* to match Allen's. In this ancient Greek text, several friends at a drinking party give definitive descriptions of love that are meant to cover all bases, ranging from jealous love to procreative desires to love of a teacher. Since love between old and young partners is the Greek ideal, the *Symposium*'s definitions are particularly relevant to *Manhattan* and *Limelight*, whose relationships are essentially teaching ones. In Greece, the older man was attracted by the innocence and beauty of the younger, while the boy was attracted to the older man's wisdom, contacts, and potential to teach him. Although the relationships in the two movies are heterosexual, their age disparity links them to the ancient Greek model in significant ways.

In our own time, we condemn May-December romances, which are usually a female May to a male December, because of an assumption that the older man has greater power (financial, social, intellectual) than the young woman, which creates an imbalance in their relationship. We may also condemn the younger woman's apparent greed in marrying for money, or the man's willingness to pay for her affection, calling her a *gold digger* and him a *sugar daddy*. Yet *Manhattan* and *Limelight*'s relationships are not based on financial factors. In each case, the female either comes from a family with greater wealth than her boyfriend's (Tracy) or is herself earning more than he does (Terry). Instead, the rationale for these attractions is the Greek one, in which the older person is attracted to the beauty and innocence of youth, while the youth is attracted to the experience and wisdom of the elder. The premise of this chapter is that when the elder lacks confidence in his own superior wisdom or nobility of character, he resents the inferiority he feels, and seeks to leave the relationship.

Cultural trends of the times of these films, the early 1950s and late 1970s, respectively, also inflect the characters' and directors' perceptions of love. The early 1950s in America was a period of conformity in people's romantic and marital expectations. The booming postwar economy fostered a flight to the suburbs, and the middle class made an exodus from city centers. The little-house-with-white-picket-fence dream became a reality for many. Access to this idealized lifestyle came, however, at a cost. The Red Scare frightened Americans into stringent anti-communism, and also into normative love relationships with so-called appropriate race, class, age, and gender object choices. The American Dream was supposedly realizable by everyone just as long as you followed all the rules. The late 1970s were quite the opposite. The idealistic dreams of world peace and free love fostered by social movements of the Sixties had deteriorated, allowing the culture of narcissism to take their place. Second-wave feminism challenged men and women to rethink gender roles. A woman should be fulfilled in sex and love, just as a man expects to be. Normative sexuality became something to be ridiculed rather than obeyed (seventeen-year-old Tracy tells her forty-two-year-old lover, "Let's do it in some strange way that you've always wanted to do, but nobody would do with you"). Yet liberated sexual expression is only one aspect of love. Love is not only the thing for which "whales are churning, worms are squirming," as Calvero croons. Closely connected to the concept of conscience that we explored in the previous chapter, love is the greatest motivator of human goodness, an inducement of shame if one feels inferior to the love object, and an unconscious attempt to complete the psyche and become whole.

Limelight opens with titles proclaiming "the glamour of limelight, from which age must pass as youth enters," and "London, Summer of 1914," the same year that Chaplin began his cinematic career. In the film, Chaplin is returning to the scene of his childhood, recalling both his father's vaudeville profession and his fatal alcoholism, from which he died at thirty-eight. Calvero (Chaplin) is a 62-year-old vaudeville comedian who has given in to alcoholism out of despair over losing his comic touch. Returning dizzy-drunk to his tenement one evening, he smells gas coming from the ground floor tenant's door. Terry Ambrose (Claire Bloom) has taken pills, turned on the gas, and blocked the drafts. Shocked to sobriety, Calvero carries her to his own two-room apartment to nurse her back to health. The landlady grudgingly allows Terry to stay in Calvero's rooms, as long as they pretend to others that they are a married couple. When she awakens, Terry tells Calvero her story. She was orphaned as a child and brought up by her older sister, Louise, who has since moved to South America and fallen out of touch. Though they were very poor, Louise paid for Terry's ballet lessons. Terry has been performing with the Empire Ballet, but recently fell ill with rheumatic fever. After the suicide attempt, her legs are paralyzed. Calvero suspects that the paralysis is psychosomatic; he elicits Terry's backstory to figure out what is troubling her. Terry feels guilty because her sister prostituted herself in order to support Terry's artistic aspirations. She somatizes her guilt into her paralyzed legs as a way of compensating for her sister's self-sacrifice. Calvero consistently encourages Terry to find beauty in life and the courage to fight her depression. His ministrations cause her to fall in love with him.

Over the succeeding weeks, Calvero assists Terry back onto her feet, but she remains awkward and unsteady. One day, he too becomes depressed. As soon as he needs her, they reverse roles; she nurses him while he gives in to despair. In a sense, Terry is paying back to Calvero the debt she feels she owes her sister. The reason for Calvero's depression is that he bombs during a comeback show. By helping to restore his confidence, Terry completely regains her ability to dance and gets back her job in the corps de ballet. Six months later, she is invited to try out for prima ballerina in *The Death of Columbine*. At her audition, the accompanist happens to be tall, dark, handsome Neville (Sydney Chaplin, Chaplin's second son). Years earlier, Terry had met and fixated on Neville, to whom she had once sold music paper in a stationery store. She had stood under his window listening to him compose, idealizing his role of poor, starving artist. Neville recognizes her now, but Terry, in love with Calvero, pretends not to know him. The ballet director casts Terry, and at her request, hires Calvero to play a clown. Elated by her success, Terry declares her love for Calvero and proposes marriage, which he turns down.

The ballet story is a *mise en abyme* of what has transpired between Terry and Calvero. At curtain's rise, Columbine lies dying, just as Terry was languishing when we first met her. A troupe of three clowns performs tricks to cheer her up. In Act II, she is buried in a graveyard where her distraught lover pines for her. Her spirit rises from the grave for a final *pas de deux*, just as Terry rose to dance again by virtue of Calvero's love. At the opening night reception, Calvero excuses himself, gets drunk, and goes home. Neville walks Terry home, telling her he loves her, but she insists she loves only Calvero. The clown learns that the Empire is about to recast his part because he wasn't funny. Dejected, he drafts a note to Terry and leaves her. Terry is distraught, but her career blossoms; she tours all over the world. Meanwhile, Calvero

"You know you love me!" Claire Bloom and Sydney Chaplin as Terry Ambrose and Neville in *Limelight*, 1952 (United Artists/Photofest).

rejoins his old troupe of street musicians. In a saloon, he runs into Neville, who has been seeing Terry as a friend. Neville informs Calvero that Terry has been pining for him. In the street, Calvero meets Terry. She tells him she still loves him and begs him to return to her. He insists their separation is for the best. Terry arranges a lifetime tribute performance for Calvero at the Empire, hiring a claque to laugh at the right times during his act. Calvero performs brilliantly both his flea circus act and a new act with Buster Keaton about two handicapped musicians (one myopic, the other obese) trying to overcome logistics to perform beautiful music. Once they finally begin playing, Calvero attacks his violin so passionately that he falls off the stage into a bass drum. He is wedged in tightly and has to be carried off stage. The trauma of the fall and his performance anxiety bring on a heart attack. In the wings, watching Terry dance, he dies. Old age has stepped aside for youth in the limelight.

Manhattan likewise opens with an accent on location. George Gershwin's "Rhapsody in Blue" accompanies a montage of iconic city sights in black-and-white. Scope-screen widens the angle of view, which has the effect of romanticizing the depiction of the city's skyscrapers, parks, and sidewalks.[2] In voiceover, Isaac (Allen) recites provisional openings to the Manhattan novel that he is writing, a reworking of a story about his mother called "The Castrating Zionist." The novel is meant to expound on the idea of New York as "a metaphor for the decay of contemporary culture," in which people are "desensitized by drugs, loud music, television, crime, garbage."[3] Isaac drafts out loud, discarding various versions of an opening paragraph before he settles on one that praises his sexual magnetism.

Isaac's day job is writing for a talk show about freaks, called *Human Beings Wow!* He is dating a seventeen-year-old high school student named Tracy (Mariel Hemingway), the only main character without a last name. This lack implies both the sense that youth has yet to form its character, and the function of Tracy as a symbol. Forty-two-year-old Isaac feels guilty about dating someone so young, but he is attracted by her wholesome beauty and innocence. His best friend Yale Pollack (Michael Murphy), an English professor, is trying to write a biography of Eugene O'Neill, but constantly distracts himself by fulfilling his erotic and consumerist urges. Purchasing a Porsche with money saved to found a literary journal, he betrays his profession in favor of his desire to appear young and virile. Married to Emily, Yale is currently having an affair with pseudo-intellectual journalist Mary Wilkie (Diane

The pseudo-intellectual and the novelist. Diane Keaton and Woody Allen as Mary Wilkie and Isaac Davis in *Manhattan*, 1979 (United Artists/Photofest).

Keaton). Yale offers to leave his marriage, but Mary refuses to be a home wrecker. Like Cliff in *Crimes and Misdemeanors*, Isaac rails against the moral bankruptcy of television, and quits his job to demonstrate his authenticity, then immediately despairs at the financial crisis this brings on.

Meanwhile, Yale dumps Mary, and continues to avoid his book on Eugene O'Neill (an author emblematic of Yale's difficulty with marriage and family, O'Neill neglected and abused his wives and children). Interested in having Mary for himself, Isaac dumps Tracy, hurting her in the process. In dating Mary, he feels he has traded upwards. But Yale regrets his decision, and asks Mary to come back. Mary agrees to return to Yale, and dumps Isaac. Irate, Isaac runs to Yale's English classroom to confront him about his betrayal. Yale leaves in the middle of class, pulling his friend into an empty classroom where the scene plays next to an ape-man skeleton hanging on a hook. Isaac berates Yale for offering him the opportunity to date Mary, only to take her back as soon as Isaac became involved. Where are your morals? asks Isaac. When we are dead (turns to the skeleton), we want to be known for our good deeds: "Y-you know, I'll—I'll be hanging in a classroom one day. And—and I wanna make sure when I … thin out that I'm w-w-well thought of!" (265). Yale counters that Isaac is insincere, just putting on a moral act in order to seem better than his friend.

Later, Isaac is depressed. Lying on his couch, he dictates on a tape recorder a list of things worth living for: Groucho Marx, Willie Mays, the second movement of the Jupiter Symphony, the crabs at Sam Wo's, and Tracy's face. Catalyzed by this image, Isaac realizes his error. He runs to her family's apartment just in time to confront Tracy, who is ready to depart for London and drama school. He begs her not to go. "I made a mistake, and do you still love me—or what?" Tracy tells him that if they still love each other, six months won't be that long to wait, ending with the words, "Not everybody gets corrupted. You have to have a little faith in people" (271). The last frame of the film shows Isaac wistfully half-smiling in close-up, a shot that powerfully evokes the Tramp's smile in *City Lights*' final frame, suggesting the same idea: Although I long for you, I have very little faith that you will love me. Alternatively, Isaac's smile could be interpreted as a small hope that she will return to him. Allen uses close-ups on himself more often than Chaplin does. Nonetheless, this image is unique for Allen in the same way that Chaplin's is for him: it beautifully captures his vulnerability.[4] Isaac feels he will probably lose Tracy, and most critics believe that the Tramp is sure of losing the once blind, now sighted flower girl. In *Manhattan*, the ambiguous ending lends a powerful final touch to a film that raises so many questions about love.

Both films draw substantially from their creators' love lives for their inspiration. During the making of *Annie Hall* (1977), Allen had a two-year secret affair with high-schooler Stacey Nelkin, then seventeen to his forty-

5. Limelight *and* Manhattan

Old-fashioned date. Woody Allen and Mariel Hemingway as Isaac Davis and Tracy in *Manhattan*, 1979 (United Artists/Photofest).

two, who became the model for the character Tracy.[5] He filmed Stacey in a brief sequence detailing young Alvy Singer's love life, but later cut this footage from the film. Nelkin's anguish over their breakup is recreated in the soda shop scene in *Manhattan* where we see Tracy reacting painfully to Isaac's news about dating Mary.[6] Her strong attachment to Allen matches Tracy's to Isaac. In an interview, Nelkin reported that she had been deeply in love with Allen, and that through him she had "learned a lot about music and films. I was crazy about him."[7] During the filming of *Manhattan*, Allen tried to recreate another such May-December idyll off-screen with Mariel Hemingway, who describes in her memoir his repeated requests that she travel to Paris with him. When she realized that they would not be having separate bedrooms, she woke him in the middle of the night to tell him she couldn't go (he was sleeping in the guest room of her parents' Ketchum, Idaho, home). She loved him as a friend, but was not interested in him as a lover—nor, at the age of sixteen, was she sexually interested in anyone else.[8]

Chaplin's relationship at the time of *Limelight* was different: in 1943, he had married the young woman of his dreams. By the time of making the movie he was the father of four children with Oona O'Neill Chaplin. When they married, she was eighteen to his fifty-four. The secret to his successful fourth marriage was Oona's adoration. As Charles Jr. (Chaplin's first son by

Lita Grey), wrote, "She worshipped him, drinking in every word he spoke, whether it was about his latest script, the weather, or some bit of philosophy. She seldom spoke."[9] Like Stacey Nelkin, Oona was looking for a father figure. After his divorce when Oona was four, Eugene O'Neill made no attempts to keep in touch with his daughter, communicating only his disapproval of her following in his career footsteps. Especially enraged when she was named Debutante of the Year at the Brearley School, her father cancelled a contract that Oona had signed with a film company in Los Angeles.[10] When Oona married Chaplin, Eugene O'Neill disowned her. Oona gave up her acting career and dedicated her life to Chaplin's happiness and bringing up a family of eight children. Such total dedication to a man's happiness is what Terry exhibits in *Limelight*. Like Oona, Terry hangs on Calvero's every word.[11] The clown may be too old to have children, but Terry's repeatedly iterated dream of sharing a little house in the country is code for the satisfaction she believes she will find in serving him. A wife's willingness to do so is completely in line with an American 1950s middle-class model of heterosexual marriage. The couple might not literally live in the country, since Terry is the bread-winner and would need to be near the ballet. But they would withdraw figuratively to a protected existence, immune to the opinions of those who might deem their match inappropriate.

Like Allen, Chaplin had a pattern of dating and marrying much younger women. Chaplin was twenty-nine when he married sixteen-year-old Mildred Harris, his first wife; he was thirty-five when he married sixteen-year-old Lita Grey, his second. These marriages both ended in early divorces that were costly, painful, and sensationalized by the press. Allen was fifty-six when he started dating Soon-Yi Previn, who was then twenty-one. Their successful marriage has lasted twenty years so far. They have two adopted children, whom Allen loves. The couple's rapport is evident in Barbara Kopple's 1998 documentary, *Wild Man Blues*, which documents their world tour with his jazz band. In the film, Soon-Yi ministers to Allen's neurotic needs, giving him the emotional support that he requires to be able to travel and perform, both of which he finds stressful. Allen acknowledges that he plays a father figure to Soon-Yi, but maintains that he doesn't overplay it, saying, "I was paternal. She responded to someone who was paternal. She deferred to me, and I was happy to give her an enormous amount of decision-making just as a gift and let her take charge of so many things. She flourished. It was just a good luck thing."[12] In *Manhattan*, Isaac teaches Tracy about photography, sculpture, film, and literature, but whether or not he realizes it in time to salvage the relationship, it is Tracy who teaches Isaac about love.

What is love? It is various, and its nature changes over the course of a marriage. In addition to romantic love (*eros*), there are *philia* (love of friends), *agape* (charity), and *storge* (between parents and their children). This topic is the basis of Plato's *Symposium*, where a dinner host poses that very question for his (male) guests to address: what is love?[13] The ancient *Symposium* remains relevant today because its characters speak from the heart about love problems that are strikingly similar to ours. Although the ancients were undemocratic in their political philosophy—their democracy excluded women, children, and slaves—they were excellent psychologists, calling that branch of learning by the name philosophy. I use this ancient text as a template for love definitions because it is one of the few such discussions that avoid both sentimentality and fashionable cynicism. It is also germane to the films because the ideal love that the characters describe is that between an older and younger person. In the variety of their answers, the men at the symposium cover all the bases. For the purposes of this discussion, I select only those guests whose opinions apply to the films: Phaedrus, Pausanias, Alcibiades, and Socrates (who also quotes from the prophetess Diotima).

The poet Phaedrus believes that "love is the most powerful god to assist men in the acquisition of merit and happiness, both here and hereafter" (42). This is because "love inspires shame at what is disgraceful and ambition for what is noble; without these feelings neither a state nor an individual can accomplish anything great or fine" (45). According to Phaedrus, it is only lovers who are willing to sacrifice their lives for another. Terry Ambrose is such a lover. She doesn't, however, view her offer to marry Calvero as a sacrifice. She loves Calvero for "his soul, his sweetness, his sadness"—in ancient Greek terms, for his moral beauty.[14] Phaedrus' notion that love inspires shame when the lover compares himself unfavorably to the beloved is central to Isaac's problem with Tracy. She continually makes him feel inferior with her simple assertions of truth, which I will discuss later.

The next speaker, Pausanias, explains the two basic forms of love, common (lustful) and heavenly (soulful). He identifies the homosexual love that the symposium participants considered ideal, but his distinction between lustful and soulful love is equally applicable to heterosexual love in a more egalitarian world than ancient Greece. Because women were not educated in ancient Athens, men could not construct a "heavenly love" relationship with them, one based on intellectual exchange. With women, says Pausanias, only common love is possible, based on lust. For the Greeks, heavenly love is specifically that of an older man for a younger boy. To be virtuous, the boy may yield to an older man for one reason only: to attain excellence by hearing his wisdom. Tracy and Terry of the films love their older partners for such excellence; they hope to gain wisdom by learning from them. From Calvero's speeches, Terry learns to fight guilt and depression; from Isaac, Tracy learns about various art forms and the pretentious critics who, according to her boyfriend, don't know much about art. Mary Wilkie takes heavenly love to an extreme. She married her former husband, Jeremiah (Wallace Shawn), because he was brilliant, and she believes Yale is likewise endowed. We see no evidence of the trait in either, but Allen's shorthand may be non-diegetic or meta-textual. In real life, Wallace Shawn is the author of clever plays and stories. As for Yale, perhaps associations of his forename with academic excellence, along with his research topic (Eugene O'Neill), are Allen's shorthand for brilliance. Mary describes Jeremiah's intelligence to Isaac: "Oh, God, was he brilliant. I was so crazy about him. He really opened me up sexually. He taught me everything. Women found him devastating" (222). Mary links a man's sexual prowess with his brainpower, or perhaps it is more accurate to say that her partner's perceived brilliance turns her on. Like Isaac, after hearing this encomium we are shocked to meet Jeremiah, who is short, bald, and overweight. Mary has sublimated her physical sense of beauty into her intellectual sense, and this links her to Isaac, who is also looking for something more than sheer physical appeal. The difference between Mary and Isaac, however, is associated with gender. Men consistently report that a woman's looks are the most important factor in their own feelings of attraction, whereas women include looks along with, typically, a sense of humor, intelligence, and stability. Mary willingly overlooks physical appearance in favor of brains, but Isaac demands both qualities in one person. His love choices Tracy, Mary, and Jill are evidence of his taste.

As the wisest man in Athens, Socrates is given the lion's share of the discourse. He humbly reveals that his instructress in the art and philosophy of love is a woman, Diotima, the prophetess of Mantinea. It is interesting to note that, contrary to Pausanias's male bias, this female is capable of teaching the wisest man in Athens about intellectual love. Isaac Davis has a lesson to learn from Socrates, for Isaac's young girlfriend understands love better than he does, though he cannot openly acknowledge this. Diotima tells Socrates that the object of love is not beauty, but rather it is the desire to procreate and bring forth beauty, since procreation is the nearest that mortals can get to immortality (87). Women and men have strong desires for children, but in the culture of narcissism that late-seventies *Manhattan* critiques, men want to extend their own youth, like Peter Pan.[15] To such men, having children is a threat to their autonomy. In the movie, this reluctance distresses Mary and complicates her relationship with Yale. His inability to mature creates a sterile marriage. In Greek terms, they have sacrificed their potential to bring forth beauty and approach godliness. Both Emily (Yale's wife) and Mary Wilkie want children. Mary tells Isaac he is the kind of man she can imagine having children with. Emily repeatedly tells Yale she wants children; he puts her off with irrelevant excuses, such as that they'd have to move to Connecticut, and they can't leave Isaac alone in New York. In actuality, Yale is too invested in feeding his erotic hungers to be willing to commit to a family.

Speaking to Socrates, Diotima describes the phases one must go through to arrive at the highest form of love. In Allen's world, such a high form of love—Supreme Knowledge—is greatly desired, but never achieved nor even considered possible in the fallen urban world. Allen's perennial worry about his failure to find God may be the cause of the failed relationships in his films. If we believe, like Plato, that lovers must mature through several phases, from eroticism to supreme knowledge, in order to find God, Allen's characters will never succeed. In most of his films, they fail to move beyond simple eroticism; when their sex life fails, companionship also falters.[16] They leave their partners and seek new ones, constantly setting their quest back to ground zero. Our awareness of the difference between these glorious archaic Greek archetypes and Allen's contemporary makeshift relationships is part of what makes his art ring true to a postmodern viewer.[17]

According to Diotima, the first phase of love is physical attraction toward one person; the second is the love of all persons, for the "pilgrim" will realize that passion for one "is of small account" (92). From physical love, he passes on to love for the souls of men. After loving morality, the pilgrim moves on to science, then love of wisdom, and finally to an ultimate divine beauty, which is eternal, absolute, and unique. Supreme Knowledge has Absolute Beauty as its sole object. Socrates equates absolute beauty with goodness, but by "beauty" he intends moral and intellectual beauty rather than physical. Whereas Yale operates purely in the realm of common love, Isaac shares some of the higher principles of heavenly love. He loves Tracy's innocence or moral beauty, dreading the day when "that thing I like about you" will change. As Christopher Knight points out, Tracy is the moral center of the chaotic, narcissistic late-seventies Manhattan scene.[18] Isaac is mature enough to include moral beauty in his quest for a love object, but physical beauty constantly compels him. He would not date an ugly girl. Tellingly, he describes Mary, Tracy, and Jill (his ex-wife, played by Meryl Streep) first and foremost by their stunning beauty.

Back in Athens, the famous politician and general, Alcibiades, arrives late at the party, drunk and acting aggressively toward Socrates. Alcibiades is in love with Socrates' intelligence and nobility and is very jealous of his ability to philosophize (like Mary's "brilliant men" in *Manhattan*). Socrates' discourse puts Alcibiades in a "religious frenzy," compelling him to realize that his own life is a "mass of imperfections" (101). Socrates' perfection of mind shames Alcibiades, recalling Phaedrus's statement that love inspires shame when we are unworthy of the beloved. According to Alcibiades, Socrates falls in love with good-looking young men, but beneath the surface he does not care about their beauty, rank, or wealth, only their goodness. Some time ago, Alcibiades had set out to test Socrates' principles by seducing him, but Socrates, though polite, was impervious to the pleasures of the flesh.

This proved the beloved's purity of purpose and shamed Alcibiades even more by the contrast with his own character. Alcibiades still loves Socrates and is jealous of attractive Agathon, who is sitting next to him. Alcibiades' description of love includes shame, jealousy, and testing the beloved's principles to see how strong they remain under duress.

Isaac shares the jealous and testing qualities of Alcibiades' form of love. When his marriage to beautiful Jill (a successful writer) is over, he can no more relinquish his sense of ownership than the ancient Athenian politician could. He tries to run over his ex-wife's new lover with a car. Isaac's next relationship also reveals his insecurity; his breakup with Tracy may be a test of her loyalty. Although his purported reason for the breakup was Mary's interest in him, he had been looking since the beginning of the film for any excuse to leave Tracy because of his guilt about their age disparity. His return to her at the end of the film is a test of her principles, her authenticity, and her loyalty. When he poses the question, do you still love me, it is also a test of whether she ever did love him, an issue about which he was insecure. He may believe that, if she ever did love him, she will forego her trip to London.

Phaedrus and Alcibiades state the principle that love inspires shame about one's imperfections. The idea of shame as an element of love is central to Calvero and Isaac's dilemmas about loving Terry and Tracy, both of whom, by virtue of their innocence, are purer than their loved ones. In the heterosexual love of the modern films, as opposed to the homosexual love of the ancient *Symposium*, there is an added element of challenge insofar as the male is expected to outstrip his female mate in intellectual, artistic, and financial accomplishments. At the root of Calvero's problem with Terry, and Isaac's with Tracy, may be their fear of the woman being or becoming a better artist, and in Terry's case the primary breadwinner. Calvero's first expression of repugnance at the idea of marrying Terry does not occur until he witnesses her talent during her audition for *The Death of Columbine*. "You are a true artist," he says. Their careers proceed in an obverse relationship: as her star rises, his declines. Ever since his alcoholism prevented Calvero from putting on a legitimate show, he doesn't feel like a true artist. Likewise, Isaac's appreciation of Tracy extends to what he sees as her artistic potential: "You're a wonderful actress ... you'll be the toast of the town," he tells her in reference to her trip to London (225). Moving from TV scriptwriter to novelist has left Isaac insecure about his artistic ability, so Tracy's potential as she heads toward an acting career in London may threaten him. Isaac says that Viking Press loved the first four chapters of his novel, but writers know that "loving" is a far cry from signing. Furthermore, Isaac's writing challenge goes beyond worrying about sales; he is concerned about his own authenticity.

The film's opening scene provides the key to his search for an authentic self, which is in competition with his desire to write a bestseller. Isaac tries on different voices, failing to find an authentic tone. Even when he finally settles on a version he likes, the viewer perceives its falseness. First, he tries to sound like a great romantic à la Jay Gatsby, but the disparity between his nebbish quality and Gatsby's WASPishness (etched in the viewer's mind by the image of Robert Redford playing the part in the 1974 film) is jarring. Isaac feels that the first and second drafts of his opening paragraph demonstrate a false romanticism, so he scratches the phrases "he idolized [New York]" and "he was too romantic" (181). His third try expresses his desire to be more macho, a noir-ish sentence that could belong to a gravelly-voiced actor such as Humphrey Bogart: "New York meant beautiful women and street-smart guys who seemed to know all the angles." The visual that accompanies this paragraph is a big-breasted woman walking by a construction site where men stop working to ogle her. If Isaac doesn't resemble Robert Redford, even less does he match the hardboiled sangfroid of a Humphrey Bogart. Isaac is trying to find authenticity by modeling himself on famous male personae. When these personae are too different from him, the experiment doesn't work, and the disparity is comical. Rejecting the macho version as "too corny," Isaac consciously tries for profundity: "The same lack of individual integrity to cause so many people to take the easy way out ... was rapidly turning the town of his dreams in—." Midsentence, he rejects this version as "too preachy.... I mean, let's face it, I wanna sell some books here" (181). In contrast, this is not a thought that Tracy, his model of authenticity, is likely to have.

Especially in autobiographical writing, authenticity and commercialism are antithetical. Isaac knows this; he often complains about the superficiality of pop culture. Next, he tries shifting moral responsibility from the individual to the culture: "How hard it was to exist in a society desensitized by drugs, loud music, television, crime, garbage." Still concerned about potential sales, he rejects this thought as "too angry." Finally, he arrives at a persona that he "loves" (and this is his only positive use of the word "love" in the entire film, one which is directed not at another person but at his ego-ideal). His ideal self "was as tough and romantic as the city he loved. Behind his black-rimmed glasses was the coiled sexual power of a jungle cat" (182).

Surprisingly, the film supports the view of its protagonist as sexually attractive, since both Mary and Tracy find him so. The fact that Mary finds her ex, Jeremiah, to be "this oversexed brilliant kind of animal" also supports the view of the film that homely men can be sexually attractive. However, the opening line about his coiled sexual power is funny, but not true. It amplifies the difference between Isaac's ego ideal and the reality of the nebbish that the audience sees. This device asks us to be inside the Woody persona's head, seeing the beautiful woman loving him, while at the same time the visual effect of the nerdy person we see on screen requires us to suspend our disbelief in order to make this possible. The comic quality of the image sells it.

Furthermore, male viewers can relate to the practice of building up their egos to prepare for their own hunt for a sexual partner.

Writing has its analogies to this process. As the scene demonstrates, memoirists need to try on different personae until they find one that makes them like themselves enough to perform the task. Yet Isaac's commercial savvy vies with his longing for authenticity. Isaac values artistic authenticity and has a keen barometer for when others are inauthentic. When he first meets her, Isaac rejects Mary's art criticism as "pseudointellectual garbage" (196). His TV work is so inauthentic that he finally quits. He complains to the producers, "There's not any substance to the comedy" (198). Despite the inflated persona of his narrator, Isaac's own book is about his search for authenticity in a city filled with "decaying values."

When it comes to pursuing authenticity in his relationships, however, Isaac consistently falls short. When his analyst warned him prior to his marriage about Jill's lesbian tendencies, he said to Jill, "but you were so beautiful that I got another analyst" (217). When Tracy calls him out on his inauthenticity, saying, "You keep stating it like it's to my advantage when it's you that wants to get out of it," Isaac responds, "Hey, don't be so precocious, okay? I mean, don't be so smart.... My hair's falling out.... Is that what you want?" (245). In this exchange, Isaac realizes that Tracy is right and has caught him in his sophistry, but he defaults once again to the age disparity argument in order to slip out of the relationship.

Even though Isaac does not act authentically by being honest with himself and Tracy, he is still a moral person, and this gives him enough active conscience to worry about what he is doing. His morality is evident in several of his actions. He wouldn't date Mary until Yale was tired of her. He didn't correct Emily's view that he was with Mary before Yale was, since protecting her feelings was more important than the truth. He didn't run away from Mary when, on the first night of lovemaking, she said he was someone with whom she could see having children. Most of all, Isaac's morality is apparent in the lecture he gives to Yale as they stand next to the skeleton: "You rationalize everything. You're not honest with yourself.... It's very important to have—to have some kind of personal integrity" (265). The fact that Isaac shares his friend's faults of rationalizing and inauthenticity does not lessen the moral impact of what he says, because Isaac's is an active conscience, constantly at work on his issues, whereas Yale is a sellout, telling Isaac, "You are so self-righteous, you know. I mean, we're just people, we're just human beings, you know. You think you're God!" (265). True, Isaac is judgmental about many other people, but he has a conscience that he sometimes acts on. He feels guilty about things like depriving Tracy of a normal adolescence, and he tries to practice serial monogamy as opposed to his friend's straight-out cheating. In contrast, Yale is happy to give in to his fallible human nature instead of trying to model himself on a better example.

Compared to Isaac and Yale, Tracy is a paragon of authenticity. She shares Isaac's view of the degradation of values in popular culture. She comments about a TV talk show's guests: "Why can't they just age naturally instead of putting all that junk on?" (237). Her definition of love is about getting along, not about borrowed status, sexual boasting rights, or access to money: "We have laughs together. I care about you. Your concerns are my concerns. We have great sex," she says (245). It's a far cry from Diotima's Supreme Knowledge and Absolute Beauty, but it's also more practical than Yale and Isaac's pursuit of erotic fantasies. Tracy is also wiser than Isaac insofar as she understands the value of serial monogamy; even though he practices it, he is offended to hear about it from a young woman. Tracy says, "Maybe people weren't meant to have one deep relationship. Maybe we're meant to have, you know, a series of relationships of different lengths. I mean, that kind of thing's gone out of date" (197). The idea threatens Isaac, and he tries to assert his age as an indicator of greater wisdom, boasting "I–I–I was World War Two.... I was in the trenches." Never cowed by Isaac's lies, always understanding his insecurity, Tracy merely corrects him: "You were eight in World War Two." Tracy calmly accepts the traits that his ex-wife, Jill, abhorred in Isaac—his "fits of rage, Jewish liberal paranoia, male chauvinism, self-righteous misanthropy, and nihilistic moods of despair"—making careful corrections to his utterances without preaching (259).

Like Alcibiades, Isaac compares himself to his lover and comes out inferior. In Tracy's mirror of himself, he feels ashamed. Rather than inspiring him to become "ambitious for excellence" (Phaedrus), Tracy's goodness frightens him so that he runs away from the mirror. Just as he left the analyst who told him the truth about Jill, Isaac leaves the lover who tells him the truth about himself. For Isaac, Mary is a better love choice than Tracy; like him, she is narcissistic, confused, self-indulgent, and pseudo-intellectual, though Isaac is more anti-intellectual than pseudo-intellectual. He regularly curtails with a joke any line of analytic thought that arises from his musing, anxious to defuse the intensity of authentic discourse. In Mary's mirror, Isaac recognizes himself, which is a more comforting situation.

Some critics offer a third possibility (after age disparity and narcissism) for Isaac's failure of love, saying Tracy is a symbol or metaphor, and *Manhattan* an allegory. This does not really solve the problems of two little people in this crazy world because it removes the discourse to a literary-genre realm, turning them into ideas. This allegorization does, however, clarify the May-December romance as archetypal in the male psyche. For Nancy Pogel, Tracy may be "only a fiction, an incarnation of Isaac's longing, an unobtainable ideal."[19] To Christopher Knight, *Manhattan* is an allegory about the ethical law of renunciation. Often, in order to protect others from harm and to increase one's own chance for happiness in the future, one needs to renounce one's immediate lusts and satisfactions. In Knight's allegory, Tracy is the hero of the film, for she is the one with "the greatest respect for the law of renunciation."[20] For Joanne Rapf, women in Allen's films are metaphors for the artist's persona. Rapf underlines Isaac's objectification of Tracy, who "exists for Isaac on the surface."[21] When extolling her virtues during the Central Park carriage ride, he points to her, saying, "God made one of these." For Sander Lee, Tracy symbolizes "an innocence so overwhelming that Isaac spends most of the film fleeing her."[22] For Douglas Brode, Tracy is "a symbol, a grail, an image of radical innocence and allegorical figure of purity."[23] Because Isaac is such a nuanced figure, identifying his problems as simple narcissism doesn't do full justice to his psychology. Whether *Manhattan* is an allegory about innocence and experience, or a realist drama about one man's incapacity to love, its appeal to our sense of the complexity in all love relationships makes it meaningful for many viewers.

In *Limelight*, Calvero is less complex. The aging clown is stymied in his love affair by his own narcissism. It is hard for him to see Terry's love because he no longer loves himself as he did when he was a successful performer. When the audience laughs at his act, he can love himself, and only when he loves himself can he love another person. When Terry proclaims she loves him, he cannot believe it, because he has not performed for her. While nursing her back to health, he removes his comic persona to reveal the sad philosopher underneath. Terry has seen his despair and loves him for it: "It's his soul, his sweetness, his sadness. Nothing will ever separate me from that." But Calvero performs as a clown, not a sage. André Bazin states that Calvero's happiness depends on performance success: "Calvero exists only for others. He knows himself only as reflected in the public mirror.... [T]he artist is

"You love *me*? I don't think so!" Claire Bloom and Charlie Chaplin as Terry Ambrose and Calvero in *Limelight*, 1952 (United Artists/Photofest).

incomplete without his public.... This approval constitutes the theatrical personality."[24] In the musical act with Buster Keaton, Buster stares at his sheet music, but Calvero looks at both the theatre audience and the camera, seeking affirmation through his relationship with the audience.[25] According to Ira Jaffe, the ending is so satisfactory because Calvero "dies beloved. Even more fortunate is that he dies in love [with his audience]. Even when he bitterly calls the public a monster without a head, he concedes his longing: 'Maybe I love them'" (205). Donna Kornhaber deflects Calvero's narcissism back onto Chaplin himself, who she says is giving himself a compliment when Calvero calls Terry a "true artist," because it was he who wrote the music and choreographed the dance that she has just performed.[26] It is clear that Terry is beginning a successful career while Calvero is washed up, which is no incentive for romance from a man's point of view.

Another angle from which to examine Calvero's relationship to Terry is that of an analyst. Jean-Max Méjean uses the concept of transference to explain why Calvero doesn't love Terry. According to Méjean,

> The clown isn't in love with the dancer. Chaplin stages a paternal relationship, that of a man who remembers his youth. Chaplin is in the position of the analyst. By means of transference, he brings healing to the woman and afterwards, dies. Symbolically it's about the death of the analyst, his retreat at the end of the cure.[27]

This interpretation does not necessarily ennoble Calvero's character via an implied ethics of renunciation because his role-playing as a psychoanalyst is natural for the wise old man. In a psychoanalytic reading, the characters are seen as symbolic of fundamental psychoanalytic processes; note Méjean's phrasing, that Chaplin "stages" a relationship. If Terry transfers her ambivalent feelings about her father and mother onto Calvero, then Calvero either accepts them and loves her in his own counter-transference to the analysand, or, as Méjean suggests, rejects her love because it arises from an analytic relationship and is therefore unethical for him to pursue her. Calvero does feel a strong, loving urge towards Terry. He finds her beautiful, and he is changed by their relationship. At the beginning, when she is still healing, he says, "You know, preaching and moralizing to you has really affected me. I'm beginning to believe it myself. I haven't taken a drink since I've known you." At the end, his dying words—"The heart and the mind ... what an enigma"—indicate the split between his heart's love for young Terry and his mind's belief that he is not good enough for her.

We have reviewed evidence that Isaac loves Tracy but refuses the relationship out of shame and narcissism, and that Calvero loves Terry but refuses her out of narcissism and paternalism, or a failure to achieve counter-transference. Now we will examine the feelings of these two talented and noble female characters towards their mentors. I believe that Tracy loves Isaac, because she repeatedly tells him so. Also, she defines their love in a believable, non-idealized manner ("your concerns are my concerns ..., we have laughs together"). She stays with him despite his pushback ("I'm not hung up on you; I love you"). She invites him to accompany her to London when she first learns of the drama school acceptance. At the end of the film, she even implies that there is a possibility for a renewal of their relationship upon her return from London ("Well, I mean, what's six months if we still love each other?") As Christopher Knight indicates, Tracy renounces other relationships because her relationship with Isaac is special.

Likewise, there is no question for me that Terry's feelings for Calvero are those of a special, exclusive love. She loves him not only for his help or because of the debt of the saved towards their savior, but for his qualities: "I love you. I've wanted to say it for so long. Ever since the day you thought I was a woman of the street. You took me in, cared for me, saved my life, inspired it. But above all that, I just love you." She loves him because his philosophy enabled her to fight against the challenges of her life and her sensitive temperament. As Donna Kornhaber points out, Terry internalized Calvero's optimistic words, turning them into expressive dancing.[28] Terry credits her survival and career success to Calvero. But beyond that, "she just loves him." In addition to these utterances, the structure of the film and its genre (melodrama) require that she love him, as is also the case with Tracy loving Isaac. Otherwise, how would either director build and maintain suspense in the dramatization of his May-December love thesis, if true love were not involved?

Yet nearly all the male critics I've read deny the existence of Tracy and Terry's love for their men. Like Calvero and Isaac, the critics substitute their own judgment (of what love is, of whether a woman feels it) for that of the female characters. In Criterion Collection's *Limelight* DVD "Special Feature," Bernardo Bertolucci looks directly at the camera and says, "She lies, she lies, and Calvero knows that she lies and she knows that he knows that she lies. It is not love she feels, but pity. To even contemplate such a match is humiliating for Calvero."[29] Dan Kamin writes: "Terry's love for Calvero is really pity and a sense of obligation."[30] Julian Smith proclaims: "Terry lies constantly in the name of love or sympathy."[31] André Bazin chimes in: "Thereza believed that her love was only a profound pity."[32]

Critics are somewhat less bothered about whether Tracy really loves Isaac, but Peter Bailey says, with regard to the characters' final conversation, "Tracy's response to Isaac conveys dissimulation more than love." Bailey does not believe that Tracy loves Isaac (any more) but that she is lying to end a painful moment: "the disparity between what she knows and what she says in order to get away from him to the airport elicits the sadly bemused smile on Isaac's face in the film's final dramatic frames: in telling him disingenuously that not everybody gets corrupted, she's proving that she has been."[33] Bailey finds it corrupt that Tracy might be protecting Isaac's feelings.[34] If this is the case (which we don't know), such an impulse is not corrupt, but kind. Within the narrative itself, there is no reason to disbelieve Tracy's suggestion that she might come back to Isaac, but viewers will impose their own interpretations on the ending, depending on their own experiences of love and relationships. Any corruption implied in the scene is in Isaac's mind, the fear of Tracy's finding another boyfriend in London. "Corruption," then, is Isaac losing her to someone he fears will be better than him. Could "corrupted" also mean that she doesn't obey Isaac's request that she forego drama school to stay with him? In all these possibilities, a male perspective insinuates male desire for control over a woman's sexuality, a key element of the way in which patriarchy seeks to keep women under male dominance. Asking Tracy to give up her career because he has decided he loves her is Isaac's last selfish move. If anyone in the scene is corrupt, it is Isaac. Tracy remains the same kind person she was before the breakup.

Several critics who objectify Tracy as a symbol or allegory of innocence are likewise detracting from her viability as the realistic character of a young woman who is involved in her first romance. One thing these critics agree upon is that an innocent woman is a fabrication of a male mind. In his early writings, Sigmund Freud theorized a Madonna-whore complex, an aspect of the unresolved Oedipal complex that results in the splitting of a man's conception of womanhood into an object who is either pure or corrupt.[35] It implies that entry into sexual knowledge violates a woman's integrity, and turns her into a corruptor of men. The notion underscores men's patriarchal fear of women's sexuality. The Madonna/whore complex is an important symptom within the Oedipal complex stemming from the male need to desexualize Mother by keeping her separate from the child's erotic desires.

Because we go through different socialization processes and hold different roles in a patriarchal society, men and women view many things differently. The cinematic medium speaks so directly to our unconscious and conscious fears and desires that a given film can evoke predictably contrary reactions in men and women spectators. In her 1975 article, "Visual Pleasure and Narrative Cinema," Laura Mulvey establishes the groundwork for a feminist critique of traditional cinema. According to feminist film theory, the male gaze dominates Hollywood film. The male gaze appears in three guises: 1) The male protagonist looks at the female lead. 2) The male cameraman looks at and films the female lead. 3) The male spectator looks at the woman and at the man looking at her, identifying himself with the male character. Woman characters are created for their "to-be-looked-at-ness," or qualities of beauty and sexuality that are available for male consumption. However, to men, the image of woman on the screen signifies castration. In Mulvey's words, "Phallocentrism depends on the image of the castrated woman to give order and meaning to its world; it is her lack that produces the phallus as a symbolic presence."[36] In response to the image of a woman on film, male castration anxiety induces voyeuristic or fetishistic mechanisms intended to circumvent the threat. The male spectator has two options: he can investigate and ultimately judge the female character in order to contain her threat, or he can objectify her, turning her into a fetish so that she becomes reassuring rather than dangerous. Mulvey draws examples from Hitchcock films in which the male is powerful, the woman guilty, and "true perversion is barely concealed" (812). In *Vertigo*, Scottie stalks one woman until she dies (or so he mistakenly thinks); then he sadistically forces another woman to become the woman he was obsessed with. In *Marnie*, Rutland stalks the *femme fatale*, becomes obsessed with her guilt, exposes her buried childhood trauma, and saves her from herself. In *Rear Window*, Jeffries is bored with his girlfriend, Lisa, until he watches her through a telescope in a dangerous situation, which sexually excites him and activates his desire to save her and prove his masculinity.

Applying Mulvey's theory to the romances in *Manhattan* and *Limelight*, we see that Terry and Tracy are also investigated, judged, and fetishized by the male gaze. Isaac and Yale conceive Tracy as an object of innocence, whereas Mary sees through the secret of her charm (for Isaac): "Oh, sure, I understand, believe me. Sixteen years old and no possible threat at all" (207). Mary knows it is easy for a man to bask in the admiration of a girl who has until now been eating at the children's table, unaware of the thrills and weaknesses to which adults are prone. Calvero likewise fetishizes Terry by seeing her as a symbol of youth (and of his bygone success) rather than a flesh-and-blood woman who truly loves him.

Fortunately, the camera does not fetishize either woman. Mariel Hemingway's beauty is powerful because she is so wholesome. Dividing a body into parts, or fixating on parts rather than the whole, are two aspects of fetishizing. Whereas Sam Girgus sees the partial bodies of *Manhattan* cut up by tight framing, I see Tracy as exempt from that fragmentation; Mary and Yale's bodies are truncated by the frame, but Isaac and Tracy's faces, at least, are always whole, as befits the male and female leads.[37] Only in the final scene do we view Tracy through a glass door with two horizontal bars that visually cut her body in three. We are seeing her from Isaac's viewpoint, outside the foyer door. When he opens the door, Isaac's vision of Tracy, whole and elegant in her 1980s grownup skirt-suit brings a rush of wellbeing. For Isaac, she is a vision of beauty; for many, she is a wholesome young woman ready for her first career adventure.

Like *Vertigo*'s Scottie, who attempts to transform Judy into the nobler (seeming) Madeleine by dressing her and staging her appearance, Isaac wants to freeze Tracy in an imaginary moment to preserve her innocence: "I just don't want that thing about you that I like to change"(271). But her youthful innocence is only one part of Tracy. Isaac and the aforementioned male critics refuse to embrace the totality of Tracy's character, especially her intelligence. As Brianne Brenneman writes, Allen likes his woman characters submissive, and no more intelligent than he is. "Allen portrays an intelligent woman in a very negative light" [she is referring to Mary]. "Instead of refined, her mannerisms are dismissive. Instead of sophisticated, her interests are snobbish." "You're not such a genius," Isaac tells Mary. Instead of reacting to his rudeness, "she begins to transform herself into the woman he wants her to be."[38] In my view, Tracy is smarter than Mary because she combines her emotional intelligence with her willingness to learn, but she does not change herself in order to fit her boyfriend's needs. When Isaac initially finds Mary pretentious, Tracy realizes she is just nervous, and says so. When Isaac tries to pretend he's breaking up with Tracy for her own good, she calls him on his fallacy: he's trying to make it look like he's doing it for her, when it's not what she wants. Finally, she has the wisdom to know that their relationship failed because of Isaac's uncertainties, not her own inadequacies, and when he asks her, post-breakup, whether she still loves him, she knows her answer is contingent on him: "Do *you* love *me*?" (emphasis mine).

Many male viewers fetishize Tracy in order to contain male anxiety, whereas in Terry's case, they interrogate and judge her. As evidenced by the critics' resounding denial of Terry's love, the male gaze attempts to contain the anxiety occasioned by Terry's love by judging it to be false. It is not love, only pity, say these critics. Terry lies, while Tracy dissimulates. As Isaac tells Tracy, "You don't know what love means" (245). Neville says the same to Terry about her loving Calvero: "This devotion is idealistic. Your youth! But it isn't love." He also informs her that she loves him. Neville: "You're as helpless as I am. We love each other." Terry: "I never said I loved you." Neville: "Every look, gesture says it!" And Calvero rejects her declaration of love as "nonsense." By identifying with the male characters, these critics may be protecting themselves from what they see as the likelihood that the young woman will reject the older man. Additionally, if they define love as primarily an erotic attraction, these critics may not understand that some women value moral beauty over physical, or that they actually find older men physically attractive.

As we have seen, male viewers have a tendency to believe the words of the male characters in the films, while they disbelieve the words of Tracy and Terry. As Mulvey points out, "we identify the screen persona as our ego ideal. The spectator's fascination with and recognition of his likeness" is what makes the narrative convincing (808). Budd Boetticher makes it clear that women play a secondary role in traditional film, as they do in patriarchy at large. "In herself, the woman has not the slightest importance," writes Boetticher.

Instead, "the love or fear she inspires in the hero, or else the concern he feels for her, makes him act the way he does" (in Mulvey, 809). In traditional film, a woman is the catalyst for men's actions. It is interesting to note that in Woody Allen pictures, the women are the change agents for men, but they are also the ones who change the most. Joanne Rapf argues that the character who changes the most in *Manhattan* is Tracy. "Even though the film is structured around a male point of view, it is the woman who embodies a positive perspective." Allen's genders are the reverse of Mulvey's: "whereas Laura Mulvey once described women in film as passive and men as active, the reverse tends to be true for characters in Allen films."[39]

Sam Girgus and Joanne Rapf both comment on the complexity of gender role-playing in Allen's film and relate it to the culturally charged moment at the end of second-wave feminism in which it takes place. According to Rapf, "*Manhattan* conveys the uneasy situation for women at the end of second-wave feminism" (260). The female characters represent different positions with regard to feminism. Yale's wife, Emily, is pre-feminist; she wants only to preserve her marriage at any cost. Mary is active in the feminist movement, but can't live without a man. Rapf does not mention whether she considers Tracy a feminist, but I think there is much evidence for such a case. For example, Tracy challenges her twenty-five-years-older boyfriend, correcting him when he lies. She also pays for the groceries and initiates sex. She refuses to quit her career training just because he asks her to. Rapf concludes that Allen's perspective is an honest one with regard to how men view women, and, even though women are there to promote men's growth, she concedes that Allen "allows women to struggle with their specular identity"(260–61). *Specular* here refers to Mulvey's description of women characters' key function of "to-be-looked-at-ness." In his assessment of the film, Sam Girgus tries to move beyond gender difference: "The inherent instability of sexual organization continually disrupts the relationships of desire [in the film], constructing a radical dialogue of desire in which the most basic questions about love and identity are asked but never answered with finality"(79). Allen's inability (and our own) to answer the most basic questions is not a drawback, I would argue, but a symptom of our postmodern ways of thinking and existing in the contemporary world. His accurate reflection of our times is what makes Allen a great filmmaker.

Yet it is not possible, nor very helpful, to take gender out of a discourse on desire, because desire means different things to different people. It is not the case that female viewers always identify with women characters and male viewers always identify with male characters. Such a paradigm is complicated by the fact that one's gender-identity may differ from the sex assigned to one at birth. It is true, however, that most men in a patriarchy identify with men on screen because it is disempowering to be seen as a woman, or an object.

But many women in a patriarchy might identify with a male character on screen because he is the protagonist. I believe that herein lies the appeal for women viewers of both the Tramp and Woody's personas. Because of the strong female aspects (worried, reflective, underdog, sensitive) of each persona, it is relatively easy for a woman to identify with them. Furthermore, both personas' mode of surviving is through comedy. Women identity strongly with such a strategy for coping with patriarchy; if one has to be the underdog, it is easier done with a smile and a laugh. Most importantly, the ability to find the irony, paradox, and hypocrisy in most situations helps a woman to critique the dominant power structure of the world, and—at least in a literary or rhetorical way—to try to get around it.

Limelight and *Manhattan* compare well because their central relationships involve a young woman loving an older man who loves her back but rejects her. We noted common critical tendencies regarding these films. Male critics tend to deny that the young woman loves the protagonist, and to fetishize youth rather than normalizing the relationships. But there are important differences between the films. The time periods of their making, which are separated by more than twenty-five years, produce significant differences in the tone, dialog, and range of their cinematic worlds. Chaplin's *Limelight* is a melodrama centered on the conflicting desires of two people. It uses exaggerated characters and exciting events (suicide, death, unrequited love) to appeal to the emotions. The stereotype of the pure woman in love with the cynical man is an old one, but Chaplin reenergizes it with autobiographical particularity. The audience is aware that the film relates to the director's life insofar as he is on the downward side of his career trajectory and has been reviled by American puritans for his sexual choices and political affiliations (whereas Calvero's faults are intoxication and inept performances). We also recognize in Calvero certain key aspects of Chaplin Sr., Charlie's father, whose vaudeville career was destroyed by alcoholism. Yet Chaplin keeps our interest by reversing the trajectory of Calvero and Terry's love affair vis-à-vis his own love story with Oona, his thirty-five-years-younger wife. Whereas Calvero disengages with his ingénue, Chaplin engages and marries his, enjoying a successful and harmonious bond for the rest of his life. It is 1952, the days of the Red Scare, and mainstream Americans want conformity; they don't want to see December-May marriage, and they especially don't want to see Chaplin getting away with yet another impropriety.[40] So Calvero leaves Terry, melodrama achieves its heightened emotions, and the hero manages to save the heroine in the course of a nonsexual relationship.

In 1979, on the other hand, Woody Allen felt the need to address the complicated mores of the new sexual liberation and changing roles for women. Combined with the culture of narcissism, these trends made it hard for men to keep the upper hand in relationships. Many of them must have distrusted the constancy of their female partners at a time when narcissism and serial monogamy constituted the predominant Manhattan ethos. In *Limelight,* the certainty that Calvero saved Terry's life and that Terry loves him contrasts with the postmodernist chaos of relationship terrain in *Manhattan.* Isaac rejects love because he doesn't know what it is until—possibly—too late.

6

Nobility and Ambiguity in Modern and Postmodern Endings

Allen and Chaplin's comic visions are based on strong class- and ethnicity-related feelings of alienation. Largely because of their different time periods, their modes of dramatizing this condition are quite different. As a Modernist, Chaplin critiques socioeconomic hierarchies, capitalism, and dictatorship, giving his little men the dignity he feels they deserve. As a postmodernist, Allen questions the possibility of meaning in a universe without absolutes. For the purposes of this discussion, I call the period prior to 1945 "modern" and the period after 1945 "postmodern." I choose 1945 because it is the date of the first detonation of an atomic bomb in Alamagordo, New Mexico, soon to be followed by the atomic bombing of Hiroshima and Nagasaki. Although theorists disagree as to the exact moment of transition, all agree that elements of both modernism and postmodernism appear in works of both periods.[1] Most designate midcentury as a turning point, and are in consensus that the Second World War effectuated the shift to postmodernism, with the immediately ensuing Cold War providing an emblematic condition of the postmodern. The postmodern condition denotes a state of constant suspicion of others—whether nations, institutions, or individuals. Compounding this feeling of alienation is a profound self-doubt; we do not know ourselves. Whereas modernism's major philosophical question was epistemological (how do we know things?), postmodernism asks the ontological question of what things really are (what is the nature of existence and non-existence?). Modernism is an artistic reaction to the horrors of World War I, industrialization, secularization, and the women's and workers' movements. Postmodernism responds to the traumas of ethnic cleansing, the state of constant war, economic globalization, neocolonialism, and the threat of nuclear annihilation.

More than finite historical periods, modernism and postmodernism are descriptions of ways in which artists respond to world events, especially disasters such as war and extermination. In film, modernism was most powerfully expressed in three subgenres: German expressionism, Russian montage, and Spanish and French Surrealism. Expressionism held that the exaggerated expression of the auteur's feelings, rather than the story, was of paramount importance. Eisenstein's montage theory posits that the artful juxtaposition of two shots creates a third effect; the mind works powerfully to create meaning out of the sequencing of images. Surrealist art tried to access unconscious states such as dreams and hallucinations in order to show a far wider range of human perception than strict rationality and conscious feelings. These three artistic modes were connected with the realm of high art, rather than the low or popular culture in which Chaplin and his cohorts were steeped. Genre films, silent films, and slapstick are considered low art. But Chaplin had a decidedly modernist, experimental sensibility; he adopted many of the innovations of the film modernists such as symbolic dreams (*The Kid, Shoulder Arms*) and montage (symbolic cross cutting in *The Great Dictator*).

In modernism, a set of philosophical assumptions prevailed. There was a teleological belief in the design and purpose of the world, an assumption that social and political progress was inherent in the very nature of human life. There was a faith in the autonomy of the individual. High and low art forms were distinct, and were informed by different values. People believed in the existence of reality and its accessibility in works of fiction. Claims to knowledge and expertise tended to be trusted.[2]

With the advent of World War II, the nuclear bomb, the Holocaust, fascist governments, the Cold War, decolonization, the global economy, advertising, and new levels of shameless consumerism, these beliefs in truth and reality have failed. Postmodernism resists and subverts the tenets of modernism, offering opposing views. There is no faith in the master narrative of history; there is only a belief in uncertainty and contradiction. The self is not an autonomous subject but the product of social and biological conditioning. Good art mixes the high and low registers. Absolute reality doesn't exist; all meaning is deeply subjective.

In classic narrative film, continuity editing aims to create a seamless story without emphasis on the artificiality of the medium. Chaplin's style is not strictly classical, for he often breaks the fourth wall and looks directly into the camera. His narrative structures do, however, follow modernist dictates, especially insofar as they contain a hero who (excepting Monsieur Verdoux) exhibits either noble, self-sacrificing qualities, or admirably clever ones. In Chaplin's films, we find a clear belief in autonomous individuality. Through his innate superiority, the Tramp defies mainstream prejudices and hypocrisies. In contrast, postmodern films may find the medium as interesting as the message, or the medium may be the message (as in Allen's *Zelig*). A postmodern film brings attention to itself as film; its metanarrative and self-reflexive properties define it. A mixture of several genres may appear in one film; there may be references to other films, books, or media figures; and the narrative structure is often achronological. There may be moviemaking going on within the film itself, a *mise-en-abyme* style of reflexivity. Allen gives us easy-to-follow narratives, but his toolkit includes all the tricks of postmodernism: genre-mixing, parody, parallel worlds, and above all, self-consciousness about making art, which is apparent in his willingness to reflect on everything about the process.

Though modernist in his choice of narrative content and classic storytelling elements, Chaplin is a surprisingly self-reflexive, and in that sense, postmodernist artist. Reflexivity is present when a film comments upon the conditions of its making. In other words, references are made to the art of filmmaking, to other films, or to the lives of the auteur and his cohorts. Such films recognize that art is a construct, not a reproduction of reality. Dan Kamin's assertion, discussed in Chapter 2, that *Modern Times* is really about its maker's fear of being swallowed up by the machinery of Hollywood classical-style filmmaking, exemplifies the reflexivity that can be found in Chaplin's films.

Regardless of historical period, reflexivity is an attribute of auteur films. By the time filmmakers reach auteur status, they have created a canon of works to which they and their audience continually refer. As an audience accumulates familiarity with the auteur's films over time, it also gains a basic familiarity with their lives and careers. Audiences' disapproval of Chaplin's evil Verdoux arose from their love of the previous iterations of Charlie as the Tramp. Verdoux's morality was antithetical to that of the Tramp who, for all his bravado, would never harm an innocent being (or course, actors were apparently made of rubber in the time of slapstick, and could take quite a bit of abuse). Similarly, Allen cannot play a Judah Rosenthal who orders a hit on his mistress because we know his characters are conscience-ridden—as in the instances of Max Kleinman, Miles Monroe, and Leonard Zelig. True auteurs, as defined in the Introduction, put their personality and their personage into their films; reflexivity is an aspect of this closeness between life and art.

The film selections in this book address a variety of issues that are central to the auteurs' personal lives and artistic ideas. How do low art forms, such as the circus, function as social critique? What are the effects of mechanization and bureaucratization on humans' ability to care for one another? Why do people follow corrupt leaders, and what can be done to fight such tyrants? What is conscience, and is the possession of it a universal trait? What is love, and why is it so difficult to sustain?

Like all great art, Chaplin and Allen's films do not answer such profound questions definitively. Instead, they investigate and dramatize possible answers. Chaplin's answers are more solid while Allen's are more ambivalent, in keeping with their historical moment. When the Tramp smiles at the flower girl at the end of *City Lights*, the image refers to our recognition of an ideal called True Love, but when Isaac half-smiles at Tracy at the end of *Manhattan*, the image causes us to reflect on the true doubts of the character, his radical uncertainty about whether he merits Tracy's love, regardless of whether she comes back to him. Despite being a reaction to the chaos of World War I and the breakdown of traditional institutions, modernism posits the existence of order and meaning. Because of the untrustworthiness of institutions (such as marriage, social class, gender norms, governments, and corporations), it is incumbent upon the individual to discover and/or create this order and meaning for himself. Romantic individualism is the answer that many modernist narratives supply for the challenge of living in a broken system.

Postmodernism fears more than a broken system; it posits a chaotic universe in which the very category of "knowledge" is suspect. Absolute reality doesn't exist; meaning is deeply subjective. Individuals are not autonomous; therefore, romantic individualism is not a solution. Moral relativity, ambivalence, and contingency are the attributes of postmodern consciousness. Postmodern narratives demonstrate these qualities by using polyphony (many voices) and double plotting to represent the variety of human experience. The antihero—perhaps lacking in courage, idealism, or morality, but relatable precisely because he is so human—does not win the battle against the indifferent universe; resolution of a narrative usually entails his or her momentary relief from the struggle, which is presented as temporary escape rather than solution. The same temporary escape could be said to apply to Chaplin's Tramp who walks away from the circus, from undignified work, even from the fascist prison in *The Great Dictator*, but with this difference: he achieves a literary or narrative victory over his circumstances that the antihero of Allen's films never can. Allen's characters appear to live in the real world of contingency, uncertainty, and terror, not an idealized world of fiction genres.

Each film pairing demonstrates this distinction. The circus films demonstrate the liberating effects of carnival. *The Circus* creates a material world that is structured on the basis of socioeconomic class. It has a social hierarchy that the Tramp momentarily defies, thanks to his resourcefulness and acrobatic skill. The modernist narrative does not question how this world works, since it is assumed that competition is the rule of the land. The Tramp gains status in the hierarchy by outwitting his rival, putting on a better show. *Shadows and Fogs*, on the other hand, asks us to consider parallel worlds and realities other than the socioeconomic, such as the world of Irmstedt's magic and the shadow world of anti-Semitism in a town haunted by an unknowable monster of Death. Postmodernity is apparent in the film's ambiguities; it doesn't ask, what is the meaning of death or evil, so much as, which world are we in? Is the whole political structure of this town really anti-Semitic? To what extent do the town leaders know about and condone anti-Semitism? Is it really the vigilantes rather than the mayor and police who control this town? And what about Irmstedt's realm? Why is he able to chain Death, if only for an instant? Is there a magic world that allows us to escape calamity?

Our next pairing, the anti-technology films, demonstrates the human fear of being taken over by our own technologies; the distinction again is in the degree to which the films present an opportunity to control or escape their pernicious effects. At the end of *Modern Times*, Charlie once again walks away from the troubles of one town to start afresh in the next, suggesting a belief in the individual solution to the problems of modernity. When the factory was literally consuming him, he found better work as an artist. The film critiques socioeconomic hierarchy, as in *The Circus*. But in this film, the lower echelon is also at fault; the workers' resistance is careless and dangerous. Certain individuals, such as the Gamin, her father, and the Tramp, are nobler than the mass of workers. Yet theirs is not an absolute purity, only an honor among thieves, that underdog dignity that characterizes the Tramp's existence.

In similar fashion, Allen's character Miles Monroe argues that there is no political, spiritual, or technological solution to economic and political inequalities; only love can give a temporary sense of relief in this world. But *Sleeper* differs from *Modern Times* in asking the ontological question—what world is this (what is real)? This question is the foundation of all science fiction, a genre that attempts to create an imaginary world in order to dissect, by implication, the foibles of our own world. In *Sleeper*'s dystopia, Allen recreates the same human problems of competition and greed in the future world that he suffers in the present. Like Aldous Huxley (*Brave New World*) and Margaret Atwood's (*A Handmaid's Tale*) dystopias, Allen's new world placates its citizens with drugs and brainwashing. Miles's solution to the predicament in which he finds himself is temporary and unstable; love will not protect him and Luna from the next dictatorship that he predicts will commence in six months' time. Allen's world is existentially dangerous; his postmodern inability to even imagine a meaningful order is different from Chaplin's world of primarily physical danger. The way in which the Tramp leaves the "machinery" of the corrupt world is to walk out. But Miles cannot walk far enough. Even two hundred years into the future is not distant enough to escape the existential angst of his creator.

The Master/Slave films address the frightening fact that totalitarian rhetoric appeals to a majority of citizens (or, they are just too afraid to revolt).

The world that Chaplin creates is immediately recognizable as Hitler's Third Reich. In *The Great Dictator*, Chaplin satirizes fascism, using Hitler and Mussolini character types to deflate the pompous, insidious megalomania of these two world leaders. On the other hand, the worlds of Allen's *Zelig* are multiple, the film being one of his most reflexive artworks. It critiques talking heads for being out of touch with reality: psychoanalysts who project their own illnesses onto their patients, talk show hosts who impose their own narrative on their guests' stories, intellectuals who interpret history via their own pet theories, and the media (news, biopics, documentaries, advertisements) that lie and distort the truth in order to sell their product. As with political propaganda and party platforms, "reality" is not an absolute, but is framed by different media and public relations men. No one is telling the truth; everyone has an agenda. In such a world, Zelig's personality gets lost and he becomes a *tabula rasa* for anyone to write on. The problems of Hitler and the Holocaust are in the background of this film; they are used as the *reductio ad absurdum* of what a culture of lies can, and did, lead to. Even the documentary within the documentary, or, the making of a film about Zelig, becomes suspect when we realize that biographical pictures are themselves a target of satire in this film. The film *Zelig* demonstrates all of the tenets of postmodernism enumerated above: There is no faith in the master narrative of history because each expert tells it differently according to his or her personal agenda. The only belief is in the prevalence of uncertainty and contradiction: witness the tides of public opinion that alternately lionize and persecute Zelig, or the contradicting diagnoses of his condition by several doctors and psychiatrists. The self is not an autonomous subject but the product of social and biological conditioning: before his cure, Zelig lacks all autonomy; he molds himself to every persona he meets. Good art mixes the high and low registers: Allen combines several rhetorical styles and informational media to tell Zelig's story, ranging from the low (yellow journalism) to the high (Bruno Bettelheim's psychological theories). Absolute reality doesn't exist: each character in the story tells a different story about the events and meanings of Zelig's life.

In the murder films, the directors take on the problem of morality in a fallen world: what are the source and rationale for morality in a world where religious faith is eclipsed by rationalism and narcissism? In *Monsieur Verdoux*, Chaplin strains credulity and genre in trying to portray a psychopath as a likable, cultivated gentleman. Although The Girl contests his cynical view of humanity, the film presents the criminal's view as the correct one, giving our hero a purportedly rousing speech that condemns the evils of capitalism. In contrast, *Crimes and Misdemeanors* presents the ethical problem of murder through several competing and viable viewpoints, while simultaneously undercutting the capacity of any one of them to finally solve the problem for all people. Following Aunt May, Judah believes that godlessness is a pass for getting away with crime. Ben believes there is a moral structure to the universe, but his blindness suggests he is merely naive. Sol believes that God punishes all sins, but he is an ineffective, neglectful father. Levy believes in lovingkindness, but kills himself. Cliff posits murder as a literary question, possibly because he himself is so moral that he could not conceive of a conscience-free murderer. The range of the film extends beyond the ethical problem of murder. Its female characters make us wonder why women love narcissists (Halley loves Lester; Miriam loves Judah) and cause us to question the shaky foundation of many marriages. Can the Rosenthal marriage survive a secret as disgusting as murder? Whereas Chaplin fails to justify his protagonist's misdeeds, Allen uses them to attempt to answer a philosophical question: what is conscience? While Chaplin's film is a materialist social critique ("look what capitalism made me do"), Allen's is a metaphysical and psychological inquiry. He asks: if there is no moral structure to the universe, then what gives humans a conscience? Also, is there a type of psyche that is not psychotic, but that nonetheless accepts murder as a solution to problems?

In the May-December love films, Allen and Chaplin interrogate a specific kind of love relationship, that between a young woman and a much older man. Can love exist in such a bond, or is it always suspect, necessarily insinuating a hidden agenda? Chaplin's film has the auteurist characteristic of taking for granted that the author's life is a fascinating subject for artistic examination. In modernist fashion, only two viewpoints receive serious consideration, those of the two leads, Calvero and Terry—and ultimately, the male view prevails. Chaplin's modernist narrative posits the hero's as the correct viewpoint, ennobling his quest as it undermines all opposition. On the other hand, *Manhattan* tackles the complexity of the modern jungle of dating and love. In the postmodern chaos of the film's setting, the law of the jungle applies: every man (and woman) for him- or herself. Several lifestyle choices are illustrated, but none provides a magical solution to the problem of love's short duration. Yale practices serial infidelity. Tracy argues for the value of serial monogamy. Jill finds satisfaction with a female partner, but vindicates her failed marriage and her anger at patriarchy with a tell-all memoir.[3] Mary uses sexuality as an attempt to boost her low self-esteem; fidelity is not as important as momentary release from her neuroses. Isaac is engaged on a quest for the perfect mate, but his guilt and anger keep him from accepting the love he receives. Although Tracy's definition of love and her constancy are the most salubrious, they are not presented as the answer to adult problems, since they are the products of her inexperience. Befitting postmodernism, *Manhattan* offers no individual solution to the problem of love, only dramatizes the highs and lows of several characters' search. In contrast, *Limelight* posits the existence of an abstract and ideal love, only to deny its possibility between young and old partners. Nostalgia for a lost ideal or lost innocence is a quintessentially modernist subject.

In comparing modernity and postmodernity in narrative films, there is no better place to look than their endings. How the auteur resolves the story tells much about how he or she sees the world. In Allen's endings, ambiguity prevails. They are open endings, which leave the viewer with questions. In *Shadows and Fog*, we're left wondering how long Max will be safe from the Nazis, since magic may be "as necessary as the air we breathe," but does not provide a long term solution to human cruelty. In *Sleeper*, how long will Miles and Luna's love last, and when will a new dictatorship arise? Miles gives it six months till the revolutionaries are replaced. The spectator might give the Miles/Luna relationship an even shorter life expectancy, given their extreme irritability. In *Zelig*, has the human chameleon really fulfilled his potential for being his own man, when he has not even been able to finish reading *Moby Dick* before his death, the very problem that gave rise to his illness in the first place? In becoming a complacent bourgeois married to a Gentile doctor, Zelig relinquished, rather than regained, his ethnic identity. *Crimes and Misdemeanors* closes on the hopeful words of Dr. Levy voiced over Ben's waltz with his loving daughter, but the final image of Judah and Miriam casts doubt, as their marriage is predicated on a lie. This raises the question of whether Judah really got away with murder. What intimacy is possible with Miriam when he hides the worst part of himself? In *Manhattan*, it is completely unpredictable whether Tracy will take Isaac back at the end of six months. What does Isaac's quizzical smile mean—that he thinks she'll want him, or that he's sure she'll meet someone better?

In each of Allen's endings, the premises of the films are undermined by final, ambiguous moments. Judah got away with murder (or did he?) and Lester made Halley love him (or does she?). Miles gets the girl and the promise of a new government for the Federation, but is either of these outcomes as valuable as it seems? Allen's ambiguity is rich and true to life; such endings are the mark of a good postmodernist auteur. Art, like life, offers no certainty, but performs an ironic undermining of the human longing for stability, justice, and truth.

Chaplin's endings are uneven; appropriate closure was one of his greatest challenges as a filmmaker. The early films' endings are driven by the requirements of the genre in which he works. Melodramas have artificially happy endings, where good triumphs over evil. In this sense, Chaplin's narrative structures sometimes appear more Victorian than modern, as they reward virtue and punish vice. *City Lights* moves beyond Victorian dichotomies; it has a good, wistful ending, insofar as we feel the Tramp's desire for the flower girl's love, even though nearly all commentators believe she will not love him because he is poor. *The Circus* and *Modern Times* are picaresques: their heroes engage in episodic mini-stories rather than a quest for meaning or personal

6. Nobility and Ambiguity 157

improvement. Both of their ending scenes are visually effective insofar as they accentuate the pathos of the indomitable outsider, the circus performer moving away from the ring for new adventure, and the Tramp setting out with the Gamin for a better life. In *Modern Times*, Chaplin exposes the inhumanity of the mechanized world, but the Tramp is by no means equipped to fight the system at large. In *The Great Dictator*, the same incapacity pertains to the Jewish barber, though he momentarily ignores his quality of littleness in order to speak truth to power, risking death in the process.

With *The Great Dictator* begins a period of improbable endings for Chaplin's films. He continues to strive for the incisive narrative closure of the Victorian novel, wherein the little man defeats the rich and powerful in a Dickensian reversal of fortune. In his next film, *Monsieur Verdoux*, all attempts at genre classification prove futile. The film purports to provide moral closure by revealing Verdoux's motives, but fails to create enough empathy for the killer to make us care about his execution. The murderer's rhetoric is fallacious, his crimes unpardonable, and his final speech ridiculous. This struggle with appropriate endings reflects Chaplin's difficulty in adapting to new, postmodern sensibilities. *Verdoux* (1947) comes out shortly after World War II ends; it is a critique of the U.S. government as a killing machine. But Chaplin has not developed the postmodernist polyvocality required to present complex problems that lack concrete solutions. His one-voiced narrative falls flat, the condemned murderer unable or unwilling to provide reasonable answers to the interrogations of the priest and journalist who confront him in his last hour. His epigrams, though reductive, invite comparison with the existential philosophy of Camus's stranger, whose temperamental likeness to Verdoux should not go unnoticed.[4] With *Limelight*, Chaplin returns to melodrama, and the film's ending is entirely appropriate to the rest of the film. As in *Monsieur Verdoux*, Chaplin once again kills the Tramp. In this case, however, he provides a congratulatory sendoff rather than an execution, when Calvero "kills" with comedy in the last show of his life.

Chaplin's endings are self-referential; they underline the character and his creator's nobility—though it is a nobility of the modern, not to be confused with the chivalry of the medieval knight. The prominent quality of the Tramp and of his later, wealthier iterations is that of grit. He has what it takes to survive in the cruel world, keeping his dignity and humor intact. Allen's endings, on the other hand, push outside the borders of the self, seeking artistic expression of the postmodern condition at large. They are about the condition of the world, and the question whether any notion of love, peace, or fairness can survive in postmodern times. After Auschwitz, only black humor. Chaplin's modernity renders his little man noble; Allen's postmodernity fosters a sense of ambiguity, in which our only solace is in knowing that other people (characters) feel as we do.

The atom bomb and the Holocaust represent the moral nadir of human ingenuity. The awareness that "we are like this" darkened our world as we entered the second half of the twentieth century. After Auschwitz, it is difficult to have faith in the morality of other humans; we live in a state of justified paranoia about the potential for evil or harm to come to us (or that we may commit). Comedy provides a joyful release of such tension, especially comedy of the absurd, which acknowledges the cruelty and irrationality of the world. With its seriocomic tone, comedy of the absurd confronts the terrifying human condition but momentarily lightens its terror with irony and a self-deprecating laugh.

Modernism and postmodernism are ideologies that express our fears and desires, as well as our coping strategies. Chaplin's films demonstrate the modernist desire for certainty and closure, with their (usually) closed endings, individual solutions to universal problems, quiet heroism, romantic idealism, heteronormative couplings, single plots, monovocality (one viewpoint), physical mastery over physical threats, and their repeated use of Chaplin as the protagonist-hero. Allen's films demonstrate the postmodernist view that closure and certainty are not possible, with their open endings, ambiguous morality, double plots, polyvocality, reflexivity, sexual variety, metaphysical as well as physical threats, self-deprecatory antiheroes, and the auteur sharing the lead with other actors.

Allen and Chaplin are artists of their own eras; it was not possible or desirable for Chaplin to anticipate all the postmodern devices that would come to express the sense of anxiety characterizing the postwar world. Despite Chaplin's narrative conundrums and the reductive philosophizing of some of his later films, he is considered the master of narrative cinema. Federico Fellini called him "a sort of Adam from whom we are all descended"; Vittorio De Sica said he "discovered everything"; Jean Renoir called him the "master of masters."[5] Allen holds similar status in his own time, though detractors as prominent as Pauline Kael weaken it, and many recent commentators temper their praise with politically correct condemnation of his attraction to young women. Allen's is a fame that should strengthen posthumously, as did Chaplin's. When he is gone, the world will miss that very particular sense of humor—the comical way he confessed his existential angst and left us feeling less alone. Despite the repetitive and shallow nature of many of his later films and the public's disapprobation attached to his sex scandal, Allen has received encomiums equivalent to Chaplin's, albeit couched in quieter terms that are more typical of our era. Vincent Canby called him "our most important comedic director," Rob Eshman, "the Chaplin of our time, the greatest living filmmaker in the world."[6] Sander Lee recognized the "enormous import" of films "obsessed with issues of contemporary metaphysical concern."[7] In *Woody on Rye*, Tom Morris describes Allen's unique voice: "No one can lead us to the edge of the cosmic abyss like Woody, and then hit us with a joke that somehow makes it all easier, and even more memorable."[8] As Broadway Danny Rose says, "It's important to have some laughs, but you got to suffer a little too, because otherwise you miss the whole point of life."[9] Allen and Chaplin knew how to make us laugh and suffer along with their characters; they are the comic geniuses of their times.

Appendix:
Sex Scandals and the
Role of the Critic

Scholars and critics who work on Woody Allen in recent times cannot avoid addressing a question that is currently in the news: Is Allen a child molester? Because of the ubiquity of the news and the seriousness of the subject matter, I am going to discuss the case at some length. The material is so abundant because there are many details and conflicting testimonies about events that occur over a period of twenty-six years. Simply put, because the participants have different stories, and the legal and psychological experts have different opinions, it is not possible to know what actually happened. Therefore, I will not offer an opinion, but will try to present some of these views in a neutral manner.

In December 2017, what is known as the Dylan-Mia-Woody scandal re-erupted, causing many filmgoers to reevaluate their appreciation of Woody Allen's movies. Dylan Farrow wrote an article in the *Los Angeles Times*, called "Why Has the #MeToo Revolution Spared Woody Allen?"[1] In this piece, she exhorted actors to boycott him because, according to her allegation, he molested her when she was seven years old. To review briefly the sequence of events: in 1992, Mia Farrow claimed that Woody Allen molested their adopted daughter, Dylan, on one occasion in the attic of Farrow's Connecticut farmhouse. Allen denied this occurrence, providing several reasons why it was impossible: there were half a dozen people in the house; it was on his "raging adversary's turf"; he was in the "blissful early stages of a happy new relationship"; he had a claustrophobic fear of attics; and no child molester starts his activities at such a late age (he was fifty-six at the time).[2] He passed a lie detector test regarding the incident. On the other hand, Allen had recently been seeing a counselor, at Farrow's suggestion, for help with his overly intimate relationship with Dylan. Before the alleged incident, Allen had worked with Dr. Susan Coates regarding inappropriate behaviors such as letting the child suck his thumb and putting his head in her lap. Dr. Coates reported that he had made progress.[3]

After six months' investigation that included forensic tests of Allen's hair, medical examinations, and nine interviews with Dylan by the Yale–New Haven Hospital Child Abuse Evaluation Clinic, Allen was exonerated from the charge of child molestation. The director of the investigation, Dr. John M. Leventhal, stated that Dylan was "emotionally unstable" and that there was evidence that Mia Farrow had "coached her to accuse Woody Allen."[4] As soon as she learned of the alleged incident, Mia had "taken a video camera and taped an interview with a naked Dylan about what had transpired."[5] Because there were many breaks in the sequence, it appeared that Farrow had corrected the child's story. There were also "important inconsistencies" in Dylan's story in the videotape and in her statements to the investigators, who reported that her statements had a "rehearsed quality" and "she told the story in a manner that was overly thoughtful and controlling."[6] Allen filed in New York State court for custody of Dylan and his two sons, Moses and Ronan (then known by his first name, Satchel). Judge Elliott Wilk denied him custody and visitation rights, saying he was "less certain than is the Yale–New Haven team that the evidence proves conclusively that there was no sexual abuse."[7] Various testimonies "prove that Mr. Allen's behavior toward Dylan was grossly inappropriate and that measures must be taken to protect her."[8] In addition to the hospital investigation, Connecticut prosecutor Frank Maco ordered another investigation that lasted fourteen months. In his opinion, there was no question that Dylan had been molested. He made the unusual and unprofessional choice to accuse Allen in a public statement, but to drop the charges "in order to spare Dylan the trauma of a criminal trial."[9]

Twenty years later, between 2013 and 2018, Dylan publicized in several venues her belief that Allen had molested her when she was a child. In the 2017 *Los Angeles Times* article, thirty-two-year-old Dylan equates her mother's ex-partner with sexual predators such as Harvey Weinstein. She calls for actors to publicly denounce him in order to demonstrate support for the rights of sexual abuse victims. So far, her appeal has been effective. Actors who have expressed solidarity with Dylan by denouncing Woody Allen include Griffin Newman, Kate Winslet, Ellen Page, Colin Firth, Greta Gerwig, Mira Sorvino, Rebecca Hall, Timothée Chalamet, and Peter Sarsgaard.[10] Their statements contain one or more of the following: they condemn Allen, apologize to Dylan for working with him, pledge to donate their salaries to charity, and promise never to work for him again. On the other hand, some actors do support and respect Allen, including Alec Baldwin, Javier Bardem, Jude Law, Alan Alda, and Diane Keaton. In 2016, Blake Lively said that working with Allen is empowering to women.[11] Negativity tends to outweigh the positive in the #MeToo climate, however, and because of the magnitude of negative publicity that Allen has received, Amazon Studios refuses to distribute his 2018 film, *A Rainy Day in New York*, claiming it is unmarketable. Allen is suing Amazon Studios for breach of contract. Fortunately, Allen has found a Barcelona-based financer—Mediapro—for his 2019 film, *Qué Lástima! (What a Shame!)*. The production company's justification for working with Allen is their positive ten-year history with him and their belief in "judging the creator by his work."[12]

What should a film critic do with such information and speculation about her subject? A critic's job is to evaluate art using the tools of her training. In my case, that training is an education in literary theory and film studies acquired during several decades of study and teaching. A fundamental principle of critical theory informs my approach to this book: judge the art separately from the artist. There are at least three reasons for this fundamental principle. First, art is produced from one's conscious and unconscious desires and fears; as such, it expresses not what should be believed or felt or valued, but what actually is believed, felt, and valued. If artists strangled their creativity in order to appease public taste or attain commercial success, there would be no innovation in art, nor truth or beauty. Second, in art as in life, we cannot know with certainty the intentions of the artist or of any other person. What someone says is not necessarily what they think.[13] In literature, for a critic to second-guess the writer's intention is usually considered a fallacy.[14] In certain critical approaches, such as the psychoanalytical, it is acceptable to speculate or explore possibilities of the artist's motivation, but it is not acceptable to claim the truth of the speculation. In post-structural literary theory, even the author is said not to know his or her own intentions.[15] Third, if we were to censor (in academic curricula, movie theatres, art museums, publishing houses, etc.) the works of all artists whose morality is suspicious, we would be left with very little art to enjoy. Sigmund Freud taught us that all artists are neurotic, that art is their way of working through their pain. People don't create great works of art without tapping into sources of sadness, pain, aggression, or despair. In order to appreciate art, it is helpful at times to suspend moral judgment. This does not mean that every work of art is accessible or meaningful or morally acceptable to every viewer, only that one's range of experience will be broadened by judging the art separately from the artist.

The moral issue regarding both Chaplin and Allen is their love of very young women (Chaplin married sixteen-year-olds, one when he was twenty-nine and another when he was thirty-five; Allen dated a seventeen-year-old when he was forty-one and a twenty-one-year-old when he was fifty-six. The latter relationship is complicated by the fact that his girlfriend was the adoptive sister of children he had adopted.). Controversy over Chaplin's personal life still exists today, but critics seem to have detached it from their assessments of his films, since he has been dead for forty years—which is why I dedicate less space to Chaplin scandals in this appendix, though I do make reference to them throughout the book. In Chaplin's case, most film buffs are able to separate the art from the artist. But Allen is a living artist who is still producing a film each year and who may live and work for another ten years (he is eighty-three). Moreover, moral disapproval of his dating history is compounded by Dylan Farrow's accusation of child molestation, which she is now re-publicizing in the sensitive climate of the #MeToo movement. Watching all of his fifty films made from 1965 to 2017, it is hard to miss Allen's characters' uncomfortably frequent jokes about the desire to have sex with minors. Taking into consideration the fundamental principles of film and literary criticism mentioned above, as well as certain fundamental principles of legal procedure, such as presumption of innocence, and circumstantial versus direct evidence,[16] I believe we must not infer from these jokes that the filmmaker molested a seven-year-old. We cannot help feeling, however, that the jokes suggest an unhealthy sexual interest in young females.

We will never know with certainty what happened on August 4, 1992. We can speculate that each of the key players had motives to say what they did about the purported incident. Allen had reason to deny the charge in order to save his reputation and career. Mia Farrow had reason to coach Dylan to accuse Allen because he betrayed Farrow by falling in love with her daughter, Soon-Yi Previn. "You took my child, I'm going to take yours," she said and wrote to Allen and repeated to his sister, Letty Aronson, on a number of occasions.[17] She also told him on the phone, "I have something very nasty planned for you."[18] As a child, Dylan had reason to accuse her mother's ex-boyfriend in order to please her mother. In a court of law, however, speculative motives are not admissible. To better understand the legal procedures, social work investigations, and possible motives of the players, it is necessary to read full-length biographies, even while knowing that these cannot provide definitive answers about what happened.

Because I am a feminist who likes Woody Allen movies, I came to the research question with an open mind, ready to weigh both sides. I stand firmly against child molestation and the abuse of power that occurs in male-dominated industries such as Hollywood, and I admire the women who have spoken out about the abuse they have endured in the course of their film careers. My impression of Allen, after reading his essays and watching all his films and the documentaries about him, is that he is a strongly moral man. His conscience is a key feature of both his jokes and his serious subject matter. He or his characters often assert that they would like to do something but that their conscience would kill them if they did. There can, of course, be moral men whose compulsions are so strong that they outweigh their ability to withstand them. Most molesters begin their pattern of behavior while still in their teens, but Allen had no apparent history of sexual abuse before this case arose when he was fifty-six. Allen's therapist, Dr. Susan Coates, testified in the custody trial that his relationship with Dylan was "inappropriately intense" but not sexual.[19] The fact that New York State judges allowed Allen and Soon-Yi to adopt two children indicates that Allen was again put through stringent evaluation regarding his appropriateness as an adoptive father, and passed that evaluation. On the other hand, we have testimonies of babysitters and friends of Mia Farrow that corroborate her opinion that Allen touched Dylan too often and too intimately. We cannot know whether Allen molested Dylan, but we can gain extensive background about the players and the case. The following is a brief description of biographies and memoirs that I read as research for this project.

What Falls Away: A Memoir by Mia Farrow is most interesting when it recounts her childhood traumas about a philandering, alcoholic father; the death of her brother Michael in an airplane crash; and a severe bout of polio when she was nine. At least one-third of the book addresses her difficult relationship with Allen, the scandal, and Allen's suit for custody. Farrow writes convincingly about her childhood and young adult experiences, but her rationalizations for staying with Allen, when she claims he mistreated her and her children, tend to weaken her overall credibility. For five years, she had considered his behavior to Dylan inappropriate, but did not stop seeing him or stop his petition for joint custody in 1991. She wrote, "I feared that if I denied him the adoptions, it would end our relationship. He had already suggested that I might find it difficult in the real world to work and support the children" (270). She did feel guilty after Dylan made her allegation, and sought to put her failure to protect her daughter into the context of her relationship with one of the world's foremost directors: "I could argue that the world I had occupied with him for a quarter of my life was so utterly removed from any other that it was impossible for me to envision a life for myself beyond it" (260). Without his films, she would have no other income with which to support fourteen children. After *Husbands and Wives* wrapped, and the molestation allegation was made, she even had plans to work for Allen in *Manhattan Murder Mystery* at the same time she was making death threats to him on the telephone.[20]

Another woman's account of Allen's life adopts a judicious balance in its treatment of both Mia Farrow and Woody Allen. In *The Unruly Life of Woody Allen*, Marion Meade alternately empathizes with Allen's situation and criticizes his general behavior and temperament. Her account is engaging because of its unrestrained honesty about the unsavory behavior of "media sharks" and celebrities, the possible motives of judges and prosecutors, and the good and bad behaviors of Farrow and Allen. Her treatment of the scandal is one of the most detailed, and she is willing to describe the personalities of the players without sacrificing objectivity or predicting the likelihood that they would commit malicious or criminal acts.

It is also useful to consult accounts by women who knew and worked with Allen when they were young, to learn whether they experienced inappropriate sexual behavior by him. In her memoir, *Out Came the Sun*,[21] Mariel Hemingway tells of her positive experience with Woody Allen while making *Manhattan* (she was sixteen at the time). She appreciated the fact that he listened to her ideas, when her teachers never had. Unlike many actors, Mariel asserted that Woody "kept his set loose and fun—he would go to lunch with some of the cast and the crew members ... and we would sit and order food while everyone told jokes" (96). When she realized that Allen's joking invitations to Paris probably entailed the desire to have an affair, Mariel refused to take the journey. Allen did not drop her when he learned that the relationship would not become sexual. Through the years, he continued to consult her—for instance, asking her whether he had captured correctly the WASPy world of repressed emotions and dysfunctional family dynamics in his film *Interiors*.

In his biography *Woody*, David Evanier is particularly good on the ways in which the media and public opinion fanned the flames. He makes a careful distinction, which most people overlook, between Allen's relationship with his adopted child Dylan, and his other, quite different relationship with Mia Farrow's older daughter Soon-Yi. On the one hand, when his interest in Mia had waned after twelve years, Woody dated and (much later) married Soon-Yi Previn, one of Mia Farrow's many adopted daughters toward whom he had not acted as a father (Soon-Yi's adoptive father was André Previn). This relationship started in 1991, when Soon-Yi was twenty-one years old. On the other hand, he had loved his adopted daughter Dylan Farrow from infancy (Mia Farrow adopted her at two weeks old; Allen co-adopted her six years later, in 1991). Evanier writes, "These different events seem to be indistinguishable from one another for those inclined to indict him for a sex crime without evidence" (45). He also notes that people often use characters in Allen's films as evidence for the crimes they think he committed at home: "Inferring from the ample evidence of his protagonists' fondness for young girls in his films, they overlooked the right of the artist to fantasize in his art and chose unfairly to conclude that he was therefore capable of monstrous acts in his private life" (42-3). Making distinctions between life and art is very important for a critic who wants to retain his or her objectivity.

Another biography that focuses on the media storm around the scandal is *Woody Allen: A Biography* by John Baxter. He discloses some of the financial and public relations aspects that made the scandal into "a melodrama." A week after the incident, Farrow's lawyers met with Allen's, asking for approximately seven million dollars, "whether as child support or hush money remained vague," as Baxter noted (404). The immediate financial fallout due to the public's moral outrage included boycotting by movie industry organizations and individuals: Blockbuster refused to distribute his latest movie, the Italian Catholic Co-Op Nordemilia cancelled a contract for commercials, and his Italian dubbing artist refused to dub *Shadows and Fog* (407). But Baxter believes that Allen could have minimized damages if he had been a different sort of person, capable of acting in the way many public figures have done: "Had he gone on the *Johnny Carson* show to confess his wrongs, offered to make amends, perhaps broken down in tears ... the scandal could have been defused. But Allen, true to his roots in the Me Decade of the seventies, elected to tough it out, a challenge the Caring, Sharing eighties couldn't ignore" (408). Citing Adam Gopnik, Baxter shows where Allen went wrong:

> He made his best comedy by recognizing that the sexual revolution had opened a vast space between abstract belief and real life—between what the fifties had taught you to say and what the sixties and seventies allowed you to do. But when a new abyss began to open in the last decade—one in which sex was separated from the realm of comedy and taken over almost exclusively by that of confession—he couldn't plumb it, or perhaps even see that it existed. When the new gap widened, he fell right in.[22]

My last biographer, Eric Lax, is as supportive a Woody fan as one can find in Allen scholarship. A longtime friend of the director, Lax has written four books on Allen (in 1975, 1991, 2007, and 2017), including a biography. He has been allowed unprecedented access to Allen's film sets, accompanied him on location scouting and casting calls, and conversed with Allen while he wrote and edited his films. Lax's most recent book, *Start to Finish*, follows the making of *Irrational Man* (2015) all the way from pre- to post-production. It also addresses the re-eruption of the scandal, adducing new evidence that tends to exonerate Allen.

As part of his research, Eric Lax spoke with Moses Farrow, adopted son of Mia, who came to the United States from Korea in 1991. Crippled with cerebral palsy, Moses had been abandoned in a telephone booth, taken to an orphanage, and adopted by Farrow at age two. He is seven-and-a-half years older than Dylan. Now a family therapist, Moses speaks frankly about the atmosphere of his own family home. He says it was frightening to live with Farrow because of her fierce temper and bullying tantrums. Moses and the other adopted children learned to cope by giving Farrow the stories she wanted them to tell. They were afraid they would otherwise be sent away. "My biggest fear was that we would be rejected, excommunicated rather, from the family.... When you are an adopted child, there is no bigger fear than to lose your family."[23] Farrow had a pattern of accusing Moses of small peccadillos, most of which he had not committed, then scripting his apology, and not letting up till he had recited it perfectly. Once as a young child, he had cut a couple of belt loops off his jeans. Farrow spanked him "all over," then had him strip and stand naked in the corner.

The humiliation of stripping for one's bad behavior is disturbing in light of Mia Farrow's videotape of Dylan. Farrow filmed her naked seven-year-old daughter while she prompted her to tell her story about Allen molesting her. It is possible that Mia Farrow was reenacting some terrible memory or half-memory from her past (this is speculation, not fact). Untreated victims become abusers. In "A Son Speaks Out," Moses wrote of "a deep and persistent darkness within the Farrow family," meaning Mia's family of origin. Mia Farrow told Moses "she was the victim of attempted molestation within her own family."[24] Her brother John was convicted of sexual abuse of two young boys in 2013 and sentenced to twenty-five years in prison. Mia Farrow's brother Patrick shot himself in the head in 2009. Their father, John Villiers Farrow, was an alcoholic "womanizer of legendary proportions," according to Mia, with "an almighty temper." He "whacked her across the room" and caned her with his walking stick when angry.[25] This is not direct evidence that Mia Farrow abused her children, but it creates an inference that she had not overcome the traumas of her upbringing by the time she birthed or adopted fourteen children. In Moses' account, she reenacted her father's bullying upon her own adopted children, adding a bizarre "directorial" twist. She would "coach, drill, script and rehearse" them to tell the stories she wanted to hear about their naughtiness (Lax, 124). Young Dylan once told Moses, "Mom wants me to say something I don't want to say," but she did it anyway, in order to get the Attic Kids doll she wanted (126). The only occasion on which young Moses contradicted Mia about a lie she wanted him to tell resulted in severe punishment: "she hit me uncontrollably all over my body" (126). About the scandal, Moses said, "Based on my own experience, I believe it's possible that Mia rehearsed with Dylan what she ended up saying on video" (126).

In response to Moses's statements, his brother Ronan Farrow denied their truth, and supported their sister Dylan's molestation claim. Ronan is a bright, successful journalist, lawyer, book author, and former government advisor, now thirty-one years old. He is two-and-a-half years younger than his adoptive sister Dylan. His series of *New Yorker* articles on Harvey Weinstein's sexual assaults won the Pulitzer Prize for Public Service in 2018. He looks nothing like Woody Allen, but is strikingly like her ex-husband Frank Sinatra, whom Mia Farrow admits may have been his biological father. Ronan characterizes his brother's words as "part of a repeated campaign to discredit my sister, often by attacking our mother [who] ... did an extraordinary job raising us, and none of my siblings with whom I've spoken ever witnessed anything but love and care from a single mom who went through hell to keep her kids safe."[26]

Soon-Yi confirms Moses's characterization of their mother: "She just liked to pick on people. She chose the easy, vulnerable targets. She had a fierce temper. On one occasion she kicked me and hit me again and again with the phone. She was regularly mentally and physically abusive to Moses."[27] In a September, 2018 interview with Daphne Merkin,[28] Soon-Yi expatiated on the traumatic experience of growing up in Mia Farrow's household. Farrow showed a clear preference for Ronan because of his good looks and sharp mind, whereas she ridiculed Soon-Yi's mental capacity and threatened to send her to an insane asylum (Soon-Yi has a learning disability that affects her spelling, but is extremely quick-witted and articulate, according to her interviewer). Echoing her brother's account of child abuse, Soon-Yi says that Farrow slapped her in the face, threw blocks and a porcelain pig at her, called her a *moron*, and held her upside down to "make her smarter." Despite Soon-Yi's learning disability, Farrow did not provide tutors or other extracurricular activities for her daughter, but instead stopped paying any attention to her after Ronan was born. Another event—one that is eerily reminiscent of Farrow's videotaping of a naked Dylan speaking of Allen's abuse—is Farrow putting her young daughter Soon-Yi in front of her camera to say she was beaten by her prostitute-mother before she ran away at age five. Soon-Yi did not remember such an event and refused to make the video for Farrow. Soon-Yi's summary of her upbringing by Mia Farrow is that her adoptive mother was never kind nor civil to her. She echoes her brother Moses's opinion that Farrow was jealous of Soon-Yi's relationship with Woody Allen and that Farrow wanted to vindicate herself and put the blame on Allen for abuse.

This is not the Mia Farrow that fans know and love. From her first Allen film, *A Midsummer Night's Sex Comedy*, where she is a chaste Victorian ingénue, to the pitiable housewife who returns to her abusive husband in *Purple Rose of Cairo*, to the baby-adopting innocent of *Shadows and Fog*, Mia Farrow in Woody Allen movies is synonymous with sweetness. As established in Chapter 1, Woody Allen was also beaten throughout his childhood and, in turn, could be harsh or cold towards friends and lovers. Farrow's memoir relates several incidents of this behavior. In short, Allen's difficult childhood obviously led to ongoing trust issues that he has spent over thirty years of therapy trying to resolve. Whether these trust issues could lead to his becoming a child molester is a question that maybe not even psychiatrists and social workers can answer.

In comparison to Woody Allen, public scandal about Charlie Chaplin was of an even larger magnitude insofar as it combined a political as well as sexual element. I don't mean to suggest that sex and gender are not political subjects; I simply mean that Chaplin engaged with controversial politics in ways that Allen had no interest in doing. Given the paranoid atmosphere of post–World War II America, Chaplin's pro-Russia pronouncements were so strong that Immigration Services, the House Un-American Activities Committee, and the FBI wanted him deported. In 1952, Chaplin was effectively invited to consider his permission to live in the United States revoked. To qualify for re-entry, he would have had to undergo investigation that he knew from experience would be hostile and based on fabrications that he was a Communist. Although he was resilient about the exile, and continued working, the quality of Chaplin's films decreased from that point forward: *A King in New York* (1957) and *A Countess from Hong Kong* (1967) are uneven pictures, with some barbed satire, but lacking the pathos and physical comedy of earlier work.

In addition to his politics, Chaplin's marriages with much younger women (two aged sixteen, one aged eighteen) eventually alienated the American public. Just as the media did with regard to Allen, America's first gossip columnists, Louella Parsons and Hedda Hopper, took advantage of the moral climate to sensationalize Chaplin's "sordid" love life. These journalists capitalized on America's taste for salacious stories about revered movie stars. Jilted lover Joan Barry jumped into the fray with a fake paternity suit against Chaplin, which she won despite blood tests proving that he was not the father of her child. Chaplin's fame and infamy say as much about American cultural history as they do about the sexual proclivities of a movie star; Charles Maland's *Chaplin and American Culture: The Evolution of a Star Image* is a thorough investigation of the rise and fall of Chaplin's popularity against the background of American cultural politics. In *Charlie Chaplin's Little Tramp in America*,[29] Lisa Stein Haven expands Maland's area of research by tracing the resurrection of Chaplin's American reputation starting in the late forties and fifties, especially by fans such as the Beat poets, film collectors, and biographers.

With the passage of time, perhaps someday scholars will have gained enough perspective on Woody Allen's own rising and falling star to write a book on the ways in which his life and work interacted with American cultural politics. In the meantime, I, for one, hope he continues his practice of making a film every year, since each new one surprises and delights me, despite the recurrent themes and character types. Many female viewers continue to enjoy Woody Allen films because of their astute depictions of women.

Chapter Notes

Preface

1. Charles L.P. Silet, ed., *The Films of Woody Allen* (Lanham, MD: Scarecrow, 2006).
2. Peter Bailey and Sam Girgus, eds., *A Companion to Woody Allen* (Malden, MA: Wiley-Blackwell, 2013).
3. Frank Scheide and Hooman Mehran, *Chaplin: The Dictator and the Tramp* (London: British Film Institute, 2004).
4. Donna Kornhaber, *Charlie Chaplin, Director* (Evanston: Northwestern University Press, 2014); Lisa Stein Haven, *Charlie Chaplin's Little Tramp in America, 1947–1977* (London: Palgrave Macmillan, 2016).
5. Charles Maland, *Chaplin and American Culture: The Evolution of a Star Image* (Princeton: Princeton University Press, 1989); David Robinson, *Chaplin: His Life and Art* (New York: McGraw-Hill, 1985); Richard Carr, *Charlie Chaplin: A Political Biography from Victorian Britain to Modern America* (London: Routledge, 2017); John Baxter, *Woody Allen: A Biography* (New York: Carroll & Graf, 1998); Eric Lax, *Woody Allen* (New York: Knopf, 1991) and *Start to Finish: Woody Allen and the Art of Moviemaking* (New York: Knopf, 2017); David Evanier, *Woody* (New York: St. Martin's, 2015).

Introduction

1. William Hutchings, "Woody Allen and the Literary Canon," in *A Companion to Woody Allen*, eds. Peter Bailey and Sam Girgus (Malden, MA: Wiley-Blackwell, 2013), 358–380, 379.
2. Gerald Mast, *The Comic Mind: Comedy and the Movies* (Chicago: University of Chicago Press, 1979), 314.
3. John Lahr, *Show and Tell* (Woodstock, NY: Overlook Press, 2000), 3. Chaplin began moviemaking at the same time that Freud was developing his theories. *Jokes and Their Relation to the Unconscious*, published in 1905, would have shed light on motives and signs of Chaplin's rebellious motifs and the strange anality of his slapstick humor, if his fans had cared to read it. Freudian concepts would not saturate popular culture (and the movies), however, until much later. Allen's work easily integrates Freudian references into his dialog with a combination of sarcasm and seriousness.
4. There is an exception. In *A King in New York* (1957), Chaplin gives the mouthpiece to his son, Michael, who plays ten-year-old Rupert Macabee, a precocious anarchist with a winning rhetorical style. But Rupert is not the sole or best orator of the film; Chaplin's character, King Shadov, has that distinction.
5. David Robinson, *Chaplin: His Life and Art* (New York: McGraw-Hill, 1985), 529.
6. Richard Schickel, *Woody Allen: A Life in Film* (Chicago: Ivan R. Dee, 2004), 105–106.
7. Eric Lax, *Conversations with Woody Allen: His Films, the Movies, and Moviemaking* (New York: Knopf, 2009), 66.
8. Lax, *Conversations*, 355–56.
9. Later in his career, Allen did achieve artistic wholeness in the drama form; however, it was the films' thriller plots and good acting that carried them, whereas the existentialist sadness of the chamber films had made them too still or too depressing for most viewers' taste. *Match Point* (2005) and *Cassandra's Dream* (2007) achieve wholeness and authenticity while creating suspense and raising serious philosophical questions. My Chapter 4 analyzes the philosophical question of how one's conscience handles murder in Chaplin's *Verdoux* and several Allen films.
10. Some well-known auteurs are Alfred Hitchcock, Francois Truffaut, Ingmar Bergman, Pedro Almodóvar, Bernardo Bertolucci, Luis Buñuel, Francis Ford Coppola, Federico Fellini, Vittorio De Sica, Stanley Kubrick, Howard Hawks, Terry Gilliam, Sidney Lumet, F. W. Murnau, Jean Renoir, and Alain Resnais.

Chapter Notes—Introduction

11. Chaplin starred in all but two of his films, *A Woman of Paris* (1923) and *A Countess from Hong Kong* (1967). Allen starred in thirty-one of the forty-nine films that he also directed.

12. Simon Louvish wrote that Charlie's Tramp is recognizable to people who have never seen a Chaplin film, and in places where his films are never shown (*Chaplin: The Tramp's Odyssey*. London: Faber and Faber, 2010, *xvii*). Andrew Sarris called Chaplin "the single most important artist produced by the cinema, certainly its most extraordinary performer and probably still its most universal icon" (*You Ain't Heard Nothin' Yet: The American Talking Film—History and Memory, 1927–1949*. New York: Oxford University Press, 1998). And *Time Magazine* included Chaplin in its list of "100 Most Important People of the 20th Century." He is loved for the "laughter he brought to millions" and because he "more or less invented global recognizability and helped turn an industry into an art" (Joshua Quittner, "*Time* 100: Charlie Chaplin," *Time Magazine*, 8 June 1998, accessed June 15, 2018).

13. Sadly, Woody Allen is well known at the present time not so much because of his films, but due to the scandal surrounding his relationship with Dylan Farrow. See the Appendix for an extensive discussion of the scandal.

14. It is important to distinguish true auteur status from the casual adoption of the term *auteur* to indicate that a fan respects or idolizes a director. The term *auteur* has begun to be used so indiscriminately that it is important to define exactly what I mean by it, which is why I've described the trifecta of directing, writing, and acting as its most salient feature. This is not to suggest that the quality of the work does not play an equally important part in determining which filmmakers merit auteur status; however, such a criterion is of course more subjective than the trifecta criterion.

15. This ratio of directing to acting is explained by the fact of Allen's aging (he is eighty-two). Since he continues to work primarily in the romantic comedy genre, he may not be the most appropriate actor for the lead part, and has gradually taken himself out of that role, which he used to consistently play. In the past twenty years (since *Celebrity*), he usually plays supporting roles instead. Occasional attempts to return to leading man status are not very successful, such as in a musical opposite Julia Roberts in 1996 (*Everyone Says I Love You*), and in *Hollywood Ending* (2002), where Allen's character is loved by Téa Leoni.

16. The Little Man persona is not to be confused with the Little Man or Short Man Syndrome, also known as the Napoleon complex, which Chaplin might have had. He was fascinated by Napoleon's story, and had wanted to film it for years; he wrote a screenplay (never produced), he dressed up as the emperor at costume parties, and studied Napoleon's biography. But Chaplin was altogether too independent to suffer from the full-blown complex, in which one attaches oneself to authority figures. Chaplin did hobnob with the rich and famous, as will be discussed in Chapter 2. But he did not directly seek power through working with them; he learned from them, borrowed ideas, and enjoyed the press and the photo opportunities of meeting with them. Since Chaplin very quickly became a leader in his field, he did not need to curry favor with other leaders, and was, in any case, temperamentally unsuited to doing so.

17. Some examples of the Little Man in literature include the protagonists in Nikolai Gogol's "The Overcoat," Alexander Pushkin's "Bronze Horseman," Fyodor Dostoyevsky's "Poor Folk" and "The Double," Nikolay Nekrasov's "The Clerk" and "The Chatterbox," and Herman Melville's "Bartleby, the Scrivener."

18. Nancy Pogel, "Little Men and Dialogues," in *Woody Allen* (Boston: Twayne, 1987), 4.

19. Pogel, "Little," 5.

20. See Menachem Feuer, "Woody Allen's Schlemiel: From Humble Beginnings to an Abrupt End," in *Woody on Rye*, eds. Vincent Brook and Marat Grinberg (Waltham, MA: Brandeis University Press, 2014), 79–99, 81.

21. Examples of these include *Vicky Cristina Barcelona*, *You Will Meet a Tall Dark Stranger*, *To Rome with Love*, and *Magic in the Moonlight*.

22. Woody Allen, *Without Feathers* (New York: Random House, 1975).

23. *Hannah and Her Sisters*, directed by Woody Allen (1986; Los Angeles: Orion Pictures, 2013), DVD.

24. Hannah Arendt, "The Jew as Pariah: A Hidden Transition." *The Jewish Writings*, ed. Ron Feldman and Jerome Kohn (New York: Schocken, 2007), 275–98.

25. Morris Dickstein, "Urban Comedy and Modernity: From Chaplin to Woody Allen," *The Partisan Review* 52.3 (1985), 271–81, 277.

26. Dickstein, *Urban*, 273.

27. As of 2014, roughly a quarter of the Upper East Side's residents were Jewish, but with wealth tends to come assimilation and disassociation from Jewish religious institutions. Of the 56,000 Jews living in the neighborhood in 2014, "only 15,000 affiliated in some way [to the Chabad, or Orthodox Jewish movement]." See Baila Olidort, "Jewish Identity Grows on Manhattan's Upper East Side," February 14, 2014. www.lubavich.com. Accessed July 9, 2018.

28. See Stephen Weissman, *Chaplin: A Life* (New York: Arcade, 2008): Because he could not save his mother from madness, his alter-

ego screen character's "rescue of physically stricken or socially fallen or oppressed women would become the recurrent theme echoed and re-echoed in his films" (110).

29. See Charles Chaplin, Jr., *My Father, Charlie Chaplin* (New York: Random House, 1960). Charles Jr., wrote, "My grandmother's illness must have preyed greatly on my father's mind for he spoke of it often to Syd and me in later years. 'Thank God ... that you're normal, because sometimes you know.... And of course you could have been this other way. There's something in the family, something.... Oh, you had me definitely worried.' He spoke jokingly, but he would then knock on wood as though the very mention of that family specter had brought it nearer than was comfortable to him" (10).

30. Allen expresses this sense of confusion, mystery, and perhaps betrayal in *Woody Allen: A Documentary*, directed by Robert Weide (New York: Whyaduck Productions, 2011). The young Woody character in *Radio Days* also expresses dismay at the fact that whenever he asks his father what he does for a living, he is denied an answer.

31. Weide, *Documentary*.

32. Weide, *Documentary*. The information in the remainder of this paragraph and the next is also from the Robert Weide documentary.

33. Sigmund Freud, 1931 letter to Friedrich Schiller, in Richard Carr, *Charlie Chaplin: A Political Biography from Victorian Britain to Modern America* (London: Routledge, 2017), 33.

34. Weissman, *Life*, 157–58.

35. Charles Chaplin, *My Autobiography* (New York: Simon and Schuster, 1964), 104.

36. Chaplin, *Autobiography*, 104.

37. Lita Grey Chaplin, with Jeffrey Vance, *Wife of the Life of the Party* (Lanham, MD: Scarecrow Press, 1998), 41–42.

38. Woody Allen, "Random Reflections of a Second-Rate Mind," *Tikkun*, Jan./Feb. 1990, 13–15, 71–72.

39. Lax, *Woody Allen: A Biography* (New York: Knopf, 1991), 150, 224, 227.

40. Douglas Brode, *Woody Allen* (Secaucus, NJ: Citadel Press, 1987), 18.

41. Chaplin, Jr., *My Father*, 263.

42. Carr, *Political*, 113.

43. Louvish, *Odyssey*, 237.

44. Eric Lax, *Conversations with Woody Allen: His Films, the Movies, and Moviemaking* (New York: Knopf, 2007), 113–14.

45. Chaplin, Jr., *My Father*, 233.

46. Ibid.

47. The first commercial, public screening of narrative films was ten Lumière Brothers shorts, which took place in Paris in 1895. The beginning date of modernism is subject to interpretation, but the 1890s are generally considered to be the starting point, depending on which artistic or intellectual discipline is involved. Freud's first publication (co-authored with Joseph Breuer), *Studies on Hysteria*, came out in 1895. His theories—about the unconscious, the sexual life of babies, and female hysteria as a response to repressed memories of sexual molestation in early childhood—contributed to the modernist sense of revolution. Old assumptions were wrong and entire fields of knowledge were being rewritten.

48. Tony Wilson, "Reading the Postmodern Image: A Cognitive Mapping," *Screen 31.4*, December 1990, 390–402, 402.

49. For a synopsis of literary and film theory relevant to postmodern film, see Mary Alemany-Galway, Chapter 1, "Toward a Postmodern Film Theory" in *A Postmodern Cinema: The Voice of the Other in Canadian Film* (Kent, UK: Scarecrow, 2002), 1–24.

50. For a full description of the shifts in gender roles, or "sexchanges" that took place during and after the First World War, see Sandra Gilbert and Susan Gubar, *No Man's Land: The Place of the Woman Writer in the Twentieth Century* (New Haven: Yale University Press, 1996).

51. Dino Felluga, "Modules on Jameson: On Postmodernity." *Introductory Guide to Critical Theory*, Purdue University. Accessed July 25, 2018

52. Frederic Jameson, *Postmodernism, or, the Cultural Logic of Late Capitalism* (Durham, NC: Duke University Press, 1990), x.

53. In a worrisome comparison to Freud's stages of infant development—where the oral stage should occur *before* the anal stage—we might read the reversal of this order in these two films to suggest that our contemporary world has lost faith in the teleological progress of civilization.

54. John Lahr, *Show and Tell*, 7.

55. Mast, *Comic*, 313.

Chapter 1

1. French psychoanalyst Jacques Lacan theorizes the existence of three orders of the psyche: the Real, the Imaginary, and the Symbolic. The Real is the area that cannot be represented through language, a realm of death and the unknowable, of instinct, id and horror. The Imaginary is the internalized image of the self as a whole, un-fragmented entity; like the Freudian ego, it is the intermediary of external and internal worlds. The Symbolic is the area of language and meaning made through language. I am not equating Kleinman's life in the town as the Real, for reality is not the same as the Real. However, the unknowability of evil,

the lurking presence of the Nazis, the unfathomability of their intent and motive—these appear to me to belong to the Lacanian Real. See Jacques Lacan, *The Seminar, Book XI: The Four Fundamental Concepts of Psychoanalysis*, ed. Jacques-Alain Miller, trans. Alan Sheridan (New York: W.W. Norton, 1977).

2. The Hays Code was abolished in 1968, and replaced by the MPAA rating system, opening the door for sex scenes and innuendos. R-rated films can show partial frontal nudity, full rear nudity, discussion about lust, and partially covered bodies or parts of bodies engaging in intercourse. Post-Hays, even sexual perversions can be the subjects of films and can be joked about. Allen's *Everything You Always Wanted to Know about Sex* (But Were Afraid to Ask)* (1972) takes full advantage of the new freedom.

3. See Menachem Feuer, "The Schlemiel in Woody Allen's Later Films," *A Companion to Woody Allen*, eds. Peter Bailey and Sam Girgus (Chichester: John Wiley, 2013), 403–423. Kleinman is a perfect example of the schlemiel in the Yiddish tradition, in that he is poised between optimism and skepticism. Speaking to the Doctor, he implies his belief in the existence of a soul, but he admits to Jack and Irmy, in separate conversations, that he finds it hard to believe in the existence of God when he can't even believe in the existence of himself (this is similar to trauma sufferers' perception of the unreality of their existence). Another example of optimism is Kleinman's inquiry at police headquarters about the Mintz eviction, implying that he believed they would care. He exhibits a momentary faith in the honesty and morality of law enforcers.

4. See William Hutchings, in "Woody Allen and the Literary Canon," *A Companion to Woody Allen* (Malden: Wiley-Blackwell, 2013), 359–380, 376. Hutchings says the town is clearly recognizable as Kafka's native Prague due to its distinctive bridges and streetlights and its angular streets.

5. See Iris Bruce, "Lurking in Shadows: Kleinman's Trial and Defense" (in Bailey and Girgus, 339–59). Bruce establishes links between conditions in the Weimar Republic and those in the unnamed city of *Shadows and Fog*. The social unrest fomented by the post–World War I economic recession created the perfect climate for Nazism to flourish: "In the midst of unrest the mastermind/murderer thrives, as Hitler and his consorts had been lurking in the shadows waiting for their opportunity to pounce" (352).

6. Hannah Arendt, "The Jew as Pariah: A Hidden Tradition," *Jewish Social Studies* 6.2 (1944). In this essay, Arendt likens Charlie, as a "little person," to the Jewish pariah, both of whom learned to survive on their wits. Such a person was always suspect: "Chaplin portrayed the chronic plight of the little man who is incessantly harried and hectored by the guardians of law and order—the representatives of society" (110).

7. Bruce, "Lurking," 350.

8. See Paul Nathanson, "Between Time and Eternity: Theological Notes on Shadows and Fog," in *The Films of Woody Allen*, ed. Charles L. P. Silet (Lanham: Scarecrow Press, 2006), 284–98.

9. *Shadows and Fog*, directed by Woody Allen (1991; Beverly Hills: MGM, 2001), DVD. All quotations from the movie are from this version.

10. Iris Bruce regards the whorehouse differently. She does not see it as the communitarian place of female solidarity that I describe. For Bruce, the brothel is a metaphor for "boundless fantasies of perversion" and the "universe divested of illusions, in which man feels an alien," à la Camus's stranger (354). Kleinman's impotence with a whore results in his loss of agency. When the students claim the whorehouse atmosphere is more stimulating than university classes, Bruce believes it "turns the place into a circus, a perverse comedy which allows the students to escape by indulging in stimulating 'metaphors of perversion,' as Jack puts it" (355).

11. In Barbara Tuchman, *A Distant Mirror: The Calamitous Fourteenth Century* (New York: Alfred Knopf, 1978).

12. Mikhail Bakhtin, *Rabelais and His World* (Bloomington: Indiana University Press, 1965), 308.

13. Occasional references to fellatio occur in the works and lives of both auteurs. In Allen's *Celebrity* (1998), Robin seeks a lesson in fellatio from a prostitute who almost dies from choking while demonstrating on a banana. This comic business may reflect Allen's squeamishness about his own body, if we can imagine that he is putting himself in the place of a person performing fellatio. The incident sets up a foreboding relationship between sex and death. In Chaplin's case—and the contrast points up the difference between pre- and post-sexual revolution mores—Chaplin's demand for fellatio was one of the charges in Lita Grey's divorce complaint. Fellatio with a minor was a misdemeanor in California at the time. From Divorce Petition, LASC/LGLP, 7, quoted in Richard Carr, *Charlie Chaplin* (New York: Routledge, 2017), 121.

14. For extensive analysis of Chaplin's transformations of objects, body parts, and people, see Dan Kamin, *The Comedy of Charlie Chaplin: Artistry in Motion* (Lanham: Scarecrow Press, 2011).

15. William Paul, "Charlie Chaplin and the Annals of Anality," *Comedy/Cinema/Theory*, ed. Andrew Horton (Berkeley: University of California Press, 1991), 117.

16. David Robinson, *Charlie Chaplin; His Life and Art* (New York: McGraw-Hill, 1995), 360.

17. For other instances of Allen's use of food in relation to sex and death, see Ronald D. LeBlanc, "Love and Death and Food: Woody Allen's Comic Use of Gastronomy," in *The Films of Woody Allen*, ed. Charles Silet (Lanham: Scarecrow Press, 2006), 100–111.

18. Carl Gustav Jung, *Mandala Symbolism* (Princeton: Princeton University Press, 1972), 73.

19. Stark Young, "The Circus," in *The Essential Chaplin*, ed. Richard Schickel (Chicago: Ivan Dee, 2006), 183–187, 186.

20. Kyp Harness, *The Art of Charlie Chaplin* (Jefferson, NC: McFarland, 2008), 134.

21. Richard Carr, *Charlie Chaplin: A Political Biography from Victorian Britain to Modern America* (London: Routledge, 2017), 108.

22. Charles Maland, *Chaplin and American Culture: The Evolution of a Star Image* (Princeton: Princeton University Press, 1989), 109.

23. This circling, hand-held camera movement also appears early in *Husbands and Wives* (1992), when Sally and Jack Simmons tell Judy and Gabe Roth that they are going to split up. Judy takes this information badly, fearing that her own marriage is breaking up too. Carlo Di Palma was cinematographer on this film as well as *Shadows and Fog*; his award for *Shadows and Fog* may have led him to think that this was a good technique. In *Husbands and Wives*, however, the effect is even more nauseating and exaggerated, thereby distracting from rather than enhancing the story.

24. D. H. Lawrence, *Women in Love* (Cambridge: Cambridge University Press, 1987), 187.

25. Peter Bailey, *The Reluctant Film Art of Woody Allen* (Lexington: University Press of Kentucky, 2001), 157.

26. Sander Lee reads the ending of *Shadows and Fog* differently. He thinks that Kleinman's soul is redeemed in the act of joining the circus. In the course of the film, Kleinman transforms from the inauthentic little man who seeks to fit into the anti-Semitic community by passing as Gentile, into the authentic seeker who finds existential redemption by following the path of the magician: "Kleinman's choice to believe in the magician and learn from him is a commitment to join a new community of faith in which he can discover a more authentic identity" (307). *Woody Allen's Angst* (Jefferson, NC: McFarland, 1997).

27. Allen said in an interview, "Human existence is a brutal experience to me ... and so it's what can you do to alleviate the agony of the human condition. ... I continue to make the films because the problem obsesses me all the time ... and I think by making films as frequently as I do I get a chance to vent the problems. There is some relief." In Robert Lauder, "Whatever Works: Woody Allen's World," *Commonweal Magazine*, www.commonwealmagazine.org/woody (accessed June 7, 2018).

28. See Jean-François Lyotard, *The Postmodern Condition: A Report on Knowledge* (Minneapolis: University of Minnesota Press, 1984).

29. D. H. Lawrence, *Sons and Lovers* (Cambridge: Cambridge University Press, 1992).

30. James Joyce, *A Portrait of the Artist as a Young Man* (Oxford: Oxford University Press, 2008).

31. Mark Twain, *The Adventures of Huckleberry Finn* (New York: Penguin, 2002).

Chapter 2

1. Karl Marx, *Economic and Philosophic Manuscripts of 1844* (New York: Simon and Schuster, [1932] 2013), 74.

2. Richard Schickel, *Woody Allen: A Life in Film* (Chicago: Ivan R. Dee, 2003), 100.

3. Schickel, *Life*, 95.

4. *What's New, Pussycat?* (1965) was a commercial hit, but Allen disowns the film due to the aesthetic ruination caused by the producer's interference; it was not "his" film.

5. David Robinson, *Chaplin: His Life and Art* (New York: McGraw-Hill, 1985), 466.

6. Theodor Adorno, "Cultural Criticism and Society," *Prisms*, trans. Samuel and Shierry Weber (Cambridge: MIT Press, 1967), 19.

7. Andrew Hodges, *Alan Turing: The Enigma* (Princeton: Princeton University Press, 2014).

8. By expressing negative values associated with the development of artificial intelligence in our time, I do not mean to promote a Luddite position or imply that all technological development is deleterious to our moral and mental health. Rather, I am following a line of humanitarian reasoning that has critiqued our rapid changes in the Digital Age. This argument records and reflects upon the loss of memory, intimacy, and cognitive ability that characterizes our age of screen-connections to screen-others.

9. Walter Kerr, *The Silent Clowns* (New York: Alfred A. Knopf, 1975), 359.

10. Walter Kerr argues convincingly that the Gamin is Charlie's alter ego, the part of him that yearns to settle down and believes it possible, while Charlie himself does not believe he can ever find a home (362).

11. Robinson, *Life*, 459.
12. *Sleeper*, directed by Woody Allen (1973; Beverly Hills: Twentieth Century Fox, 2012), DVD. All quotations are from this edition of the film.
13. The orgasmatron is a parody of the fraudulent "orgone accumulator" designed by Wilhelm Reich (1897–1957), a German psychoanalyst who claimed that sitting in the box would develop one's "orgastic potency." Reich's theories and products were popular in the United States until they were exposed as charlatanism and Reich was sentenced to prison.
14. Rod McKuen was a very bad poet popular in the late 1960s. His poetry was schmaltzy, smarmy, kitschy, and sentimental (not to put too fine a point on it).
15. Margaret Keane (b. 1927) was McKuen's counterpart in the painting world. Her big-eyed waif canvases enjoyed popularity as kitsch art. Allen is using these two pop icons as examples of the shallowness of the regime's inhabitants. The Great Leader will not allow his subjects to think or feel; consequently, they think bad art is good.
16. It is interesting to reflect that, in 1973, it was common for the media to stereotype homosexuals. Homosexuality began to be accepted in Hollywood in the 1990s. Shows like *Will and Grace* (1998 to the present) offered playful parodies of camp that differ from the gay robot in *Sleeper* insofar as the TV show's narrative explores various issues confronting homosexuals rather than offering them as flat stereotypes. Except for Isaac's ex-wife in *Manhattan*, Allen does not write LGBT roles, or cast known-to-be-LGBT actors. (Lily Tomlin and Jodie Foster, who played whores in *Shadows and Fog* in 1992, did not come out as lesbians until 2013.) This may have something to do with Alan's heterosexual obsessions, rather than to homophobia.
17. Like the throwaway aspersions of homosexuality, the misogyny of this construction is both hilarious (beauty contestants *are* taught to hide their intelligence) and disturbing in light of the more progressive social practices and cautious phraseology of our times. Why, for instance, shouldn't Miles receive dumbing-down from male brain waves instead of female? The answer, of course, is that the stereotype of beautiful women in 1973 was that they were necessarily stupid. By contrast, intelligent women would be stereotyped as ugly because they would not fashion themselves in ways intended to please men.
18. See Laura S. Brown, "Not Outside the Range: One Feminist Perspective on Psychic Trauma," in *Trauma: Explorations in Memory*, ed. Cathy Caruth (Baltimore: Johns Hopkins, 1995), 110–112.
19. Lawrence Howe, "Charlie Chaplin in the Age of Mechanical Reproduction: Reflexive Ambiguity in *Modern Times*," in *College Literature* 40.1 (Spring 2013), 47.
20. Eric L. Flom, *Chaplin in the Sound Era: An Analysis of the Seven Talkies* (Jefferson, NC: McFarland, 1997), 105.
21. Dan Kamin, *The Comedy of Charlie Chaplin: Artistry in Motion* (Lanham: Scarecrow, 2008), 137–38.
22. Umberto Eco believes "I love you" is a phrase too clichéd for a postmodernist novelist to use: "I think of the postmodern attitude as that of a man who loves a very cultivated woman and knows that he cannot say to her 'I love you madly,' because he knows that she knows (and that she knows he knows) that these words have already been written by Barbara Cartland. Still there is a solution. He can say, 'As Barbara Cartland would put it, I love you madly.' At this point, having avoided false innocence, having said clearly it is no longer possible to talk innocently, he will nevertheless say what he wanted to say to the woman: that he loves her in an age of lost innocence." *Reflections on the Name of the Rose* (London: Minerva, 1994), 67–68.
23. Woody Allen and Marshall Brickman, *Annie Hall* screenplay, *Four Films of Woody Allen* (New York: Random House, 1982), 47.
24. Charles Chaplin, *My Autobiography* (New York: Simon and Schuster, 1964), 325.
25. I leave out of this discussion *Play It Again, Sam* (April 28, 1972), released just three months before *Everything You Wanted to Know About Sex* But Were Afraid to Ask* (August 6, 1972), because Woody Allen was not the director of that picture. Herbert Ross directed; Allen wrote the screenplay.
26. Richard Carr, *Charlie Chaplin: A Political Biography from Victorian Britain to Modern America* (London: Routledge, 2017), 104, 108, 96.
27. Sigmund Freud, 1931 letter to Friedrich Schiller, quoted in Carr, *Political*, 33.
28. Chaplin, *Autobiography*, 234.
29. David Robinson, *Chaplin: His Life and Art* (New York: McGraw-Hill, 1985), 444.
30. Robinson, *Life*, 429.
31. Letter to Thomas Burke, in Robinson, *Life*, 456.
32. Chaplin, *Autobiography*, 383.
33. Howe, "Mechanical," 49.
34. Schickel, *Life*, 95–96.
35. In "Film Form: New Problems" (1935), Sergei Eisenstein describes the "inner monologue" and "sensual thinking" by which the viewer interprets film: "We know that the basis of the creation of form lies in sensual and imagist thought processes. Inner speech is precisely at the stage of image-sensual structure,

not yet having attained that logical formulation with which speech clothes itself before stepping out in to the open." *Film Form: Essays in Film Theory* (London: Dennis Dobson, 1951), 130.

36. Gerald Mast, *The Comic Mind: Comedy and the Movies* (Chicago: University of Chicago Press, 1979), 115.

37. Allen used a stunt double in a few of the most dangerous sequences, including the flying harness and the Hydrovac water escape.

38. Graham McCann, *Woody Allen: New Yorker* (Cambridge: Polity Press, 1990), 44.

39. Chaplin, *Autobiography*, 366.

40. Cathy Caruth, *Unclaimed Experience: Trauma, Narrative and History* (Baltimore, MD: Johns Hopkins University Press, 2010), 12.

41. Jeffrey Vance, *Chaplin: Genius of the Cinema* (New York: Harry N. Abrams, 2003), 26.

42. The three preceding quotations are from Douglas Brode, *Woody Allen: His Films and Career* (Secaucus, NJ: Citadel Press, 1991), 137.

43. *Woody Allen: A Documentary,* directed by Robert B. Weide (New York: Whyaduck Productions, 2011), DVD.

44. The Cryonics Institute in Clinton, Michigan, vitrified its first human patient in 2005. Dr. Robert Freitas, author of *Nanomedicine*, said he would not be surprised if the first cryonics revival would be attempted by 2040–2050.

45. In Roland Barthes, "The Death of the Author," in *Image-Music-Text* (New York: Hill and Wang, 1978), 142–48, Barthes describes a literary text as being distinct from its creator's intentions. It is the reader who gives it life, on the one hand; on the other, the text could be said to have a life of its own.

46. In Eric Lax, *On Being Funny: Woody Allen and Comedy* (New York: Manor Books, 1977), 122.

47. Robinson, *Life*, 463.

48. Robinson, *Life*, 459.

49. George Potter, "The Tramp and the Culture Industry: Adorno, Chaplin, and the Possibility of Progressive Comedy," *Arizona Quarterly* 69.1 (2013), 77.

Chapter 3

1. Theodor Adorno, "Chaplin Times Two," in *The Essential Chaplin*, ed. Richard Schickel (Chicago: Ivan R. Dee, 2006), 270.

2. These include May Reeves and Claire Goll, *The Intimate Charlie Chaplin* (Jefferson: McFarland, 2001); Charles Chaplin, Jr., *My Father, Charlie Chaplin* (New York: Random House, 1960); Lita Grey, *My Life with Chaplin: An Intimate Memoir* (New York: Grove Press, 1966); Lita Grey Chaplin and Jeffrey Vance, *Wife of the Life of the Party* (Lanham: Scarecrow Press, 1998); Jane Scovell, *Oona: Living in the Shadows* (New York: Warner, 1998); Georgia Hale: *Charlie Chaplin: Intimate Close-Ups* (Lanham: Scarecrow Press, 1995); Michael Chaplin, *I Couldn't Smoke the Grass on My Father's Lawn* (New York: Ballantine, 1969); Patrice Chaplin, *Hidden Star: Oona O'Neill Chaplin: A Memoir* (London: Trafalgar Square, 1996).

3. See Stephen Papson, "Critical Theory and the Cinematic World of Woody Allen," in *A Companion to Woody Allen*, eds. Peter Bailey and Sam Girgus (Chichester, Wiley-Blackwell, 2013), 147–167. Papson cites Karl Marx, Eric Fromm and David Riesman to present a cultural picture of the 1920s, when a new form of conformity arises from the development of a middle class of managers who were not owners of the means of production. In this social class, "to be successful means to fit in" (151). Advertising contributed to the anxiety that individuals felt when they were constantly judged by a model of success derived from Protestant bourgeois culture. Jews and other ethnic and racial groups could either assimilate or be destroyed.

4. May Reeves, *The Intimate Charlie Chaplin* (Jefferson, NC: McFarland, 2001), 98, 105.

5. Woody Allen, "Random Reflections of a Second-Rate Mind," *Tikkun: A Bimonthly Jewish Critique of Politics, Culture and Society,* January/February 1990, 71–72.

6. This definition is provided by William Hutchings, "Woody Allen and the Literary Canon," *A Companion to Woody Allen* (Malden: Wiley Blackwell, 2013), 397.

7. G. W. F. Hegel, *Phenomenology of Spirit* (Oxford: Oxford University Press, 1977), 111.

8. Master/Slave Dialectic, *Internet Encyclopedia of Philosophy.* www.iep.utm.edu. Accessed 30 April 2018.

9. Friedrich Nietzsche, *Beyond Good and Evil* (New York: Vintage, 1966), 204–05.

10. Nietzsche, *Beyond*, 204.

11. Charles Chaplin, *My Autobiography* (New York: Simon and Schuster, 1964), 399.

12. Nietzsche, *Beyond*, 115–16.

13. Jeremy Hawthorn, *A Glossary of Contemporary Literary Terms* (London: Arnold, 1998), 207.

14. Hawthorn, *Glossary*, 165.

15. In *Beyond Good and Evil*, Nietzsche writes: "The Jews are the strongest, toughest, and purest race now living in Europe; they know how to prevail under the worst conditions by means of virtues that today one would like to mark as vices—thanks above all to a resolute faith that need not be ashamed before 'modern ideas'" (187).

16. Iris Bruce, "Mysterious Illnesses of Human Commodities in Woody Allen and

Franz Kafka," in *The Films of Woody Allen*, ed. Charles Silet (Lanham: Scarecrow, 2006), 171–197, 176.

17. Ruth Johnston, "Ethnic and Discursive Drag in Woody Allen's Zelig," *Quarterly Review of Film and Video*, 24 (2007): 297–306, 297.

18. Ruth Perlmutter, "Woody Allen's Zelig, An American Jewish Parody," in *Comedy/Cinema/Theory*, ed. Andrew Horton (Berkeley: University of California Press, 1991), 206–221, 215, 214.

19. James Caryn, "Auteur Auteur!" *New York Times Magazine*, January 19, 1986, 25.

20. Letty Aronson in *Woody Allen, A Documentary*, directed by Robert Weide (New York: Whyaduck, 2012), DVD.

21. Eric Lax, *Woody Allen: A Biography* (New York: Knopf, 1991), 43.

22. *Wild Man Blues*, directed by Barbara Kopple (Burbank, CA: Fine Line Features, 1997), DVD.

23. David Evanier, *Woody: The Biography* (New York: St. Martin's Press, 2015), 28.

24. Evanier, *Woody*, 122.

25. Allen, "Random Reflections," 71.

26. Eric Lax, *Conversations with Woody Allen* (New York: Knopf, 2007), 83.

27. Papson, "Critical Theory," 154.

28. See note 5.

29. Woody Allen, *Zelig* screenplay, in *Three Films of Woody Allen* (New York: Vintage, 1987), 79.

30. Mary P. Nichols, *Reconstructing Woody Allen: Art, Love and Life in the Films of Woody Allen* (Lanham, MD: Rowman & Littlefield, 1998), 104.

31. Virginia Woolf, *A Room of One's Own and Three Guineas* (Oxford: Oxford University Press, 2008), 59.

32. It is interesting to note one of many occasions on which male and female viewers read a scene differently. Dan Kamin writes, "The audience is left to imagine his facial expression as Hannah chatters on, until finally she bursts into tears, her words futile in the face of such senseless violence. With this moving little scene Chaplin once again reasserts the expressive power of the body." While Kamin focuses on Chaplin's inert body, and finds an "expressive power" there, I focus on Goddard's active face and her courageous message that there is an escape route. To this viewer, Hannah is not "chattering," and her words are not futile. In fact, they are what prepares the Barber to give his famous democracy speech at the end of the film. Dan Kamin, *The Comedy of Charlie Chaplin: Artistry in Motion* (Lanham: Scarecrow, 2008), 163.

33. Chaplin, *Autobiography*, 398.

34. May Reeves, *The Intimate Charlie Chaplin* (Jefferson: McFarland, 2001).

35. Charles Maland, *Chaplin and American Culture: The Evolution of a Star Image* (Princeton: Princeton University Press, 1989), 177.

36. Eric Flom, *Chaplin in the Sound Era: An Analysis of the Seven Talkies* (Jefferson: McFarland & Company, 1997).

37. Lax, *Conversations*, 290.

Chapter 4

1. In 1941–42, aspiring actress Joan Barry and Chaplin had a brief affair. When he attempted to end it, she stalked him, broke into his house, brandished a gun, and threatened suicide. Then she sued him for child support. Although blood tests proved that Charlie was *not* the father of Barry's child, this was inadmissible evidence under California law. The court ordered him to pay $75.00 per week in child support until Barry's daughter reached the age of 21. Barry had visited Chaplin in New York, and federal prosecutors charged him with violation of the Mann Act, which prohibits the interstate transport of a woman or girl for "debauchery, prostitution or any other immoral purpose." He was acquitted by the law court, but not by the court of public opinion. Gossip columnists Hedda Hopper and Florabel Muir solicited unsavory information about him and submitted it to the FBI. Their press campaigns severely damaged Chaplin's star image. See Charles Maland, *Chaplin and American Culture* (Princeton: Princeton University Press, 1989), Chapter 7.

2. HUAC (House Un-American Activities Committee) had been suspicious of Chaplin's Communist involvements since 1922. Along with some members of the Hollywood Ten (blacklisted artists and producers), HUAC subpoenaed Chaplin for a September 24, 1947, hearing, which they later cancelled. Because of his friendships with émigré artists from Eastern Europe, Germany, and Russia (Hanns Eisler, Vsevolod Pudovkin, Sergei Eisenstein, Bertolt Brecht, Thomas Mann, Leon Feuchtwanger), some of whom were Communists, HUAC suspected that Chaplin was at least a sympathizer. His involvement with progressive politics also fueled HUAC's suspicions. On May 18, 1942, Chaplin spoke in San Francisco on behalf of the Russian War Relief, advocating that the Allies open a Second Front in Russia to stop Germans from invading. On July 22, he gave another Second Front speech over the radio to a gathering at Madison Square Garden. On October 16, he addressed a large crowd at Carnegie Hall as "comrades." In November 1947, Chaplin asked Pablo Picasso, a known Communist, to arrange a protest at the U.S. Embassy in Paris against the deportation of his

friend Hanns Eisler. These activities raised the suspicion of congressmen. Two months after the release of *Monsieur Verdoux*, Representative John Rankin (R-Mississippi) demanded that the administration deport Charles Chaplin. Rankin was to have his wish granted in 1952, when the U.S. Attorney General denied Chaplin re-entry to the United States, subject to interrogation by the INS.

3. *Monsieur Verdoux*, directed by Charles Chaplin (1947; New York: The Criterion Collection, 2013), DVD. All further quotations from the film are from this source.

4. Eli Sagan, *Freud, Women, and Morality: The Psychology of Good and Evil* (New York: Basic Books, 1988).

5. Peter Carr, *A Political Biography from Victorian Britain to Modern America* (London: Routledge, 2017), 250.

6. Paul Bloom, "The Moral Life of Babies," *New York Times Magazine*, May 5, 2010.

7. Some selected books and an article about pre-Oedipal development of a conscience are the following: Carol Gilligan (*In a Different Voice: Psychological Theory and Women's Development*), Dorothy Dinnerstein (*The Mermaid and the Minotaur*), Nancy Chodorow (*The Reproduction of Mothering: Psychoanalysis and the Reproduction of Gender*), Margaret Mahler (*The Psychological Birth of the Human Infant: Symbiosis and Individuation*), Eli Sagan (*Freud, Women and Morality: The Psychology of Good and Evil*), Donald Carveth (*The Still Small Voice: Psychoanalytic Reflections on Guilt and Conscience*), Elisabeth Young-Bruehl and Faith Bethelard (*Cherishment: A Psychology of the Heart*), and Karen Horney ("The Dread of Women: Observations on a Specific Difference Felt by Men and Women Respectively for the Opposite Sex," *International Journal of Psychoanalysis*, vol. 13 (1932), 348–60).

8. Young-Bruehl and Faith Bethelard, *Cherishment* (Washington, D.C.: Free Press, 2002); Donald Carveth, *The Still Small Voice: Psychoanalytic Reflections on Guilt and Conscience* (London: Routledge, 2013).

9. Sagan, *Freud*, 62. One of Freud's most sexist theories is this: since girls don't fear castration by the father, they have an underdeveloped superego and consequently, females have a weaker morality than males have. The desire to correct Freud's view is the motivation for most of the studies referred to in note 8, above.

10. Eric Lax, *Conversations with Woody Allen* (New York: Knopf, 2007), 125.

11. *Crimes and Misdemeanors*, directed by Woody Allen (1989; Los Angeles: Orion, 2001), DVD. All subsequent quotations from the movie are from this DVD.

12. Although Woody Allen denies any connection, the story of Professor Levy parallels that of Primo Levi, an Italian chemist who survived Auschwitz, became director of his family's paint business, and wrote a memoir/testimony about the depravity of the death camp, *Se questo è un uomo* (1947). When Levi retired, he wrote several more prize-winning books. He began to suffer depression; then, at the age of 67, committed suicide by falling from a third floor landing (similar to Levy's "going out the window"). Aware of the long-term effects of the camps upon the health of prisoners, Elie Wiesel said, "Primo Levi died at Auschwitz forty years later" (https://www.newyorker.com/magazine/2002/06/17/a-hard-case. Accessed May 8, 2018).

13. Imago therapy is based on the belief that, in order to work out issues from our past, we unconsciously choose a partner who has the good and bad attributes of both of our parents.

14. See Mary Nichols, *Reconstructing Woody* (Lanham, MD: Rowman and Littlefield, 1998).

15. See John Pappas, "It's All Darkness: Plato, The Ring of Gyges, and *Crimes and Misdemeanors*," in *Woody Allen and Philosophy* (Chicago: Open Court, 2004), 203–217.

16. Noam Zion, *A Guide for the Perplexed: Clarifying the Roles of the Leader of the Seder* (https://shi-webfiles.s3.amazonaws.com/Article_NoamZion_nd. Accessed April 25, 2018).

17. Mark Roche, "Justice and the Withdrawal of God in Woody Allen's *Crimes and Misdemeanors*," in *The Films of Woody Allen*, ed. Charles P. Silet (Lanham, MD: Scarecrow, 2006), 268–83, 279.

18. F. Scott Fitzgerald, *The Great Gatsby* (New York: Scribner, 2004).

19. Nichols (*Reconstructing*) accuses Lester of "womanizing, egotism, and crassness," especially with regard to his idea that the assassination of Lincoln could be a funny topic for artists, now that sufficient time has passed since its occurrence (164).

20. Sander Lee, *Woody Allen's Angst: Philosophical Commentaries on His Serious Films* (Jefferson: McFarland, 1997).

21. Roche (in "Justice") identifies the classes of morality slightly differently, calling Sol and Ben the "naïve camp"; May, Judah, Jack, and Lester the "nihilists"; and Cliff, Ben, and Levy the "idealists" who believe in caring, understanding, and forgiveness. But all three positions are undermined by their spokespeople, who fail to live up to their credos. Levy kills himself, Cliff is a "loser," Ben is "blind" to reality. Says Roche, "The film, like Judah, is morally confused" (280).

22. Sam Girgus, in *The Films of Woody Allen* (Cambridge: Cambridge University Press, 2007), is the only critic I've come across who recognizes something amiss in the uncle/niece relationship, but he uses the term *compulsion*

rather than the more loaded *perversion*: "His compulsive passion for fleeing to daily afternoon movies masks his real resistance to competition and achievement and feeds into another compulsive need, for the attention and adulation of his young niece, Jennifer" (143).

23. Peter Bailey, *The Reluctant Film Art of Woody Allen* (Lexington: University Press of Kentucky, 2001), 141.

24. Girgus, *Films*, 143.

25. Gregg Bachman, "*Crimes and Misdemeanors*: Reflections on Reflexivity," in *A Companion to Woody Allen*, eds. Peter Bailey and Sam Girgus (Chichester: Wiley-Blackwell, 2013), 170–87, 179.

26. See, among others, Bailey (*Reluctant*), Bachman ("Reflexivity"), and Claire Sisco King, "Play it Again, Woody: Self-Reflexive Critique in Contemporary Woody Allen Films," in *A Companion to Woody Allen* (Malden: Wiley-Blackwell, 2013).

27. Some other Allen films contain murderers, but they are left out of this discussion because either they are not the main characters, or Allen is uninterested in the state of their conscience. Nevertheless, he remains as fascinated by murder as he is by sex and love. Since his break with Mia Farrow, killers are regular features of his films. In *Manhattan Murder Mystery* (1993), the Allen character's neighbor kills his wife in order to run away with his girlfriend. *Bullets Over Broadway* (1994) features a Mafioso killer-cum-playwright. *Scoop* (2006) involves a handsome, gentlemanly serial killer (like Monsieur Verdoux), played by Hugh Jackman. In *Wonder Wheel* (2017), Ginny (Kate Winslet) knows about the mob's hit, but does not prevent the mob from killing her sexual rival. Allen's fascination with murder as a heroic motive for "getting the girl" begins early in the canon. *Sleeper*'s (1973) hero (Allen) kills the dictator's nose, from which a whole person was about to be cloned. In *Love and Death* (1975), Woody's character reluctantly agrees to kill Napoleon because his wife (Diane Keaton) thinks it would be noble to save the world from his tyranny.

28. Elliot Shapiro, "Toot, Toot, Tootsie (Goodbye): Disposable Women in the Films of Woody Allen," in *Woody on Rye*, eds. Vincent Brook and Marat Grinberg (Waltham, MA: Brandeis University Press, 2014), 190–214, 191.

29. Marat Grinberg, "The Birth of a Hebrew Tragedy: *Cassandra's Dream* as a Morality Play in the Context of *Crimes and Misdemeanors* and *Match Point*," in *Woody on Rye: Jewishness in the Films and Plays of Woody Allen*, eds. Vincent Brook and Marat Grinberg (Waltham: Brandeis University Press, 2014), 37–57.

30. *Take the Money and Run* and *Zelig* do address the childhoods of the burglar Virgil and the mentally ill Zelig in order to give a backstory to their development, including salient features of Allen's own childhood (he gives Virgil the same birth date as himself, and Zelig the same argumentative family environment as his own). When Allen reveals his protagonists' childhood environments, they usually share features of his own, especially yelling parents, economic pressure, parental misunderstanding, and a sense that the child was born into the wrong family.

31. André Bazin, "The Myth of Monsieur Verdoux," in *Monsieur Verdoux* DVD booklet, Criterion Collection, 2013.

32. Donna Kornhaber, *Charlie Chaplin, Director* (Evanston: Northwestern University Press, 2014), 258.

33. Bazin, "Myth."

34. Charles Maland, *Chaplin and American Culture* (Princeton: Princeton University Press, 1989), 230. Maland thoroughly analyzes the Barry trials, Chaplin's Second Front speeches, his suspicious friendships with Communists, and the effects that these events had on his films' reception and the FBI's growing determination to deport him.

35. Ignatiy Vishnevetsky, "Sympathy for the Devil," *Monsieur Verdoux* DVD booklet, Criterion Collection (2013), 5–11, 7.

36. *1 Kings 19:12, King James Bible*. The phrase "still, small voice" describes the communication of God to Elijah, and is often interpreted to mean that God talks to us quietly. "Still, small voice" is sometimes understood as synonymous with conscience.

37. Stephen Weissman, *Chaplin: A Life* (New York: Arcade, 2008); David Robinson, *Chaplin, His Life and Art* (New York: McGraw-Hill Book Company, 1985).

38. Weissman, *Chaplin*, 97.

39. Weissman, *Chaplin*, 34.

40. Dozens of memoirs by Chaplin's coworkers and intimates provide evidence of these characteristics. See Chapter 3, note 2, for a partial list.

41. *Woody Allen: A Documentary*, directed by Robert Weide (New York: Whyaduck Productions, 2012), DVD.

Chapter 5

1. Tom Morris, *Woody Allen and Philosophy*, eds. Mark Conard and Aeon Skoble (Peru, IL: Carus Publishers, 2004), ix.

2. Sam Girgus, *The Films of Woody Allen* (Cambridge: Cambridge University Press, 2002), 67. Girgus notes that in contrast to exterior shots where Scope-screen increases the romanticism of the city, the use of Scope-screen tends to decrease the romanticism of interior

shots, emphasizing instead the loneliness and isolation of the characters, especially in an early scene in Isaac's loft, where Tracy and Isaac communicate across a large space divided by an interior wall.

3. Woody Allen, *Manhattan* screenplay, *Four Films of Woody Allen* (New York: Random House, 1982), 182.

4. Chaplin claims his *City Lights* smile as one of his favorite cinematic images of himself. He portrays the Tramp's vulnerability in a facial expression, as opposed to the physical invulnerability that he usually projects: "I've had that [magic] once or twice.... I'm not acting.... Almost apologetic, standing outside myself and looking.... It's a beautiful scene, beautiful, and because it isn't over-acted." (David Robinson, "Filming *City Lights*," 2004, charliechaplin.com, accessed July 10, 2018)

5. John Baxter, *Woody Allen, A Biography* (New York: Carroll & Graf, 1998), 226.

6. Baxter, *Allen*, 253.

7. Baxter, *Allen*, 249. After the relationship ended, Nelkin acted in soap operas and B-films such as *Halloween III*. She wrote the book *You Can't Afford to Break Up: How An Empty Wallet and a Dirty Mind Can Save Your Relationship* (2009). In 2014, Nelkin told an interviewer that she had been a very willing partner to Allen, as she had been seeking a father figure. He was a "wonderful man," and she had been completely in love. https://www.youtube.com/watch?v=GeRgfnepYdE

8. Mariel Hemingway, *Out Came the Sun: Overcoming the Legacy of Mental Illness, Addiction and Suicide in My Family* (New York: Regan Arts, 2015), 103–104.

9. David Robinson, *Chaplin: His Life and Art* (New York: McGraw-Hill, 1985), 519.

10. Jane Scovell, *Oona—Living in the Shadows: A Biography of Oona O'Neill Chaplin* (New York: Grand Central Publishing, 1999).

11. Donna Kornhaber writes that Terry "internalizes Calvero's words and turns them into art." His "bit of philosophy" heals her from paralysis and depression. It inspires her to excel at dancing. *Charlie Chaplin, Director* (Evanston: Northwestern University Press, 2014), 216.

12. Derrick Bryson Taylor interview with Woody Allen, July 30, 2015. https://pagesix.com/.../woody-allen-soon-yi-responded-to-me-because-i-was-paternal/. Accessed May 14, 2018.

13. Plato, *The Symposium*, trans. Walter Hamilton (London: Penguin, 1951).

14. *Limelight*, directed by Charles Chaplin (1952; New York: Criterion Collection, 2015), DVD.

15. See Christopher Lasch, *The Culture of Narcissism: American Life in an Age of Diminishing Expectations* (New York: Norton, 1979); and Dan Kiley, *The Peter Pan Syndrome: Men Who Have Never Grown Up* (New York: Dodd Mead, 1983).

16. In *Husbands and Wives* (1992), Jack and Sally try to mend their marriage after he has strayed due to her frigidity. But the characters' hollow-sounding promises to love each other despite their sexless union, spoken directly to the camera, leave the viewer unconvinced that they would be able to construct a solid bond based on anything but sex.

17. Allen's *Mighty Aphrodite* (1995) makes explicit this contrast by introducing the present action via a Greek chorus in an ancient amphitheater. The juxtaposition of our contemporary godless state with a classical world of faith is utilized by modernists such as T.S. Eliot (*The Wasteland*) and James Joyce (*Ulysses*) to bemoan our loss (Eliot) or laugh at our pretensions (Joyce).

18. Christopher Knight, "Woody Allen's *Manhattan* and the Ethicity of Narrative" in *The Films of Woody Allen*, ed. Charles P. Silet (Lanham, MD: Scarecrow, 2006), 145–155.

19. Nancy Pogel, *Woody Allen* (Boston: Twayne, 1987), 123.

20. Knight, "Ethicity," 149.

21. Joanna E. Rapf, "It's Complicated, Really: Women in the Films of Woody Allen" in *A Companion to Woody Allen*, eds. Sam Girgus and Peter Bailey (Chichester, Wiley-Blackwell, 2013), 259.

22. Sander Lee, *Woody Allen's Angst* (Jefferson, NC: McFarland, 1997), 104.

23. Douglas Brode, *Woody Allen* (Secaucus, NJ: Citadel Press, 1985), 196.

24. André Bazin, "The Grandeur of Limelight," in *What Is Cinema?* Vol. 2 (Berkeley: University of California Press, 1971), 128–139, 132.

25. Ira S. Jaffe, "Chaplin's Labor of Performance: *The Circus* and *Limelight*," in *Literature/Film Quarterly* 12.3 (1984), 202–210.

26. Kornhaber, *Chaplin*, 266.

27. Jean-Max Méjean, "La Psychanalyse à Hollywood: Entretien avec Elisabeth Roudinesco autour de deux films: *Marnie* de Hitchcock (1964) et *Limelight* de Chaplin (1952)," *Philosophie et cinéma* (Corlet-Télérama, 2000), 194–198, 197. Translation my own.

28. Kornhaber, *Chaplin*, 261.

29. *Limelight* (DVD), Special Features, *Chaplin Today: "Limelight."*

30. Dan Kamin, *The Comedy of Charlie Chaplin: Artistry in Motion* (Lanham, MD: Scarecrow, 2008), 198.

31. Julian Smith, *Chaplin* (Boston: Twayne Publishers, 1984), 133.

32. Bazin, "Grandeur," 135.

33. Peter Bailey, *The Reluctant Film Art of*

Woody Allen (Lexington: University Press of Kentucky, 2001), 56–57.

34. Email correspondence between Peter Bailey and the author, July 10, 2018.

35. Sigmund Freud, "A Special Type of Choice of Object Made by Men" (1912) in *The Standard Edition of the Complete Psychological Works of Sigmund Freud*, Volume XI (London: Hogarth Press, 1957), 165–175.

36. Laura Mulvey, "Visual Pleasure and Narrative Cinema," *Film: Psychology, Society and Ideology* (Oxford: Oxford University Press, 1985), 803–816, 803.

37. Girgus, *Films*, 67.

38. Brianne Brenneman, "Play It Again, Diane," *Film International* 14.1 (2016), 24–34, 30.

39. Rapf, "Complicated," 274

40. The American Legion were so anti-Chaplin at this point that they arranged a boycott of *Limelight*, "urging theater owners not to show any Chaplin films until the matter of Chaplin's political and moral fitness to return to the country was cleared up." Charles Maland, *Charlie Chaplin and American Culture* (Princeton: Princeton University Press, 1989), 308.

Chapter 6

1. See for example, Brian McHale, *The Cambridge Introduction to Postmodernism* (Cambridge: Cambridge University Press, 2015); Jeremy Hawthorn, *A Glossary of Contemporary Literary Theory* (London: Arnold, 1998); and Niall Lucy, *Postmodern Literary Theory: An Introduction* (Oxford: Blackwell, 1997).

2. These modernism and postmodernism tenets were compiled by readings in Mary Alemany-Galway, *A Postmodern Cinema: The Voice of the Other in Canadian Film* (Kent: Scarecrow Press, 2002); Brian McHale, *The Cambridge Introduction to Postmodernism* (New York: Cambridge University Press, 2015); Niall Lucy, *Postmodern Literary Theory: An Introduction* (Oxford: Blackwell, 1997); *Modernism: Challenges and Perspectives*, eds. Monique Chefdor, Ricardo Quiones and Albert Wachtel (Urbana: University of Illinois Press, 1986); Peter Childs, *Modernism* (London: Routledge, 2000); Perry Meisel, *The Myth of the Modern: A Study in British Literature and Criticism after 1850* (New Haven: Yale University Press, 1987).

3. See Adrienne Rich, "Compulsory Sexuality and Lesbian Existence," in *Blood, Bread, and Poetry: Selected Prose, 1979–1985* (New York: Norton, 1994). Rich argues that patriarchy causes women to believe that they need to select male partners in order to avoid ostracism and death in the dominant culture.

4. In Albert Camus's novel, *The Stranger* (1942), Meursault is indifferent to the feelings of others and has repressed his own feelings. He feels no empathy, guilt, nor remorse. Meursault feels nothing at his mother's funeral, and nothing when he kills an Arab. He defies the French customs of respect for one's mother, for God, and for the Church. Like Verdoux, he speaks his mind, and when he does get in touch with his feelings, he finds that he is enraged at the absurdity of the human condition.

5. Federico Fellini, quoted in Vincent Canby, "The Charlie Chaplin Centennial: A Genius Is Revisited," *New York Times Archives*, April 14, 1989, C16. Vittorio De Sica, quoted in Roy Armes, *Patterns of Realism: A Study of Italian New-Realist Cinema* (New York: A. S. Barnes, 1971), 144. Jean Renoir, *My Life and My Films* (New York: Atheneum, 1974), 205.

6. Vincent Canby quoted in Vincent Brook and Marat Grinberg, "Introduction," *Woody on Rye* (Waltham, MA: Brandeis University Press, 2014), xxii–xxiii. Rob Eshman, in "Send Woody on Birthright," *Jewish Journal*, June 27–29, 2012, 4.

7. Sander Lee, *Woody Allen's Angst: Philosophical Commentaries on His Serious Films* (Jefferson, NC: McFarland, 1997), 1.

8. Tom Morris, "Can We Not Talk about Sex All the Time?" (Foreword), *Woody Allen and Philosophy* (Peru, IL: Open Court Publishing, 2004), ix.

9. *Broadway Danny Rose*, directed by Woody Allen (1984; Los Angeles: Orion Pictures, 2001), DVD.

Appendix

1. Dylan Farrow, "Why Has the #MeToo Revolution Spared Woody Allen?" *Los Angeles Times*, December 7, 2017.

2. Woody Allen, "Woody Allen Speaks Out," *New York Times*, February 7, 2014.

3. David Evanier, *Woody* (New York: St. Martin's Press, 2015), 286.

4. Sopan Deb and Deborah Leiderman, "Woody Allen, Mia Farrow, Dylan Farrow: A Timeline." *New York Times* January 31, 2018. https://www.nytimes.com/2018/.../woody-allen-mia-farrow-dylan-farrow-a-timeline.html. Accessed June 22, 2018.

5. Evanier, *Woody*, 293.

6. Evanier, *Woody*, 304.

7. Mia Farrow, *What Falls Away: A Memoir* (New York: Doubleday, 1997), 361.

8. Farrow, *Memoir*, 363.

9. Marion Meade, *The Unruly Life of Woody Allen* (New York: Scribner, 2000), 269.

10. Deb and Leiderman, "Timeline," 4.

11. Libby Hill, "Stars Reflect On—and Re-

think—Working with Woody Allen," *Los Angeles Times*, January 29, 2018.

12. Bethy Squires, "*Qué Lástima!* Woody Allen Is Filming a New Film in Spain," *New York Magazine*, February 2, 2019.

13. In *Aspects of the Novel*, E. M. Forster contends that we can never know a person based on their statements or conversation: "In daily life we never understand each other, neither complete clairvoyance nor complete confessional exists.... We cannot understand each other, except in a rough and ready way; we cannot reveal ourselves, even when we want to; what we call intimacy is only makeshift; perfect knowledge is an illusion. But in the novel we can know people perfectly." Storyinsight.com, accessed July 10, 2018.

14. William K. Wimsatt and Monroe Beardsley, "The Intentional Fallacy," *The Sewanee Review* 54.3 (1946), 468–488.

15. See, for instance, Roland Barthes, "The Death of the Author," in *Image-Music-Text* (New York: Hill and Wang, 1978), 142–148.

16. *Circumstantial evidence* relies on an inference to connect it to a conclusion of fact. For example, the fact that Allen's characters joke about sex with minors is circumstantial, since it relies on the inference that any artist who creates characters who fantasize about sex with minors also necessarily commits those sexual acts. *Direct evidence* supports the truth of an assertion directly, without need for any additional evidence or inference. If Allen had been caught in the act of child molestation and a sworn witness testified to seeing that act, it would be direct evidence.

17. Eric Lax, *Start to Finish: Woody Allen and the Art of Moviemaking* (New York: Knopf, 2017), 131.

18. Meade, *Unruly*, 230.

19. Deb and Leiderman, *Timeline*.

20. John Baxter, *Woody Allen: A Biography* (New York: Carroll & Graf, 1998), 402.

21. Mariel Hemingway, *Out Came the Sun: Overcoming the Legacy of Mental Illness, Addiction, and Suicide in my Family* (New York: Regan Arts, 2015).

22. Adam Gopnik in Baxter, *Biography*, 408–09.

23. Lax, *Start*, 126.

24. Moses Farrow, "A Son Speaks Out," mosesfarrow.blogspot.com, May 23, 2018.

25. Farrow, *Memoir*, 20, 27.

26. Laura M. Holson, "Moses Farrow Defends Woody Allen, and His Family Pushes Back," *New York Times* Arts section, May 24, 2018.

27. Lax, *Start*, 126–27.

28. Daphne Merkin, "Introducing Soon-Yi Previn," *New York Magazine*, September 17, 2018.

29. Lisa Stein Haven, *Charlie Chaplin's Little Tramp in American, 1947–1977* (London: Palgrave Macmillan, 2016).

Bibliography

Adorno, Theodor. "Chaplin Times Two." In *The Essential Chaplin*, edited by Richard Schickel, 267–272. Chicago: Ivan R. Dee, 2006.
Alemany-Galway, Mary. *A Postmodern Cinema: The Voice of the Other in Canadian Film*. Kent, UK: Scarecrow Press, 2002.
Allen, Woody. *Four Films of Woody Allen: Annie Hall, Interiors, Manhattan, Stardust Memories*. Screenplays. New York: Random House, 1982.
_____. "Random Reflections of a Second-Rate Mind." In *Tikkun: A Bimonthly Jewish Critique of Politics, Culture and Society*, January/February 1990, 71–72.
_____. *Woody Allen Interviews*, by Kent Jones, 2011. Edited by Robert Kapsis, 224–30. Jackson: University Press of Mississippi, 2016.
_____. dir. *Crimes and Misdemeanors*. 1989; Los Angeles: Orion, 2001. DVD.
_____. dir. *Manhattan*. 1979; Beverly Hills: Twentieth Century Fox, 2011. DVD.
_____. dir. *Shadows and Fog*. 1991; Beverly Hills: MGM, 2001. DVD.
_____. dir. *Sleeper*. 1973; Beverly Hills: Twentieth Century Fox, 2012. DVD.
_____. dir. *Zelig*. 1983; Beverly Hills: Twentieth Century Fox, 2001. DVD.
Arendt, Hannah. "The Jew as Pariah: A Hidden Tradition." *Jewish Social Studies* 6.2 (1944), 99–122.
Bachman, Gregg. "Crimes and Misdemeanors: Reflections on Reflexivity." In *A Companion to Woody Allen*, edited by Peter Bailey and Sam Girgus, 170–87. Chichester: Wiley-Blackwell, 2013.
Bailey, Peter J. *The Reluctant Film Art of Woody Allen*. Lexington: University Press of Kentucky, 2001.
Bailey, Peter J., and Sam Girgus, ed. *A Companion to Woody Allen*. Malden, MA: Wiley-Blackwell, 2013.
Bakhtin, Mikhail. *Rabelais and His World*. Bloomington: Indiana University Press, 1965.
Bamps, Yvan, and Ralph Heyndels. "Modern Times in the Light of Adorno and Beckett." In *Charlie Chaplin: His Reflection in Modern Times*, edited by Adolphe Nysenholc, 119–124. Berlin: Mouson de Gruyter, 1991.
Barthes, Roland. "The Death of the Author." In *Image-Music-Text*, 142–148. New York: Hill and Wang, 1978.
Baxter, John. *Woody Allen: A Biography*. New York: Carroll & Graf, 1998.
Bazin, André. *Essays on Chaplin*. New Haven: University of New Haven Press, 1985.
_____. "The Grandeur of Limelight." In *What Is Cinema?* Vol. 2, 128–139. Berkeley: University of California Press, 1971.
_____. "The Myth of Monsieur Verdoux." In *Monsieur Verdoux* DVD booklet. New York: Criterion Collection, 2013.
Bergson, Henri. *Laughter: An Essay on the Meaning of the Comic*. 1912; Eastford, CT: Martino Fine Books, 2014.
Bloom, Paul. "The Moral Life of Babies." *New York Times Magazine*, May 5, 2010.
Braudy, Leo, and Morris Dickstein. *Great Film Directors: A Critical Anthology*. New York: Oxford University Press, 1978.

Brenneman, Brianne. "Play It Again, Diane." *Film International* 14.1 (2016), 24–34.
Brode, Douglas. *Woody Allen: His Films and Career*. Secaucus: Citadel Press, 1987.
Brook, Vincent, and Marat Grinberg, eds. *Woody on Rye: Jewishness in the Films and Plays of Woody Allen*. Waltham: Brandeis University Press, 2014.
Bruce, Iris. "Lurking in Shadows: Kleinman's Trial and Defense." In *A Companion to Woody Allen*, edited by Peter Bailey and Sam Girgus, 339—59. Malden: Wiley-Blackwell, 2013.
_____. "Mysterious Illnesses of Human Commodities in Woody Allen and Franz Kafka." In *The Films of Woody Allen*, edited by Charles Silet, 171–197. Lanham, MD: Scarecrow, 2006.
Burke, Thomas. "A Comedian." In *City of Encounters*. Boston: Little, Brown, & Company, 1932.
Carr, Richard. *Charlie Chaplin: A Political Biography from Victorian Britain to Modern America*. London: Routledge, 2017.
Caruth, Cathy. *Unclaimed Experience: Trauma, Narrative and History*. Baltimore: Johns Hopkins University Press, 2010.
Carveth, Donald. *The Still Small Voice: Psychoanalytic Reflections on Guilt and Conscience*. London: Karnac Books, 2013.
Caryn, James. "Auteur Auteur!" *New York Times Magazine*, January 19, 1986, 25.
Chaplin, Charles. "A Comedian Sees the World." *Ladies Home Companion* (September 1933-January 1934).
_____. *My Autobiography*. New York: Simon & Schuster, 1964.
_____. *My Life in Pictures*. New York: Grosset & Dunlap, 1975.
_____. *My Trip Abroad*. New York: Harper & Brothers, 1922.
_____. dir. *The Circus*. 1928; Glasgow, UK: Park Circus, 2011. DVD.
_____. dir. *Limelight*. 1952; New York: Criterion Collection, 2015. DVD
_____. dir. *Modern Times*. 1936; New York: Criterion Collection, 2010. DVD.
_____. dir. *Monsieur Verdoux*. 1947; New York: The Criterion Collection, 2013. DVD.
_____. dir. *The Great Dictator*. 1940; New York: Criterion Collection, 2011. DVD.
Chaplin, Charles, Jr. *My Father, Charlie Chaplin*. New York: Random House, 1960.
Chaplin, Lita Grey, and Jeffrey Vance. *Wife of the Life of the Party*. Lanham, MD: Scarecrow Press, 1998.
Chaplin, Michael. *I Couldn't Smoke the Grass on My Father's Lawn*. New York: Ballantine, 1969.
Chaplin, Patrice. *Hidden Star: Oona O'Neill Chaplin, A Memoir*. London: Trafalgar Square, 1996.
Chefdor, Monique, Ricardo Quinones, and Albert Wachtel, eds. *Modernism: Challenges and Perspectives*. Urbana: University of Illinois, 1986.
Childs, Peter. *Modernism*. London: Routledge, 2000.
Chodorow, Nancy. *The Reproduction of Mothering*. Berkeley: University of California Press, 1999.
Conrad, Mark, and Aeon J. Skoble, eds. *Woody Allen and Philosophy: You Mean My Whole Fallacy Is Wrong?* Chicago: Open Court, 2004.
Dickstein, Morris. "Urban Comedy and Modernity: from Chaplin to Woody Allen." *The Partisan Review* 52.3 (1985), 271–81.
Dinnerstein, Dorothy. *The Mermaid and the Minotaur*. New York: Other Press, 1999.
Eco, Umberto. *Reflections on* The Name of the Rose. Translated by William Weaver. London: Secker and Warburg, 1985.
Eisenstein, Sergei. *Film Form: Essays in Film Theory*. London: Dennis Dobson, 1951.
Evanier, David. *Woody: The Biography*. New York: St. Martin's Press, 2015.
Farrow, Mia. *What Falls Away: A Memoir*. New York: Doubleday, 1997.
Fawell, John. *The Essence of Chaplin: The Style, the Rhythm, the Grace of a Master*. Jefferson, NC: McFarland, 2014.
Feuer, Menachem. "The Schlemiel in Woody Allen's Later Films." In *A Companion to Woody Allen*, edited by Peter Bailey and Sam Girgus, 403–423. Chichester: John Wiley, 2013.
Fitzgerald, F. Scott. *The Great Gatsby*. New York: Scribner's, 2004.
Flom, Eric L. *Chaplin in the Sound Era: An Analysis of the Seven Talkies*. Jefferson, NC: McFarland, 1997.

Freud, Sigmund. *The Joke and Its Relation to the Unconscious*. New York: Penguin, 2003.
———. "A Special Type of Choice of Object Made by Men" (1912). In *The Standard Edition of the Complete Psychological Works of Sigmund Freud*, Volume XI, 165–75, edited by James Strachey. London: Hogarth Press, 1957.
Gay, Peter. *Modernism: The Lure of Heresy from Baudelaire to Beckett and Beyond*. New York: Norton, 2008.
Gehring, Wes D. *Charlie Chaplin's World of Comedy*. Muncie, IN: Ball State Monograph, 1980.
Gilligan, Carol. *In a Different Voice: Psychological Theory and Women's Development*. Cambridge: Harvard University Press, 1982.
Girgus, Sam B. *The Films of Woody Allen*, 2nd ed. Cambridge: Cambridge University Press, 2002.
Grant, Barry Keith. *Auteurs and Authorship*. Malden, MA: Blackwell Publishing, 2008.
Grinberg, Marat. "The Birth of a Hebrew Tragedy: Cassandra's Dream as a Morality Play in the Context of *Crimes and Misdemeanors* and *Match Point*." In *Woody on Rye: Jewishness in the Films and Plays of Woody Allen*, edited by Vincent Brook and Marat Grinberg, 37–57. Waltham: Brandeis University Press, 2014.
Hale, Georgia. *Charlie Chaplin: Intimate Close-Ups*. Lanham: Scarecrow Press, 1995.
Haven, Lisa Stein. *Charlie Chaplin's Little Tramp in America, 1947–1977*. (London: Palgrave Macmillan, 2016).
Hawthorn, Jeremy. *A Glossary of Contemporary Literary Terms*. London: Arnold, 1998.
Hayes, Kevin, ed. *Charlie Chaplin Interviews*. Jackson: University of Mississippi Press, 2005.
Hegel, G.W.F. *Phenomenology of Spirit*. Translated by A. V. Miller. Oxford, UK: Oxford University Press, 1977.
Hemingway, Mariel. *Out Came the Sun: Overcoming the Legacy of Mental Illness, Addiction and Suicide in My Family*. New York: Regan Arts, 2015.
Hodges, Andrew. *Alan Turing: The Enigma*. Princeton, NJ: Princeton University Press, 2014.
Horton, Andrew. *Comedy/Cinema/Theory*. Berkeley: University of California, 1991.
Hösle, Vittorio. *Woody Allen: An Essay on the Nature of the Comical*. Notre Dame, IN: University of Notre Dame Press, 2007.
Howe, Lawrence. "Charlie Chaplin in the Age of Mechanical Reproduction: Reflexive Ambiguity in *Modern Times*." *College Literature* 40.1 (Spring 2013), 45–65.
Huff, Theodore. *Charlie Chaplin*. New York: Henry Schuman, 1951.
Hutchings, William. "Woody Allen and the Literary Canon." *A Companion to Woody Allen*. Malden, MA: Wiley-Blackwell, 2013. 359–380.
Jaffe, Ira S. "Chaplin's Labor of Performance: *The Circus* and *Limelight*." In *Literature/Film Quarterly* 12(3) 1984, 202–210.
Johnston, Ruth. "Ethnic and Discursive Drag in Woody Allen's *Zelig*." *Quarterly Review of Film and Video*, 24 (2007): 297–306.
Joyce, James. *Portrait of the Artist as a Young Man*. Oxford: Oxford University Press, 2008.
Jung, Carl Gustav. *Mandala Symbolism*. Princeton, NJ: Princeton University Press, 1972.
Kamin, Dan. *The Comedy of Charlie Chaplin: Artistry in Motion*. Lanham, MD: Scarecrow Press, 2011.
Kapsis, Robert E., ed. *Woody Allen Interviews*. Jackson: University Press of Mississippi, 2016.
Kerr, Walter. *The Silent Clowns*. New York: Alfred A. Knopf, 1975.
Kiley, Dan. *The Peter Pan Syndrome: Men Who Have Never Grown Up*. New York: Dodd Mead, 1983.
Knight, Christopher. "Woody Allen's *Manhattan* and the Ethicity of Narrative." In *The Films of Woody Allen*, edited by Charles P. Silet, 145–155. Lanham, MD: Scarecrow, 2006.
Kopple, Barbara, dir. *Wild Man Blues*. 1997; New York: Fine Line Features, 1997. DVD.
Kornhaber, Donna. *Charlie Chaplin, Director*. Evanston: Northwestern University Press, 2014.
Lacan, Jacques. The Seminar, Book XI, *The Four Fundamental Concepts of Psychoanalysis*, edited by Jacques-Alain Miller. Translated by Alan Sheridan. New York: W.W. Norton, 1977.
Lahr, John. "Woody Allen, The Imperfectionist." *Show and Tell: New Yorker Profiles*. Woodstock: The Overlook Press, 2000.
Lasch, Christopher. *The Culture of Narcissism: American Life in an Age of Diminishing Expectations*. New York: Norton, 1979.

Lawrence, D. H. *Sons and Lovers*. Cambridge: Cambridge University Press, 1992.
_____. *Women in Love*. Cambridge: Cambridge University Press, 1987.
Lax, Eric. *Conversations with Woody Allen: His Films, the Movies, and Moviemaking*. New York: Alfred A. Knopf, 2007.
_____. *On Being Funny: Woody Allen and Comedy*. New York: Manor Books, 1977.
_____. *Woody Allen: A Biography*. New York: Alfred A. Knopf, 1991.
Lee, Sander H. *Woody Allen's Angst: Philosophical Commentaries on His Serious Films*. Jefferson, NC: McFarland, 1997.
Liebman, Robert. "Jewish Identity in Charlie Chaplin, Jerry Lewis, and Woody Allen." *Film/Literature Quarterly*, Vol. 12, No. 3, 1984.
Louvish, Simon. *Chaplin: The Tramp's Odyssey*. New York: St. Martin's Press, 2009.
Lucy, Niall. *Postmodern Literary Theory: An Introduction*. Malden, MA: Blackwell, 1997.
Lyotard, Jean-François. *The Postmodern Condition: A Report on Knowledge*. Minneapolis: University of Minnesota Press, 1984.
Mahler, Margaret. *The Psychological Birth of the Human Infant*. New York: Basic Books, 2000.
Maland, Charles J. *Chaplin and American Culture: The Evolution of a Star Image*. Princeton: Princeton University Press, 1989.
Maltin, Leonard. *Great Movie Comedians: From Charlie Chaplin to Woody Allen*. New York: Crown Publishers, 1988.
Marx, Karl. *Economic and Philosophic Manuscripts of 1844*. New York: Simon & Schuster, 2013.
Mast, Gerald. *The Comic Mind: Comedy and the Movies*. Chicago: University of Chicago Press, 1973.
McCabe, John. *Charlie Chaplin*. New York: Doubleday, 1978.
McCaffrey, Donald W. *Four Great Comedians: Chaplin, Lloyd, Keaton, Langdon*. London: The Tantivy Press, 1968
McCann, Graham. *Woody Allen: New Yorker*. Cambridge, UK: Polity Press, 1990.
McHale, Brian. *The Cambridge Introduction to Postmodernism*. Cambridge: Cambridge University Press, 2015.
Meade, Marion. *The Unruly Life of Woody Allen: A Biography*. New York: Scribner's, 2000.
Meisel, Perry. *The Myth of the Modern: A Study in British Literature and Criticism after 1850*. New Haven: Yale, 1987.
Méjean, Jean-Max. "La Psychanalyse à Hollywood: Entretien avec Elisabeth Roudinesco autour de deux films: *Marnie* de Hitchcock (1964) et *Limelight* de Chaplin (1952)." In *Philosophie et cinema*, 194–198. Paris: Corlet-Télérama, 2000.
Mulvey, Laura. "Visual Pleasure and Narrative Cinema." *Film: Psychology, Society and Ideology*, 803–816. Oxford: Oxford University Press, 1985.
Nathanson, Paul. "Between Time and Eternity: Theological Notes on *Shadows and Fog*." In *The Films of Woody Allen*, edited by Charles L. P. Silet, 284–98. Lanham, MD: Scarecrow Press, 2006.
Nichols, Mary P. *Reconstructing Woody: Art, Love, and Life in the Films of Woody Allen*. Lanham, MD: Rowman & Littlefield, 1998.
Nietzsche, Frederick. *Beyond Good and Evil: Prelude to a Philosophy of the Future*. Translated by Walter Kaufmann. New York: Vintage Books, 1966.
Nysenholc, Adolphe, ed. *Charlie Chaplin: His Reflection in Modern Times*. Berlin, NY: Mouton de Gruyter, 1991.
Pappas, John. "It's All Darkness: Plato, The Ring of Gyges, and *Crimes and Misdemeanors*." In *Woody Allen and Philosophy*, 203–217. Chicago: Open Court, 2004.
Papson, Steven. "Critical Theory and the Cinematic World of Woody Allen." In *A Companion to Woody Allen*, edited by Peter Bailey and Sam Girgus, 147–167. Chichester, UK: Wiley-Blackwell, 2013.
Paul, William. "Charlie Chaplin and the Annals of Anality." In *Comedy/Cinema/Theory*, edited by Andrew Horton, 109–130. Berkeley: University of California Press, 1991.
Perlmutter, Ruth. "Woody Allen's *Zelig*, an American Jewish Parody." In *Comedy/Cinema/Theory*, edited by Andrew Horton, 206–221. Berkeley: University of California Press, 1991.
Plato. *The Symposium*. Translated by Walter Hamilton. London: Penguin, 1951.
Pogel, Nancy. *Woody Allen*. Boston: Twayne Publishers, 1987.

Potter, George. "The Tramp and the Culture Industry: Adorno, Chaplin, and the Possibility of Progressive Comedy." *Arizona Quarterly* 69.1 (2013), 77.
Quigly, Isabel. *Charlie Chaplin: Early Comedies*. London: Studio Vista, 1968.
Rapf, Joanna E. "It's Complicated, Really: Women in the Films of Woody Allen." In *A Companion to Woody Allen*, edited by Sam Girgus and Peter Bailey. Chichester, UK: Wiley-Blackwell, 2013.
Reeves, May, and Claire Goll. *The Intimate Charlie Chaplin*. Translated by Constance Brown Kuriyama. Jefferson, NC: McFarland, 2001.
Robinson, David. "Audio Commentary." *Modern Times*. Directed by Charlie Chaplin. New York: Criterion Collection, 2010. DVD.
———. *Chaplin: The Mirror of Opinion*. Bloomington: Indiana University Press, 1984.
———. *Charlie Chaplin: Comic Genius*. New York: Harry N. Abrams, 1996.
———. *Charlie Chaplin: His Life and Art*. New York: McGraw-Hill, 1985.
Roche, Mark. "Justice and the Withdrawal of God in Woody Allen's *Crimes and Misdemeanors*." In *The Films of Woody Allen*, edited by Charles P. Silet, 268–83. Lanham, MD: Scarecrow, 2006.
Sagan, Eli. *Freud, Women, and Morality: The Psychology of Good and Evil*. New York: Basic Books, 1988.
Scheide, Frank, and Hooman Mehran. *Chaplin: The Dictator and the Tramp*. London: British Film Institute, 2004.
Scheide, Frank, and Hooman Mehran, eds. *Chaplin's "Limelight" and the Music Hall Tradition*. Jefferson, NC: McFarland, 2006.
Schickel, Richard, ed. *The Essential Chaplin*. Chicago, IL: Ivan R. Dee, 2006.
———. *Woody Allen: A Life in Film*. Chicago, IL: Ivan R. Dee, 2003.
Scovell, Jane. *Oona: Living in the Shadows*. New York: Warner, 1998.
Shapiro, Elliot. "Toot, Toot, Tootsie (Goodbye): Disposable Women in the Films of Woody Allen." In *Woody on Rye*, edited by Vincent Brook and Marat Grinberg, 190–214. Waltham: Brandeis University Press, 2014.
Shumway, David R. "Woody Allen: the Charlie Chaplin of New Hollywood." *A Companion to Film Comedy*, edited by Andrew Horton and Joanna E. Rapf, 130–150. Chichester, UK: Wiley-Blackwell, 2013.
Silet, Charles L. P., ed. *The Films of Woody Allen: Critical Essays*. Lanham, MD: Scarecrow Press, 2006.
Silver, Charles. *An Auteurist History of Film*. New York: The Museum of Modern Art, 2016.
Smith, Julian. *Chaplin*. Boston: Twayne Publishers, 1984.
Sobel, Raoul, and David Francis. *Chaplin: Genesis of a Clown*. London: Quartet, 1977.
Tuchman, Barbara. *A Distant Mirror: The Calamitous Fourteenth Century*. New York: Alfred Knopf, 1978.
Tueth, Michael V. *Reeling with Laughter: American Film Comedies from Anarchy to Mockumentary*. Lanham, MD: Scarecrow Press, 2012.
Twain, Mark. *The Adventures of Huckleberry Finn*. New York: Penguin, 2002.
Vance, Jeffrey. *Chaplin: Genius of the Cinema*. New York: Harry N. Abrams, 2003.
Vishnevetsky, Ignatiy. "Sympathy for the Devil," *Monsieur Verdoux* DVD booklet, 5–11. New York: Criterion Collection, 2013.
Warshow, Robert. "Monsieur Verdoux." In *Great Film Directors: A Critical Anthology*, edited by Leo Braudy and Morris Dickstein, 196–208. New York: Oxford University Press, 1978
Weide, Robert B., dir. *Woody Allen: A Documentary*. New York: Whyaduck Productions, 2011. DVD.
Weissman, Stephen. *Chaplin: A Life*. New York: Arcade Publishing, 2008.
Woolf, Virginia. *A Room of One's Own* and *Three Guineas*. Oxford: Oxford University Press, 2008.
Yacowar, Maurice. *Loser Take All: The Comic Art of Woody Allen*. New York: Frederick Ungar Publishing, 1979.
Young-Bruehl, Elisabeth, and Faith Bethelard. *Cherishment: A Psychology of the Heart*. New York: The Free Press, 2000.

Index

Numbers in **_bold italics_** indicate pages with illustrations

absurdism 1, 7–9, 12, 15, 22–24, 38, 40, 61, 71, 81, 99, 154, 158, 182n4
Adorno, Theodor 54, 78
Agee, James 100
alcoholism 72, 126, 136, 141, 147, 165, 168
alienation 1, 22, 47, 52, 58, 63, 82, 84, 149; see also outsider
allegory 32, 45–7, 66, 81, 117, 139, 140, 143
Allen, Woody **_49, 59, 60, 89, 91, 129, 131_**; abuse scandal 161–70; admiration of Chaplin 52, 56, 73; attitude to Holocaust 79, 86; childhood 17–18, 20; conscience 105, 123; depression 11, 20, 25, 87; early movies 21; existential angst 105; female characters 147; *The Floating Lightbulb* 78; godlessness and relationships 135; morality 164; persona 12–21, 25, 40, 44, 45, 64, 137, 147; physical comedy 71–2; psychoanalysis 116; "Random Reflections of a Second-Rate Mind" 79; relationship with parents 17, 62, 71, 87, 123; relationship with Soon-Yi 132; sex jokes 29; sexuality 29, 64, 164
Allen, Woody, films: *Annie Hall* 1, 10, 12, 17, 20, 21, 25, 44, 50, 66, 71, 79, 105, 130; *Another Woman* 11; *Anything Else* 19, 79; *Bananas* 14, 21, 67, 73; *Broadway Danny Rose* 159; *Bullets Over Broadway* 79, 180n27; *Cassandra's Dream* 114, 116, 171n9; *Crimes and Misdemeanors* 10, 11, 26, 53, 99–123, **_109, 111_**, 130, 154, 156; *Deconstructing Harry* 1, 15, 25, 41; *Everything You Always Wanted to Know about Sex* But Were Afraid to Ask* 14, 21, 29, 40, 67, 73; *Hannah and Her Sisters* 20, 41, 105; *Husbands and Wives* 1, 15, 165, 175n23, 181n16; *Interiors* 11, 41, 166; *Irrational Man* 115, 116, 167; *Love and Death* 11, 14, 15, 21, 29, 40, 71, 180n27; *Magic in the Moonlight* 79, 171n21; *Manhattan* 1, 3, 10, 11, 19, 26, 124–48, 152, 155, 156, 166; *Manhattan Murder Mystery* 165, 180n27; *Match Point* 114, 171n9; *Melinda and Melinda* 4, 11; *Midnight in Paris* 19, 79; *A Midsummer Night's Sex Comedy* 169; *Oedipus Wrecks* 3; *Play It Again, Sam* 14, 67; *The Purple Rose of Cairo* 79, 169; *Radio Days* 17, 79; *A Rainy Day in New York* 163; *Scoop* 180n27; *September* 11, 41, 105; *Shadows and Fog* 10, 11, 15, 19, 25, 29–50, **_44, 49_**, 53, 79, 152, 156, 167, 169, 174n5, 175n23; *Sleeper* 8, 14, 21, 25, 29, 40, 51–77, **_59, 60_**, 90, 153, 156, 180n27; *Stardust Memories* 105; *Sweet and Lowdown* 3, 79; *Take the Money and Run* 14, 67, 180n30; *What a Shame!* 163; *Whatever Works* 15, 20, 25; *What's New Pussycat?* 11, 176n4; *Wonder Wheel* 15, 180n27; *Zelig* 15, 26, 78–98, **_89, 91_**, 151, 154, 156, 180n30
ameliorism 8, 86
Annie Hall 1, 10, 12, 17, 20, 21, 25, 44, 50, 66, 71, 79, 105, 130
Another Woman 11
anti-communism 99, 122, 126
anti-Semitism 22, 30, 32, 33, 44, 45, 47, 48, 50, 79, 86, 90, 153
Anything Else 19, 79
Arbuckle, Fatty 13
Arendt, Hannah 3, 15, 32
Aronson, Letty 17, 41, 87, 164
artificial intelligence 25, 54, 62, 63, 66, 74, 77, 175n8
atom bomb 24, 54, 104, 149, 150, 158
auteur 1, 12, 13, 21, 22, 52, 53, 67, 74, 99, 150, 151, 155, 156, 158, 171n10, 172n4
authenticity 5, 12, 19, 46, 65, 88, 124, 130, 136–39, 175n26

Bachman, Gregg 113
Bailey, Peter 2, 6, 47, 112, 142
Bakhtin, Mikhail 2, 29, 34, 35, 42, 58
Bananas 14, 21, 67, 73

Index

Barry, Joan 10, 99, 104, 118, 120, 170, 178*n*1
Barthes, Roland 2, 75, 177*n*45, 183*n*15
Baxter, John 5, 166, 167
Bazin, André 100, 117, 118, 140, 141, 142
Beckett, Samuel 8, 24
Behind the Screen 13
Benigni, Roberto 13
Bertolucci, Bernardo 142, 171
Bettelheim, Bruno 154
Bloom, Claire 101, 126, **128**, **140**
Boetticher, Budd 145
Brecht, Bertolt 31, 178*n*2
Brenneman, Brianne 145
Broadway Danny Rose 159
Brode, Douglas 20, 140
Brooklyn 10, 15, 17, 87
Brooks, Mel 13
Bruce, Iris 3, 32, 86
Bullets Over Broadway 79, 180*n*27
Burke, Thomas 68

Cabinet of Dr Caligari 34
camera 2, 12, 17, 18, 31, 41, 45, 55, 65, 67, 71, 87, 91–94, 96, 99, 107, 113, 141–44, 150, 162, 168, 169, 175*n*23, 181*n*16
Camus, Albert 19, 157, 174*n*10, 182*n*4
Canby, Vincent 158, 182
carnivalesque 25, 29–50, 40, 152
Carr, Richard 5, 20, 43, 68, 174
Casanova 35
Cassandra's Dream 114, 116, 171*n*9
censorship 29, 163, 174*n*2; *see also* Hays Code
chameleonism 78, 80, 81, 86, 87, 156
Chaplin, Charles **36**, **38**, **56**, **57**, **79**, **84**, **101**, **121**, **140**; accused of Communist sympathies 64, 99, 100; challenges with genre 95; childhood fears 20; conscience 122; depression 20; difficulty with endings 156; hatred of atom bomb 104; hostility to puritanism 99; as Hynkel 94; marriages 99, 132, 170; megalomania 94; narcissism 9, 97; popularity 12; poverty 15, 18, 64, 68, 72, 122; relationship with mother 122; relationship with Oona 131, 132, 147; resistance to sound era 53, 58, 65, 67, 70, 72; self-educated 68; similarity to Calvero 147; Verdoux as vindication 120; violates classical conventions 94; world tour 68
Chaplin, Charles, films: *The Circus* 9, 14, 19, 25, 29–50, **36**, **38**, 55, 152, 153, 156; *City Lights* 9, 14, 19, 37, 43, 47, 62, 68, 130, 152, 156, 181*n*4; *A Countess from Hong Kong* 4, 122, 170, 172*n*11; *The Gold Rush* 13, 14, 18, 56, 61; *The Great Dictator* 2, 8, 9, 21, 23, 24, 26, 51, 78–98, **79**, **84**, 118, 150, 152, 154, 157; *The Immigrant* 5, 19; *The Kid* 18, 19, 43, 56, 62, 150; *A King in New York* 21, 122, 170, 171*n*4; *Limelight* 9, 23, 26, 73, 122, 124–48, **128**, **140**, 155, 157; *Modern Times* 8, 9, 19, 21, 23, 25, 51–77, **56**, **57**, 151, 153, 156, 157;
Monsieur Verdoux 9, 10, 21, 26, 99–123, **101**, **121**, 150, 151, 154, 157, 171*n*9; *Shoulder Arms* 13, 56, 150; *A Woman of Paris* 9, 14, 172*n*11
Chaplin, Charles, Jr. (filmmaker's son) 131, 132
Chaplin, Charles, Sr. 16, 126, 147
Chaplin, Hannah 16, 72, 122
Chaplin, Oona O'Neill 131, 132, 147
Chaplin, Sydney (filmmaker's brother) 16, 17, 72, 122
Chaplin, Sydney (filmmaker's son) 127, **128**
Churchill, Winston 68
circus 29–50, 151, 152, 157, 174*n*10
The Circus 9, 14, 19, 25, 29–50, **36**, **38**, 55, 152, 153, 156
City College of New York 18
City Lights 9, 14, 19, 37, 43, 47, 62, 68, 130, 152, 156, 181*n*4
Clarke, Arthur C. 74
clown 1, 11, 20, 29–50, 71, 124, 127, 132, 140, 141
Coates, Susan, Dr. 162, 165
Coen Brothers 13
Cold War 8, 64, 74, 118, 149, 150
comedy 1, 2, 7–13, 20–22, 25, 27, 40, 51–53, 62, 68, 71, 73, 81, 83, 107, 137, 138, 147, 157–59, 167, 169–72
communism 10, 56, 64, 99, 100, 117, 118, 122, 126, 170, 178*n*2
conformism 54, 64, 78, 86, 88, 96–98, 126, 147
conscience 9, 26, 49, 99, 103–06, 110, 114–16, 118–23, 126, 138, 151, 155, 164, 180*n*36
A Countess from Hong Kong 4, 122, 170, 172*n*11
Crime and Punishment (novel) 115
Crimes and Misdemeanors 10, 11, 26, 53, 99–123, **109**, **111**, 130, 154, 156

death 11, 29, 30, 32, 41, 45, 47, 48, 62, 71, 72, 92, 93, 106, 128, 141, 147, 153, 156, 157, 173*n*1, 174*n*13, 182*n*3
Deconstructing Harry 1, 15, 25, 41
depression 7, 11, 12, 16, 19, 20, 25, 30, 52, 62, 87, 92, 116, 123, 127, 130, 133, 171*n*9, 179*n*12, 181*n*11
De Sica, Vittorio 158, 171*n*10, 182*n*5
deus ex machina 95, 116
Dickstein, Morris 16
Digital Age 51–77
Di Palma, Carlo 44, 45, 175*n*23

Eco, Umberto 176*n*22
editing, film 2, 4, 5, 9, 94, 150, 167
Einstein, Alfred 68, 69
Eisenstein, Sergei 54, 150, 176*n*35, 178*n*2
Eshman, Rob 158
Evanier, David 5, 87, 166
Everything You Always Wanted to Know about Sex* But Were Afraid to Ask 14, 21, 29, 40, 67, 73

Index

existentialism 11, 17, 19, 20, 30, 46, 50, 81, 105, 113, 116, 123, 153, 157, 158, 171n9
Eyes Wide Shut 35

Farrow, Dylan 2, 3, 161–70
Farrow, Mia 35, **49**, 80, 101, ***111***, 112, 161–70; *What Falls Away: A Memoir* 165
Farrow, Moses 162, 167–69
Farrow, Ronan 162, 168, 169
fascism 8, 21, 66, 78, 79, 81, 83, 86, 88, 94–8, 150, 154
FBI (Federal Bureau of Investigation) 10, 99, 118, 170
Fellini, Federico 35, 158, 171n10, 182n5
feminism 2–4, 126, 143, 146, 164, 176n18
Ferguson, Otis 76
Feuer, Menachem 14, 15
film noir 31, 137, 158
Flom, Eric 64, 95
framing of shots 2, 4, 29, 41, 46, 55, 92, 130, 142, 144
Freud, Sigmund 2, 7, 8, 18, 68, 72, 103–05, 114, 120, 143, 163, 171n3, 173n33, 173n47, 173n53, 173ch1n1, 179n9

Gandhi, Mahatma 68, 69
gender roles 58, 71, 76, 82, 90–93, 125, 126, 134, 141, 146, 147, 152
German Expressionism 31, 34, 66, 150
Girgus, Sam 2, 6, 112, 144, 146
God 23–6, 32, 65, 69, 99, 100, 102, 103, 105–09, 115, 116, 120, 135, 138, 140, 155, 174n3, 182n4
Goddard, Paulette 4, **57**, 80, 95, 178n32
godlessness 24, 27, 54, 66, 102, 105, 116, 155, 181n17
The Gold Rush 13, 14, 18, 56, 61
The Great Depression 8, 22, 26, 54, 56, 59, 64, 67, 100, 103
The Great Dictator 2, 8, 9, 21, 23, 24, 26, 51, 78–98, **79**, **84**, 118, 150, 152, 154, 157
The Great Gatsby (novel) 110, 137
Grey, Lita 19, 43, 120, 132, 174n13
Grinberg, Marat 115
the grotesque 25, 29, 35–7, 39–41, 58

Hale, Georgia 4, 18
Hannah and Her Sisters 20, 41, 105
Harness, Kip 43
Harris, Mildred 120, 132
Hays Code 55, 174n2
Hegel, G.W.F. 2, 26, 81, 85, 86, 88, 90, 92, 93, 97
Hemingway, Mariel 129, ***131***, 166
heroism 7, 30, 33, 49, 112, 117, 150, 156, 158
Hitchcock, Alfred 34, 144, 171n10
Hitler, Adolf 32, 79, 81, 88, 95, 98, 154, 174n5
Holocaust 8, 16, 19, 22, 30, 32, 50, 54, 66, 79, 88, 102, 105, 107, 150, 154, 158
homosexuality 37, 61, 133, 135, 136, 138, 155, 176n16

Hope, Bob 71
House Un-American Activities Committee (HUAC) 99, 104, 120, 170, 178n2
Howe, Lawrence 64, 69, 76
Husbands and Wives 1, 15, 165, 175n23, 181n16
Hutchings, William 7, 9
Huxley, Aldous 63, 153

The Immigrant 5, 19
individualism 7, 22–24, 26, 30, 43, 46, 47, 49, 50, 62, 63, 65, 66, 97, 105, 150, 152, 153
Interiors 11, 41, 166
Intolerance 118
Irrational Man 115, 116, 167

Jaffe, Ira 141
Jameson, Frederic 24
Jane Eyre (film) 93
The Jazz Singer 67
Jews and Jewishness 7, 12, 14–16, 22, 25, 31–33, 36, 41, 44, 45, 48, 50, 54, 70, 71, 79, 80, 83, 85–89, 92, 93, 98, 108, 114, 115, 139, 172n27, 177n3, 177n15
Johnston, Ruth 3, 86
Jong, Erica 64
Joyce, James 49, 181n17
Jung, Carl 42

Kael, Pauline 73, 158
Kafka, Franz 19, 31, 34, 48, 86, 174n4
Kamin, Dan 6, 64, 65, 142, 151, 178n32
Karno, Fred 17
Keane, Margaret 60, 176n15
Keaton, Buster 13, 42, 52, 67, 70, 128, 141
Keaton, Diane 21, 52, 60, 73, ***129***, 162, 180n27
Kelly, Hetty 18
Kerr, Walter 56
The Kid 18, 19, 43, 56, 62, 150
A King in New York 21, 122, 170, 171n4
Knight, Christopher 135, 139, 140, 142
Konigsberg, Martin (Allen's father) 17, 123
Konigsberg, Nettie (Allen's mother) 17, 89, 123
Kornhaber, Donna 2, 4, 117, 119, 141, 142

Lacan, Jacques 2, 29, 82, 84, 85, 90, 173n1
Lambeth Workhouse 16
Langdon, Harry 13
Lawrence, David Herbert 47, 49
Lax, Eric 5, 20, 75, 105, 167
Lee, Sander 110–111, 113, 140, 158, 175n26
Lee, Spike 13
Levanthal, Dr. John M. 162
Lewis, Jerry 13, 71
Limelight 9, 23, 26, 73, 122, 124–48, ***128***, ***140***, 155, 157
Little Man 1, 12–15, 22, 46, 54, 70, 81, 97, 149, 157, 172n16, 172n17, 174n6
Lloyd, Harold 13, 38, 71
London 5, 15–18, 168, 126, 130, 135, 136, 142, 143
Louvish, Simon 20, 172n12

Index

love 11, 12, 18, 19, 25–30, 40, 43, 45–49, 54, 62, 64–69, 80–82, 86, 88, 89, 91, 94, 192–96, 110–11, 116–18, 120, 122, 124–48, 152, 153, 155–57, 163–70
Love and Death 11, 14, 15, 21, 29, 40, 71, 180n27
Lower East Side 17

Machine Age 51–77
Magic in the Moonlight 79, 171n21
Maland, Charles 5, 43, 94, 118, 170
male critics 4, 111, 124, 125, 142, 143, 145–47, 178n32
male gaze 26, 143–45
Manhattan 1, 3, 10, 11, 19, 26, 124–48, 152, 155, 156, 166
Manhattan (city) 21, 70, 71, 129, 134, 135, 137, 148
Manhattan Murder Mystery 165, 180n27
Martin, Steve 13
Marx, Groucho 71, 130
Marxism 2, 24, 48, 52, 55, 58, 61, 62, 65, 82, 177n3
Mast, Gerald 7, 70
Master/Slave (dialectic) 26, 81–85, 92–5, 97, 98, 153
Master/Slave (morality) 81, 83–94
Match Point 114, 171n9
McCann, Graham 71
McKuen, Rod 60, 176n14
Me Too movement 3, 65, 161, 163, 164
Meade, Marion 165
Méjean, Jean-Max 141
Melinda and Melinda 4, 11
mental illness 16, 20, 56, 72, 122, 172n28, 173n29
metaphysics 7, 9, 15, 27, 155, 158
Metropolis 66
Midnight in Paris 19, 79
A Midsummer Night's Sex Comedy 169
mirroring 32–4, 41, 45, 46, 48, 75, 78, 81, 82, 84, 85, 88, 90–92, 96, 120, 124, 139, 140
Moby Dick (novel) 96, 97, 98, 156
Modern Times 8, 9, 19, 21, 23, 25, 51–77, **56, 57**, 151, 153, 156, 157
modernism 1, 7, 8, 9, 22, 23, 24, 29, 30, 33, 43, 46, 48, 49, 50, 53, 65, 66, 97, 149–159, 173n47
Monsieur Verdoux 9, 10, 21, 26, 99–123, **101, 121**, 150, 151, 154, 157, 171n9
montage 54, 128, 150
Monty Python 8
Morris, Tom 125, 158
Mulvey, Laura 2, 26, 143, 144, 145, 146; "Visual Pleasure and Narrative Cinema" 143
murder 26, 34, 99–123, 154, 155, 156, 157, 180n27

narcissism 7, 9, 24, 45, 65, 97, 102, 111, 113, 126, 134, 135, 139, 140, 141, 147, 148, 154, 155

Nazis 15, 32, 41, 61, 79, 81, 86, 88, 94, 95, 96, 104, 156, 174n5
Nelkin, Stacey 130, 131, 132, 181n7
New York University 18
Nichols, Mary 2, 4, 89, 90, 91
Nietzsche, Friedrich 2, 26, 81–84, 86, 90, 108
Night and Fog 32
Normand, Mabel 4

Oakley, Jack 21
Oedipal complex 103, 104, 115, 120, 143
Oedipus Wrecks 3
O'Neill, Eugene 129, 130, 132, 134
OPEC (Organization of the Petroleum Exporting Countries) 63
Orwell, George 55, 63; *Animal Farm* 117
outsider 30, 34, 41–44, 56, 122, 157; *see also* alienation

Pappas, John 107, 113
Papson, Stephen 88
parody 16, 24, 66, 67, 74–76, 78, 87, 151, 176n13
patriarchy 4, 23, 48, 63, 65, 90, 91, 93, 103, 108, 124, 125, 143, 145–47, 155, 182n3
Paul, William 37
Perlmutter, Ruth 3, 86
Pickford, Mary 4
Plato 113; "The Ring of Gyges" 106, 107; *Symposium* 125, 133–136
Play It Again, Sam 14, 67
Pogel, Nancy 2, 139
pornography 35, 52, 74
postmodernism 1, 7–10, 15, 21, 22, 24–26, 29, 30, 33, 44, 47, 48, 49, 50, 53, 65, 66, 81, 97, 135, 146, 148, 149–159, 176n22
Potter, George 77
Pound, Ezra 23
Previn, Soon-Yi 87, 132, 164, 165, 166, 169
psychoanalysis 2, 26, 42, 45, 80, 82, 84, 85, 88, 89, 90, 96, 103, 104, 109, 116, 141, 154, 163
psychology 19, 20, 56, 68, 72, 74, 78, 80, 85, 87, 99, 116, 127, 143, 144, 155, 161
The Purple Rose of Cairo 79, 169
Purviance, Edna 19

Radio Days 17, 79
A Rainy Day in New York 163
Rapf, Joanna 3, 140, 146
Raskolnikov 115, 123
Red Scare 21, 126, 147
Reeves, May 79
reflexivity 22, 47, 53, 54, 64, 66, 96, 113, 114, 151, 154, 158
Reich, Wilhelm 176n13
reification 27, 54, 62
Renoir, Jean 158, 171n10
Robinson, David 5, 122
Roche, Mark 110
role of critic 2, 3, 161–70

Index

Rollins, Jack 20
romance, May-to-December 26, 124–48, 155, 163
Rosen, Harlene 18, 62

Sagan, Eli 103, 104
satire 8, 12, 54, 62, 63, 66, 69, 95–7, 102, 154, 170
scandal 2, 3, 15, 39, 40, 63, 76, 118, 132, 147, 158, 161–70
Schickel, Richard 11, 52, 70, 73
schlemiel 7, 10, 14, 15, 19, 20, 25, 30, 40, 41, 48, 54, 174n3
Scoop 180n27
September 11, 41, 105
sexism 41, 134, 139, 140, 143, 176n17, 179n9
sexuality 25, 26, 29, 34, 35, 36, 39–41, 45, 46, 58, 61, 63, 64, 65, 76, 126, 131, 134, 135, 137, 139, 143, 144, 155, 166
Shadows and Fog 10, 11, 15, 19, 25, 29–50, **44, 49**, 53, 79, 152, 156, 167, 169, 174n5, 175n23
Shapiro, Elliot 114
Shaw, George Bernard 68
Sherlock Holmes 17
Shoulder Arms 13, 56, 150
silent films 7, 9, 10, 13, 52, 53, 59, 65–7, 70–73, 93, 117, 122, 150
Silet, Charles 2
Sinatra, Frank 168
slapstick 7, 20–21, 37, 39, 42, 52, 61, 70, 73, 117, 150, 151, 171n3,
Sleeper 8, 14, 21, 25, 29, 40, 51–77, **59, 60**, 90, 153, 156, 180n27
Smith, Julian 142
Socrates 107, 113, 133–35
Sontag, Susan 90
sound era 8, 9, 13, 65, 67, 70, 72, 73
sound track 2, 31, 53
Stardust Memories 105
Stein Haven, Lisa 2, 170
Strangers on a Train 34
suffragism 4, 23; *see also* feminism
Sweet and Lowdown 3, 79

Take the Money and Run 14, 67, 180n30
talkies 9, 13, 21, 53, 58, 67, 70, 72, 91
Tati, Jacques 13
technocracy 21, 27, 52, 53, 59, 63, 66, 69, 74

technology 8, 21, 22, 23, 25, 26, 51–77, 153, 175n8
Toffler, Alvin 63
totalitarianism 52, 54, 59, 63, 66, 90, 153
tragicomedy 1, 7, 9–12, 15, 20, 21, 25, 53, 68, 158
The Tramp 4, 7–10, 12–21, 29–50, 53, 54, 117, 130, 147, 150, 151, 152, 153, 156, 157
trauma 16, 20, 50, 62, 63, 72, 73, 74, 77, 80, 105, 116, 122, 128, 144, 162, 165, 168, 169, 174n3
Tuchman, Barbara 34, 35
Turing, Alan 54
2001: A Space Odyssey 54, 68, 74, 75

United Artists 4, 12, 118
Upper East Side 16, 147, 172n27
utilitarianism 115

vaudeville 4, 9, 17, 18, 20, 42, 126, 147
Vietnam War 74
Vishnevetsky, Ignatiy 119

The Wasteland 110, 181n17
Watergate 63, 74
Weide, Robert 17; *Woody Allen* (documentary) 87
Weissman, Stephen 16, 18, 122
Wells, H.G. 68
What a Shame! 163
Whatever Works 15, 20, 25
What's New Pussycat? 11, 176n4
Wild Man Blues 87, 132
Wizard of Oz (film) 69
A Woman of Paris 9, 14, 172n11
Wonder Wheel 15, 180n27
Woody Allen: A Documentary 17–18
Woolf, Virginia 90
World War I 8, 22, 23, 149, 152
World War II 22, 23, 54, 66, 79, 139, 149, 150, 157, 169

Yale-New Haven Hospital Child Abuse Evaluation Clinic 162
Young, Stark 43

Zelig 15, 26, 78–98, **89, 91**, 151, 154, 156, 180n30

www.ingramcontent.com/pod-product-compliance
Lightning Source LLC
Chambersburg PA
CBHW032045300426
44117CB00009B/1201